PERSONAL CARE IN AN IMPERSONAL WORLD: A MULTIDIMENSIONAL LOOK AT BEREAVEMENT

Edited by
John D. Morgan

Death, Value and Meaning Series
Series Editor: John D. Morgan

Baywood Publishing Company, Inc.
AMITYVILLE, NEW YORK

Library of Congress Catalog Number: 92-37430
ISBN: 0-89503-110-8 (Paper)
ISBN: 0-89503-109-4 (Cloth)

Library of Congress Cataloging-in-Publication Data

Personal care in an impersonal world : a multidimensional look at
   bereavement / edited by John D. Morgan.
          p.   cm. - - (Death, value, and meaning series)
   Includes bibliographical references and index.
   ISBN 0-89503-109-4 (hard). - - ISBN 0-89503-110-8 (pbk.)
   1. Bereavement- -Psychological aspects.   2. Death- -Psychological
aspects.   3. Bereavement- -Cross-cultural studies.   4. Death- -Cross
-cultural studies.   5. Personalism.   I. Morgan, John D., 1933-
II. Series
BF575.G7P3785 1993
155.9'37- -dc20   92-37430
                                                                                    CIP

Table of Contents

INTRODUCTION

One of the most interesting changes in contemporary thinking has been the emphasis on the unique person. While the distinction between a person (a unique rational being) and an individual (one of several similar things) is as old as Boethius [1], it is in the 20th century that we seem to have become fully conscious of this distinction. In previous cultures one may have thought of him/herself primarily as a citizen of Athens, a child of God, a member of a particular religion, a citizen of a particular country, or as a cog in the economic wheel of capitalism. Today, we seem to be much more conscious of the unique character of a person's life.

There is good reason for such an emphasis today. Twice within this century, the world was engulfed in a war in which innocent persons were slaughtered in the name of some "ism." Today, we have seen mass starvation in Iraq; bombings in Lebanon, Ireland and Palestine; political kidnappings in Europe and the mid-East; and mass unemployment in both capitalist and socialist countries. In each case the person has been deemed less important than some policy. The cause of our dehumanization seems to be the reduction of the individual person to a part of a political, economic or religious system. Much of the philosophical literature of the twentieth century, the writings of Marcel [2], Camus [3], Heideggar [4], Sartre [5] and Ortega [6] emphasize that the person is not simply "one out of many," but that the person is a unique *event* in history. The death awareness/hospice movement has played an important role in counteracting an anti-person orientation.

The 20th century saw great developments in medicine. It became possible to maintain existence long after a quality of personal life was possible. The reason for this continuation of life was twofold. On the one hand, the hospitals had a need to try new techniques and to teach; on the other hand, western society was so progress and youth oriented that the idea of death was repugnant as a response. The hospice death awareness movement was begun by Cecily Saunders [7], developed by Herman Feifel [8] and emphasized by Kübler-Ross [9] as an antidote for this "mass thinking." Each of these authors, as well as Martin Luther King [10] and Mother Teresa, hold that individual persons are primary and that political, social and economic systems are there to serve people, not the other way around.

It is within the tradition of that movement that the following chapters are written. The purpose of this volume is to ask, and propose a positive answer, to the question "Can we attend to the personhood of individuals within systems and cultures which are mass oriented?"

This volume is divided into four parts. The first part deals with some considerations of what personhood means and how emphasis on personhood is a part of the hospice/death awareness tradition. The second part treats of the particular problems of special groups such as those from dysfunctional families, or those who suffer the death of a child through SIDS. The third part shows us the lessons we can gain from traditional societies and challenges us to integrate their wisdom into our culture. Finally, we end with hope. The hope is offered by Dr. Cecily Saunders, the founder of the hospice movement, as to the future of hospice.

Professor Jeanne Quint Benoliel offers us an analysis of the present health care situation in which vulnerable persons are caught in a situation of helplessness. She defines personal care and suggests personal, structural and political ways to empower vulnerable persons. John Morgan examines the the idea of personhood from a history of philosophical thought and shows how personhood is presupposed in contemporary writings about terminal care and bereavement care. Mary Ann Morgan gives an historical examination of the idea of caring as well as a critical examination of its application to terminal care. Mrs. Morgan also indicates the limits of care, or rather distinguishes between patient oriented care and caregiver oriented care. Dr. Edward Keyserlink, of the McGill Centre for Medicine, Law and Ethics, holds that the family's right to grieve is more important than the needs of the medical community to teach or research. This is particularly true in those cases where medical science has nothing more to offer the patient or family.

Deanna Edwards, songwriter and musician, tells us how she entered the field of caring for the dying and bereaved and how music has been an aid to vulnerable people. Karen Martin and Sandra Elder explain a particular method of caring for the bereaved which they have developed through their clinical practice. Martin and Elder stress "total person" involvement as well as the normality of loss. It is precisely the normality of loss which Drs. Nan Giblin and Frances Ryan examine. They believe that because of the numbers of persons coming from dysfunctional families and cultures, grief therapy more than grief counselling is required. Finally Patricia MacElveen-Hoehn examines the relationship between death and sexuality. It is MacElveen-Hoehn's contention that this unexplained area will tell us much about human personality and the reality of loss.

In the second part we turn our attention to the care that we can give to particular groups. Richard Paul shows how the funeral director can help bereaved families express their needs particularly at critical times such as Christmas. He includes nine practical suggestions. Rabbi Daniel Roberts examines the role that the clergyperson has with the bereaved in "being there," and ritual needs. While he concentrates on bereavement caused by a suicide, the information is more universally applicable. Maryse Pelletier examines the particular needs of the family who has had to make decisions about organ donation and the effect that organ donation has had on the grief of the family. Linda Ernst and John DeFrain examine the needs of the family bereaved by the sudden death of an infant. They emphasize the problems of guilt which a parent faces when a child dies. Finally, Dr. Judy Oaks examines the effect of cumulative grief which is the result of growing up in a dysfunctional family. She examines the nature of family relationships and the effect of codependency in bereavement.

In the third part of this volume, we examine what we can learn from the native cultures in the United States and in the Northwest Territories of Canada, from the black community in the United States, and from Thailand and Southeast Asia. Ronald K. Barrett applies the general view that the responses which death elicits, while universal, are shaped by the attitude of the particular culture. This theme will be seen in each of the five chapters in this section. Dr. Barrett shows that it would be an error to interpret the Black American experience outside of its historical roots. Dr. Gerry Cox believes that one can understand the aboriginal perception of the person, especially the unity of the person with his or her environment through their burial practices. We get a more specific view of native culture in Ross Gray's chapter dealing with suicide prevention in Canada's Northwest Territories. Finally, we have two views of death customs in Asia. Jiakang Wu describes her experience of discussing death with decidedly death denying young Chinese persons in Singapore. She points out the extreme of not using the number "four" in Chinese as it sounds the same as the word for "death." Michael Leming puts emphasis on the Buddhist view of the impermanance of all things in his chapter about Thailand.

It is fitting that we end this volume with a chapter by Dame Cecily Sanders, the founder of the hospice movement. Dr. Saunders reminds us of our roots—that only in doing hospice work from a personal standpoint can we be truly effective.

REFERENCES

1. Boethius, Contra Eutychen, in *A History of Philosophy: Volume II; Medieval Philosophy, Augustine to Scotus,* F. J. Coplestone, Newman, Westminster, 1955.
2. G. Marcel, *Home Viator,* E. Crawford (trans.), Regnery, Chicago, 1945.
3. A. Camus, *The Myth of Sisypus,* J. O'Brien (trans.), Vintage, New York, 1955.
4. W. Kaufman, *Existentialism From Dostoevsky to Sartre,* Meridian, New York, 1969.
5. J. P. Sartre, *Existentialism and Human Emotion,* Philosophical Library, New York, 1985.
6. J. Ortega y Gassett, *The Dehumanization of Art and Other Writings on Art and Culture,* W. W. Norton, New York, 1965.

7. S. Stoddard, *The Hospice Movement: A Better Way of Caring for the Dying*, Stein and Day, New York, 1978.
8. H. Feifel, *The Meaning of Death*, McGraw Hill, New York, 1959.
9. E. Kübler-Ross, *On Death and Dying*, Macmillan, New York, 1969.
10. M. L. King, Letter from Birmingham Jail, in *Anthology of Right and Reason*, A. Fagothey (ed.), Mosby, St. Louis, 1972.

PART I

Theoretical Considerations

CHAPTER 1

Personal Care in an Impersonal World

Jeanne Quint Benoliel

In November of 1990 I was privileged to attend the Fourth International Congress on Women's Health Issues held in Palmerston North, New Zealand. I carry from that experience two memories that are pertinent to any discussion of caregiving in modern society.

1. I had forgotten what it is like to be in a land which has not experienced the intense pressures of overpopulation. For me it was like going back in time to the California of my childhood.
2. The activities and format of the Congress on Women's Issues were organized and implemented in ways that fostered the personal empowerment of each participant. This atmosphere began in the opening session which consisted of a *powhiri*—a Maori ritual of welcome in which the hosts invite visitors into a process of sharing through welcoming speeches, touching noses and foreheads in greeting, and food and drink.

What was striking about the experience of the Congress was that women (and a few men) came from all over the world to share their ideas and learn from each other. Respect for the value of each person was a powerful theme permeating the packed agenda of three days. In a sense, the planning committee created an atmosphere that encouraged expressions of personal care among friends, colleagues, and strangers across variations in ethnicity, culture, and sexual orientation. Participation in the Congress was a moving experience of involvement— intellectually, emotionally, physically, and spiritually.

The only other time that I have experienced this intense camaraderie was during World War II. There was a kind of experienced community among the Army nurses who lived together and worked together in New Guinea and the Philippines and wondered if they would get home alive.

A SENSE OF COMMUNITY

In both of these situations there was a sense of living in the moment. The tasks and daily activities were focused, short term in nature, and oriented toward life and lifesaving goals. Even though the war experience included exposure to death, tropical diseases, the wounds of warfare, and other unpleasant parts of life in the South Pacific, the camaraderie among the nurses continued throughout their time together (even though many did not see each other again after the war ended). These two experiences illustrate what I call a spirit of community—a sense of being part of a shared commitment to something larger than the self—the well-being of the collective. A question I pose for consideration: *Is it possible to capture this shared communal spirit in caregiving environments for vulnerable people in need of personalized care on a long term basis?*

CHARACTERISTICS OF VULNERABLE GROUPS

These vulnerable groups include not solely those who are dying but also groups with these characteristics:

1. Older people with chronic long term illness and disabilities,
2. Patients with limited social power, such as women, children, members of minorities,
3. People with morally reprehensible diseases, such as AIDS, STD, leprosy, and cancer,
4. People with quality of life problems, such as chronic pain, chronic dementia, chronic dyspnea, and other ailments that make life a matter of suffering more so than living.

Some common characteristics of these vulnerable groups are:

1. They are socially dependent on other people in relation to human activities essential for survival and living the good life—getting around, feeding oneself, getting dressed, even breathing unassisted by machines.
2. They are socially disabled in one of two ways: either because of changes in mental functioning—resulting in confusion, loss of memory, extreme irritability, or other attributes that interfere with social relationships; or because of social isolation resulting from the stigma associated with the particular ailment.
3. They generally require help with daily living to some degree—more so than with medical treatments oriented toward recovery—and many for the remainder of their lives. In a sense one might say these are *people caught in the situation of helplessness.*

Current Caregiving Environments

Further, the situation of helplessness is compounded because current caregiving environments (hospitals, nursing homes) are oriented less to the human needs of the person who happens to be a patient and more to the disease or disability that has been "diagnosed to be treated." Some characteristics of caregiving environments that interfere with the delivery of person-centred care include:

1. Patient's problem of dealing with multiple providers.
2. Caregivers avoidance of situations that trigger feelings of helplessness and hopelessness.
3. Person-to-person relationships of patients and providers are affected by institutionalized values and practices,
   - Provider as expert
   - Unequal social power and influence in system
   - Differences in wants and expectations of patients and providers
   - Communication difficulties
   - Choices and decisions—whose to make?
   - Palliative care difficulties.

Caregiving Environments: Institutionalized Values

To my view it is useful to recognize that caregiving environments are reflections of institutionalized cultural values—that is, beliefs and practices that have become institutionalized by what has been called by some *the power structure*. In my opinion the form and format of current caregiving institutions reflect the legacy of patriarchy in several ways.

The values that have priority in Western societies are manifestations of the influence of Cartesian thinking and the power of science to determine what is important. These values include the importance of objectivity and detachment from involvement with the patient. The patriarchal metaphor of conquest and control has produced what might be called an ethic of lifesaving at all costs. At the same time day-to-day caregiving is undervalued and associated with the idea of woman's work. An examination of the allocation of societal resources for social and health services is a telling way to determine which values have priority. A second legacy of patriarchy shows that power and control over resources and decisions are maintained in the hands of experts who are organized in a hierarchical model with the physician in charge. Within work environments power is maintained through what some have come to call the *old boys' network* through which prerogatives and special privileges are upheld. For a glance at the power of the Old Boys Network in the Academic World, I refer you to Bateson's discussion of difficulties faced by women faculty in gaining tenure in universities [1].

All providers work in social systems in which their behaviors are influenced and controlled by powerful norms and mores (rules that become institutionalized).

At the formal level are rules, procedures, and regulations that employees are expected to follow. At the informal level are the constraining influences of peer pressures and group sanctions which, in the patriarchal model of human relationships, foster a competitive social system, encouraging rivalry more so than cooperation and collaboration.

WOMEN AND CAREGIVING: CREATIVE PIONEERS

To date models of caregiving, as in hospices and palliative care units, have been developed in small social systems with high priority given to communication and collegial relationships. Is it possible to provide personalized care in large complex institutions? My thinking about these matters has been influenced by several women who translated their life experiences with loss and pain into creative expressions that gave meaning to their lives. These women are Kaethe Kollwitz, artist and sculptor [2]; Mary Breckinridge, founder of The Frontier Nursing Service in Kentucky [3]; Cicely Saunders, leader in the development of hospice [4]; and Elisabeth Kübler-Ross, leader in care for the dying [5]. The creative efforts of these four women share some common characteristics:

1. All show a sense of community—the importance of human relationships.
2. All show a concern for the vulnerable—those unable to care for themselves or easily exploited by others.
3. All used personal power to bring something into being.
4. What they created were social phenomena (activities) that demonstrated in overt ways a human concern for human beings.

Their social expressions of creativity all demonstrated recognition of and respect for the importance of three factors: 1) interdependency among human beings; 2) the influence of context on choices and actions; and 3) a morality of responsibility and care for others.

SOME MEANINGS OF PERSONAL CARE

What do I mean by the idea of personal care? In the Oncology Transition Services program created by McCorkle and Benoliel, we defined personalized care as providing three kinds of experience for persons with advanced cancer:

1. The opportunity to know what is happening and be able to talk about its reality with someone who will listen.
2. The opportunity to participate in decisions affecting how he/she will live final days, weeks, or months, and how he/she will die.
3. The opportunity to experience the pain of loss and grief instead of having to hide feelings in order to protect others from their own [6]. Stated another way, the central goal of the OTS program was to support the integrity of the

person through helping the person seek meaning in the experience, providing help with distressing signs and symptoms, and providing opportunity to bring closure to life.

Basic Elements of Personal Care

If one attempts to operationalize these ideas into a concrete form, one might say that the basic elements of personal care include:

1. The importance of having a one-to-one caring relationship, i.e,. sharing of the lived experience of living and dying with someone who is concerned,
2. Help and assistance that is offered in a manner respectful of the person's physical, mental, and social limitations [7].
3. Opportunity to deal with the existential questions and concerns faced by all human beings—separation and connection, contemplation and action, justice and care, self and others.

Personal Care and Providers

The delivery of personal care requires caregiving environments that attend to the needs and concerns of providers as well as persons receiving care. The delivery of person-centred care needs to be viewed as a *collective enterprise* with these characteristics:

1. The mode of relationship between provider and recipient of care is equal and reciprocal, contributing to a sense of shared experience and a recognition that process is as important as outcomes.
2. The mode of action is through partnerships through which contracts and agreements are negotiated and renegotiated and purposeful voluntary bonding can contribute to the actualization of mutual goals through instrumental friendship [8].
3. Mode of delivery is by a community of colleagues in which respect, collaboration, and good will are the organizing work themes [9].

CREATION OF CAREGIVING ENVIRONMENTS

The creation of caregiving environments that are communal in orientation requires efforts to counteract the legacy of patriarchy in which 1) caregiver is expert and superior; 2) power means *power over*; 3) caregiver knows best—work done through superior-subordinate orders and relationships; 4) focus or orientation is conquest or battle; 5) work atmosphere emphasizes competition and winning. The creation of a community requires a shift in focus toward work as communal effort—in other words, attention is given to the importance of providers as persons and to the importance of their working relationships with one another. In describing her work as a hospice nurse, Lind stressed the importance of learning shared leadership and shared planning, decision making by consensus, and empowerment of self and others [10]. In her judgment the capacity for empowerment is based in power from within and a sense of the importance of honouring the other person. Examples of empowerment include: 1) willingness to talk with patients about difficult problems, such as "where do you want to die?"; 2) learning to listen to the other person's story—other providers as well as those receiving care; and 3) use of active dialogue to foster mutual growth and understanding. The use of collaboration and collective action as a way of creating a caregiving context for work might also be viewed as a form of empowerment.

Creation of caregiving environments as communities rather than hierarchical teams carries with it the need to counterbalance the current dominant emphasis on autonomy and independence, abstract critical thinking, and a morality of rights and justice (masculine perspective) with an orientation that gives credence to what have been called the feminine attributes: 1) intimacy and interdependence, 2) contextual thought, and 3) a morality of responsibility and care [11]. In other words, the creation of a caregiving community requires that attention be given to the growth and development of human connections and relationships more so than the growth and development of individuals as separate beings.

Bateson has described *creative leadership* as a form of caretaking that needs to be built into our work arenas as well as our home environments [1]. Creative leadership consists of a combination of: 1) challenge and support, 2) criticism and discipline (setting limits), and 3) no belittling or putting down of the other.

To her way of thinking Creative Leadership means working toward the creation of work environments in which *creative interdependence* replaces competition as the governing orientation. Such a social environment would be oriented toward fostering the growth and learning and creative fulfilment of all participants. One of the attributes that makes for creative leadership is what Bateson calls a central survival strategy for life in the 21st century: *The Capacity to Pay Attention and Respond to Changing Circumstances*. In her view this capacity is better developed in women than in men.

In my view creative leadership also would attend to helping providers (perhaps especially women) practice the employment of empowerment strategies through collaborative activities and collective actions to bring about change. Providers also can be helped to understand that continuity of care only functions well when it is built into the system and not left to chance [12].

PERSONAL CARE: A POLITICAL ISSUE

As human beings approach the 21st century, personal care increasingly becomes a political issue. Anyone exposed to the mass media cannot help but see that access to caregiving environments is a growing human need—in all parts of the world. To my view patriarchy has become an outmoded model for human beings in a crowded and rapidly changing world, and the metaphor of conquest needs to be replaced by a metaphor of care. Politics, it is said, is fundamentally the exercise of values in the world. To shift metaphors is no easy task for it means learning new ways of living with other people and giving up old patterns, including those of maintaining one's superior status over others. It means working for a redistribution of societal resources toward the creation of environments for caregiving.

SOCIETAL RESOURCES AND POLITICAL INFLUENCE

Collective action by concerned people is essential if societal resources are to be shifted from such patriarchal activities as armaments and warfare toward adequate provision of caregiving environments for vulnerable populations in need of assistance. Such political action would influence

1. how health care and social resources are allocated within societies and in relation to the less developed countries of the world;
2. insurance and other funding sources that determine who will have access and who will not;
3. policies governing the utilization of resources, whether these be organizations, governments, private industry; and
4. legislation that promotes the health and wellbeing of people by focusing on care needs for highly vulnerable individuals and groups.

Collective political influence can never be a one-time activity; fundamentally, it needs to be built around the concept of long-term advocacy. As Mellow has indicated, for such advocacy to be successful over the long haul, proponents need 1) to be *inclusive*, not exclusive, 2) to incorporate alternative providers as part of the community, and 3) to integrate personal and environmental health concerns as a focused issue [13]. Long-term advocacy to bring about shifts in the use of societal resources requires that individuals learn to make their wishes known through coordinated networks and other goal-oriented interpersonal transactions [14]. Societal change depends on personal awareness and shared responsibility toward common goals.

SOCIALIZATION FOR THE VALUE OF RELATIONSHIPS

Personal care depends on people who value themselves and their relationships with others. Becoming a person who cares is an ongoing and lifelong process that is developmental in character and dependent on a social environment responsive to personal needs for care and assistance. The developmental tasks associated with becoming a caring and autonomous person include: 1) finding a balance between the masculine and feminine parts of the self, 2) incorporating a moral perspective into one's view of the world, 3) dealing with the realities of choice in a world of tough decisions, 4) learning to live with differences and changes deriving from situations of conflict, authority—subordinate relationships, and loss of key attachments.

Becoming a caring person involves the incorporation of an inner sense of integrity and a willingness to assume responsibility for one's choices and actions in an imperfect world. This sense of integrity—or what Hageberg has called *personal power*—is a developmental process whereby an individual moves through six stages of personal growth [15]:

Stage	Manifestation
Powerlessness	Manipulation
Association	Magic
Symbols	Control
Reflection	Influence
Purpose	Vision
Gestalt	Wisdom

Perhaps not everyone can reach the stage of power by gestalt and wisdom, but it may not be necessary. Personal power, in Hageberg's definition refers to [15, p. xvii]:

> . . . the extent to which one is able to link the outer capacity for action (external power) with the inner capacity for reflection (internal power).

PRACTICE OF EMPOWERMENT

Human development depends on affiliation with other people, and in general, people who grow up in abusive relationships grow up to be abusive adults. We who are providers have the power to help to create environments in which each of us can grow in terms of personal power. I suggest that we need to learn to practice empowerment of self and others through

1. Working relationships that are respectful, encouraging, show concern for others, and demonstrate constructive ways of dealing with conflict; and
2. Actions that foster collaboration, communication, and support at all levels in the caregiving community. Empowerment strategies—whether for self care or other care—are concerned with self esteem building in many forms.

IMPORTANCE OF RELATIONAL ETHICS

Personal care ultimately rests on a moral position about human beings and their relationships with one another. Noddings has proposed the need for a shift in ethical orientation away from the current emphasis on the individual toward an emphasis on relationships between individuals [16, 17]. In her view there is need to shift away from the current stress on principles governing actions an individual *should* take to an emphasis on "the moral health and vigor of relations" [17, p. 184]. The importance of relationships over individualism is also central to Benner and Wrubel's position that connections to people, events, and things are essential to the human condition [7].

A relational ethic does not derive from abstract ideas but rather from natural human caring, epitomized in the mother-infant relationship. In natural caring, one acts on behalf of the other because one wants to do so. The carer responds to the needs, wants, initiatives of the other. The carer's response is one of engrossment. There is displacement of motivation from the self to a focus on the other. The receiving person contributes by recognizing and responding to the actions of the carer. In a mature relationship these responses are mutual [17].

But ethical caring differs from natural caring in that it involves the development of an attitude of caring that is learned out of our experiences of caring and being cared for and incorporates a commitment to respond to other people with an attitude of caring. In traditional ethics judgements about what is appropriate in a situation are based on how well selected actions fit with established principles relative to such concepts as autonomy, rights, and justice. In relational ethics, the response of the other person is another criterion to be considered in evaluating the morality of a given act [17 p. 184].

A caring attitude carries with it a requirement to respond to a concrete situation, but the requirement to respond does not necessarily mean always saying yes to the other person's wishes. Rather the requirement means that one's proposed actions are tested against a genuine other, rather than against a principle of generalizability.

In a sense relational ethics is built on an assumption that the evils of the world—pain, separation, and helplessness—are experiences that cannot be conquered and destroyed. They are part and parcel of the human condition, and humans have the choice of living through these experiences with others or of withdrawing from involvement in such relationships.

EDUCATION FOR COMMUNAL COMMITMENT

It is easy to feel overwhelmed when thinking about the enormity of the problem of people in need of personal care. I suggest that each of us needs to find ways and means to counterbalance the competitive influence of our educational and work environments. In the educational realm with which I am most familiar, the teacher can make deliberate use of activities that foster sharing and consensual problem-solving. These can include group projects, a variety of self-learning activities, drama as a teaching-learning modality, and course assignments that bring students face-to-face with the human problems that they encounter in the real world of practice and caregiving [18]. In teaching a course, *death influence in clinical practice*, across some twenty years, I have observed the merits of introducing students to a variety of death-related situations in the community. Such "confrontations" with real people in real situations trigger students to reflect on the meaning of death in their own lives and the meaning of death in their work situations. According to my observations, these assignments have assisted students in their development as human beings faced with the existential realities of death in their personal and professional lives [19].

To foster communal commitment in students the teacher must be willing to make a commitment to the students and be available to share with them the pangs and the pleasures of what it means to be fully human. Education for communal commitment requires a caring relationship with students, not the distanced detachment of the expert scholar.

FUTURE DIRECTIONS

This presentation has argued that the current sociocultural environment of the world is governed by the values and beliefs of patriarchy as a model of human relationships. Such an environment has fostered the development of humans as *exploiters of the earth* and *conquerors of problems and other people* as well as the limitation of viewing *man as superior to woman*. Personal care in an impersonal world requires the need to find a new metaphor—one that defines human beings as elements in a context of relationships with all of the living and nonliving elements that make human existence possible. In particular, we need to find ways of socializing future generations of people toward becoming *integrated human beings* rather than *separated individuals trapped in their stereotyped gender specific roles and relationships.*

Breaking out of the constraints and limitations imposed on human relationships by the patriarchal model means counteracting the powerful influence of gender socialization on both women and men. In the women's movement consciousness-raising groups have provided a means whereby women had opportunities to 1) learn new ways of relating with other women and 2) gain in self-esteem in the process [20]. Similarly people like Robert Bly are providing men with opportunities to get in touch with the hidden parts of themselves through affiliation with other men [21]. Both movements point to the importance of same sex mentorship to the process of finding one's identity as a person who happens to be a man or a woman.

We who work in the broad field of death, dying, and bereavement have done much to provide *personal care* to the patients and families who have come to us for assistance. I propose that we also take seriously the opportunities to make our places of work into healing environments supportive of the ongoing personal development of ourselves and our colleagues as caring persons whose interpersonal connections and shared commitments are essential to the creation of caregiving communities for vulnerable groups of people.

REFERENCES

1. M. C. Bateson, *Composing a Life,* Penguin Books, New York, 1990.
2. H. Kollwitz (ed.), *The Diary and Letters of Kaethe Kollwitz,* Northwestern University Press, Evanston, Illinois, 1980.
3. E. Poole, *Nurses on Horseback,* Macmillan, New York, 1933.
4. S. du Boulay, *Cicely Saunders,* Stodder & Stoughton, London, 1984.
5. D. Gill, *Quest: The Life of Elisabeth Kübler-Ross,* Ballantine Books, New York, 1980.
6. M. J. Tornberg, B. B. McGrath, and J. Q. Benoliel, Oncology Transition Services: Partnerships of Nurses and Families, *Cancer Nursing, 7,* pp. 131-137, 1984.
7. P. Benner and J. Wrubel, *The Primacy of Caring,* Addison-Wesley Publishing, Menlo Park, California, 1989.
8. M. Rawnsley, Of Human Bonding: The Context of Nursing as Caring, *Advances in Nursing Science, 13*:1, pp. 41-48, 1990.
9. J. Q. Benoliel, Healing Environments and Women in Transition: An Issue for Nursing, in *Proceedings of the First and Second Annual Rosemary Ellis Scholars Retreat,* J. J. Fitzpatrick, M. C. England, E. Goodman, and M. Redmon (eds.), Case Western Reserve University, Frances Payne Bolton School of Nursing, Cleveland, Ohio, pp. 131-143, 1990.
10. A. Lind, Hospitals and Hospices: Feminist Decisions about Care for the Dying, *Healing Technology: Feminist Perspectives,* K. S. Ratcliff et al. (eds.), The University of Michigan Press, Ann Arbor, pp. 263-277, 1989.
11. M. F. Belenky, B. M. Clinchy, N. R. Goldberger, and J. M. Tarule, *Women's Ways of Knowing,* Basic Books, New York, 1986.
12. L. M. Shegda and R. McCorkle, Continuing Care in the Community, *Journal of Pain and Symptom Management, 5,* pp. 279-286, 1991.
13. G. O. Mellow, Sustaining Our Organizations: Feminist Health Activism in an Age of Technology, in *Healing Technology: Feminist Perspectives,* K. S. Ratcliff et al. (eds.), The University of Michigan Press, Ann Arbor, pp. 371-395, 1989.
14. J. Q. Benoliel, *From Research to Scholarship: Personal and Collective Transitions,* American Cancer Society (Publication No. 90 25M-No 3332 OO-PE), American Cancer Society, Atlanta, 1990.
15. J. Hageberg, *Real Power,* Winston Press, Minneapolis, 1984.
16. N. Noddings, Caring: *A Feminist Approach to Ethics and Moral Education,* University of California Press, Berkeley, 1984.
17. N. Noddings, *Women and Evil,* University of California Press, Berkeley, 1989.
18. J. Q. Benoliel, Undervalued Caregiving: An Issue for the Thanatology Community, *Loss, Grief & Care, 6*:1/2, 1992.
19. J. Q. Benoliel, Death Influence in Clinical Practice: A Course for Graduate Students, *Death Studies, 5,* pp. 327-346, 1982.
20. C. Becker, *The Invisible Drama,* Macmillan, New York, 1987.
21. R. Bly, *Iron John,* Addison-Wesley Publishing, Menlo Park, California, 1990.

CHAPTER 2

The Person: Dying and Bereaved

John D. Morgan

The death awareness movement, indeed much of the 20th century, has placed great emphasis on the uniqueness of persons. Yet there has been little attempt to explore what is the fundamental meaning of "person." What is it to be person?

The philosopher, Immanuel Kant, holds that each of us in the course of our lives asks four basic questions [1]. These are: "What do I know?," "What must I do?," "For what can I hope?," and "Who am I?" It is in the last question that we are interested in this chapter. While the distinction between an individual (one instance or example of many items of the same category) and a person (a unique rational being) is as old as Boethius [2], the stress of contemporary thought has been on the uniqueness of each human being. The death awareness movement started by Cecily Saunders [3] and Herman Feifel [4], has been particularly influenced by the awareness of the importance of individual persons. It is the purpose of this chapter to explore the meaning of what it is to be a person and to show how the death awareness movement, in its concern for the dying and for the bereaved, has assumed the important distinction between person and individual.

THE PERSON: AN HISTORICAL INTRODUCTION

The idea of the unique person is particularly a Western idea. In Eastern thought, the emphasis is on the erasing of all distinction so that the individual realizes that s/he is identified with that which is beyond all distinction. The goal is to lose one's uniqueness and to be one with all. "Atman," somewhat equivalent to "soul" in Western thought, is the inner person [5]. This atman strives for union with "Brahman" [5, p. 16] perhaps the equivalent of God in Western thought. Where the Western and Eastern traditions part radically is that in Western thought we accept, indeed we delight in, the difference between persons and God; in Eastern thought the distinction between atman and Brahman is considered to be a

15

sign of ignorance [5, p. 14]. Wisdom in Eastern thought consists of the realization that individuality is illusion and that all things are one. There is only the one— persons, places and things are human interpretations of the one. Thus, happiness or nirvana [5, p. 23] consists of the realization of the non-uniqueness of the person.

In the Hebrew Bible, there was an emphasis on the individual person. While the spiritual notion of the person [6] was not fully explored in the Hebrew Bible, explications of what was truly human was always made in reference to individual persons [7]. The most important contribution of Judaism is the emphasis that the world, and thus persons, was made by God, is thus good, and is thus ordered by a divine providence [8, p. 363]. The essential understanding of the person in Judaism is that the person is on earth to do the will of God, in the here and now.

Christianity, an outgrowth of Judaism, still kept the emphasis on the unique person. The contribution of Christianity to our discussion of personhood is the personal relationship between God and the person [5] revealed by Jesus. God is available to the individual person through prayer and through grace. It is the individual who is known, loved and to be judged by God. Some forms of Christianity believe that God remains close to individual persons in a sacramental presence in churches [8]. While Judaism emphasized the obligation that persons have to serve God in this world, Christianity further developed the idea of an immortal relationship with God in heaven [8, p. 434].

It was Greek thought primarily that caused the distinction between human nature and the human person. The Greek saw him/herself primarily as a member of the *polis*, the community [9]. The Greek mind put emphasis on what is common to the human race rather than the uniqueness of individual persons. Plato believed that persons were twofold, that the real person resides in a idea-universe in the presence of absolute truth, while the shell, the body, lives in the world of physical things [10]. True happiness consists in the rejection of the physical and the contemplation of the eternal, a contemplation which will be made perfect after death [11].

Aristotle, while rejecting Plato's dualism, still put emphasis on what is common to human nature rather than what is individual in experience [12]. Aristotle believes that the soul, the source of life in the body is inextricably united with the body [13]. The soul is nothing more than the actualization of the potentiality of the body to grow reproduce, sense, think and will. The effect of Aristotle's position is a greater unity of the human and his/her world, but the rejection of the possibility of a life after death. Since the soul is so intimately connected to the body it does not seem possible to have a bodiless soul.

The 13th-century Christian philosopher Thomas Aquinas managed to unite the insights of Plato and Aristotle with Christian revelation [14, q. LXXVI]. For Aquinas, the human is a unity of spiritual, nonmaterial soul, and physical, material body, in such a way that there is a real interaction of the two. During physical life, the soul and body act as one complete person; although the soul is the root of thinking which for Aquinas is a fundamentally spiritual activity [14, q. LXXVI].

The advantage of Aquinas' position is that he maintains a real union of body and soul, and thus a union of the person and his/her physical world, but he opens the way to a post-life existence in accord with Christianity [15, book IV].

It is perhaps in ethics that we see the distinction between individual and person more clearly. For Plato [10], Aristotle [16] and Aquinas [15], the question is what is a "good" life? To them, ethics is the development of oneself into as perfect an example of a human being as can be. The emphasis here is on human perfection, a perfection common to all members of the human species. Thus, Aristotle speaks of human perfection being the accomplishment of moral and intellectual virtues, but these virtues are the same for everyone [16, book X]. *Individual creativity is not important.* What is important is being a complete human being [16, book I]. The same is true for Plato who believes that human fulfilment is contemplating eternal ideas [10, book V]. Individual differences are not important. One finds a difference in Aquinas, who holds that the destiny of the person is union with God [15]. Contrary to Eastern thought, such a destiny by nature will be personal. However, in order to attain that destiny, each person practices the same, moral, religious and intellectual virtues [15]. We see here how Aquinas unites perfection of human nature (as in Plato and Aristotle) with the personal perfection of the Judeo-Christian tradition.

The Modern period of philosophy (17th to 19th centuries), saw an even greater emphasis on the denial of uniqueness. Modern philosophy was an outgrowth of the beginnings of science [17]. Since science can function only by discovering common elements, the scientific period of philosophy put special emphasis on the common elements of human experience. Descartes [18], Hume [19] and Kant [20] defined the person primarily as a thinker and answered the question "Who am I?" with the answer, "I am a thing that thinks." Thus, the person is a thinker. However, we may define mind, the act of thinking is what defines the person. This emphasis on the person as thinker led Descartes to a mind-body split (therefore a split of the person away from his/her environment); led Hume to absolute scepticism; and led Kant to a radical distinction to what we can know of the person and what we believe about the person and his destiny.

A few final points will complete our historical analysis of what it is to be human. The thinkers Freud and Marx have greatly influenced our understanding of ourselves. Freud holds that the self is composed of the *id,* the *ego* and the *superego* [5, p. 171]. The id is the primal source of energy (eros) which causes all actions. The superego is the set of demands that we have learned from the environment. The ego is the self that we present to the world. Freud returned to the position that the person is unique. While it is true he speaks of human nature when he speaks of the basic constitution of id, ego and superego; the activity of the id, the ego and the superego produce a unique person.

Marx believed that by being alienated from our work, we are thus alienated from our surroundings [5, p. 149]. For Marx we are what we produce. Marx views the person as entirely material, indeed subject to material laws of history [5,

p. 140]. However, each of us create ourselves through our work. Work is not merely that by which we earn our daily bread, it is that by which we define ourselves. The emphasis is on the unique activity in which each of us engages.

In 20th-century philosophy we see a radical return to the uniqueness of the person. The Spanish philosopher Miguel de Unamuno holds that an existence in hell is preferable to nonexistence [21]. We are not simply a speck in the cosmic map, we are unique persons. One realizes his/her personhood precisely in the possibility of nonbeing—in the confrontation with death. No other animal has to face his own death—a dark cloud which hangs over even the brightest day [22, p. 27]. Unamuno's student Jose Ortega y Gasset defines the person as a "vocation," a project, or a "drama" [23]. Each of us has our own destiny, which may be in conflict with the traditional notions of what is human or right or wrong [23, p. 140]. The analogy which Ortega uses is that we are all actors on the stage of life. The difficulty is that no one has told us our role or even told us the plot of the story.

What conclusion can we draw about the nature of the person in light of this analysis of twenty-five centuries of thought. If we combine the insights of the great thinkers, we can say that the human person is a unique being, created both by God with built-in instincts, but also by his/her choices and values. The person is one with nature yet at the same time is unique because s/he can think. Individual personhood is created by self development, values, work, families, and religious aspirations.

CARE FOR THE DYING AND THE BEREAVED

Persons die. Persons who have grown, developed and loved. It is especially in loving that the person has created him/herself because a commitment has been made to a vision—a view of the universe—a desire for relationship. The person lying in a bed in a hospital or hospice is a combination of spiritual energy, material casing and personal history. It is for this reason that the hospice movement has insisted on volunteers and an interdisciplinary team [24]. No one person or speciality can be expected to meet all the needs of the unique history which is a person.

Much has been written about pain control. The hospice movement has been one of the great inspirations for better pain and symptom control. But the Melzak/Wall gate control theory of pain gives scientific evidence for what we all know intuitively [25], namely that pain is never merely physical. Pain includes the psychological, spiritual and the relational, and as these elements "open the gates" they control the amount of pain that the person has. The hospice movement has insisted that the unit of care is the family, not the diseased patient. One of the several reasons for this is the realization that what it is to be the person who is the patient is a unique history of relationships. Expert symptom control alone and excellent nursing alone will not be effective in relieving the pain of a whole person.

Perhaps the whole person philosophy is best illustrated in bereavement literature. Lindemann's classic study of bereavement indicates five common elements of grief [26]. They are: 1) somatic distress; 2) preoccupation with the loss; 3) feelings of guilt; 4) loss of affect; 5) disorientation.

If our culture is correct and that one should be "getting over it" in a matter of a few days, they we must assume that the relationship of the deceased to the bereaved person was merely accidental, such as the relationship between a person and his/her clothing, or his/her glasses. There would be no reason for the symptoms which Lindemann mentions. But Lindemann was correct. Our culture is wrong. The bereaved person has *literally* lost a part of oneself. *This is not mere metaphor.* Persons are composed not only of body parts, but also of history and relationships. The bereaved person who is present before a counsellor is wounded, truly as if blood were dripping from torn flesh.

CONCLUSION

Death is a physical reality; dying and grieving are psycho-social tasks in which we engage. Robert Kastenbaum has used the phrase "death system" to describe the manner in which we live out our dying and grieving [27]. The death system is the set of ideas, customs, rituals and beliefs by which we organize our death and dying attitudes. There are three components to the death system according to Kastenbaum, they are exposure to death, life expectancy and one's philosophy of life—one's view of their control over nature [27]. There is relatively little control over exposure to death and life expectancy. However, we do have control over our philosophy of life—our attitudes to death and dying.

If by a person, we mean a unique focus of knowledge and value, one can easily see that there is much in our culture which is anti-person. For example, there are many humans whom we do not treat as persons. We deny the centrality of knowledge and values to children, to aboriginals, to the aged, to prisoners, to those in the third world. We treat them as statistics, as cogs in the wheel of economic or political reality. The hospice movement has insisted that each person is unique and has rejected the possibility of treating persons as mere individuals.

To be a person is to realize that each of us is a once-in-a-lifetime event. Never before in the history of the universe has this person existed; never again will s/he exist. Death is the loss of precious uniqueness. The realization of this loss is the real terror of death and bereavement [28]. There is so much to lose. On the other hand, it is precisely the emphasis on the uniqueness of the person that has caused the improvement in care for the dying and the bereaved.

REFERENCES

1. F. Coplestone, *A History of Philosophy: Volume VI: Wolff to Kant,* Newman, Westminster, 1966.

2. Boethius, Contra Eutychen in *A History of Philosophy: Volume II: Medieval Philosophy,* F. Coplestone, Newman, Westminster, 1966.
3. S. Stoddard, *The Hospice Movement: A Better Way of Caring for the Dying,* Stein and Day, New York, 1978.
4. H. Feifel, *The Meaning of Death,* McGraw Hill, New York, 1959.
5. L. Stevenson, *The Study of Human Nature,* Oxford, Oxford, 1981.
6. J. Morgan, The Human Quest for Meaning, in *Death and Spirituality,* K. Doka and J. D. Morgan (eds.), Baywood, Amityville, New York, 1993.
7. S. Klagsbrun, Spiritual Help from Judaic and Psychiatric Perspectives, in *In Search of the Spiritual Component of Care for the Terminally Ill,* F. S. Wald (ed.), Yale, New Haven, 1986.
8. H. Smith, *The Religions of Man,* Harper and Row, New York, 1989.
9. F. Coplestone, *A History of Philosophy: Volume I: Greece and Rome,* Newman, Westminster, 1966.
10. Plato, *The Republic,* J. B. Jowett (trans.), Anchor, Garden City, 1973.
11. L. Stevenson, *Seven Theories of Human Nature,* Oxford, Oxford, 1974.
12. Aristotle, *Metaphysics,* R. Hope (trans.), Columbia, New York, 1952.
13. Aristotle, de Anima, in *Basic Works of Aristotle,* R. McKeon (trans. and ed.), Random House, New York, 1941.
14. T. Aquinas, *Summa Theologica,* A. C. Pegis (ed.), Random House, New York, 1945.
15. T. Aquinas, *On the Truth of the Catholic Faith,* C. J. O'Neill (ed.), Doubleday, Garden City, 1956.
16. Aristotle, *Nicomachean Ethics,* M. Ostwald (trans.), Bobbs-Merrill, Indianapolis, 1962.
17. L. M. Regis, *Epistemology,* Macmillan, New York, 1955.
18. R. Descartes, *Meditations on First Philosophy,* Bobbs-Merrill, Indianapolis, 1961.
19. D. Hume, *An Enquiry Concerning Human Understanding,* Scribners, New York, 1955.
20. I. Kant, *Critique of Pure Reason,* M. J. Adler (ed.), Great Books of the Western World, Britannica, Chicago, 1955.
21. J. D. Morgan, *The Conception of Man in the Writings of Spanish Existentialists,* University Microfilms, Ann Arbor, 1957.
22. E. Becker, *The Denial of Death,* Free Press, New York, 1973.
23. J. Ortega y Gassett, *The Dehumanization of Art and Other Writings on Art and Culture,* R. Trask (trans.), Doubleday, Garden City, 1965.
24. D. A. E. Shephard, Principles and Practice of Palliative Care, in *Thanatology: A Liberal Arts Approach,* M. A. Morgan and J. D. Morgan (eds.), King's College, London, 1987.
25. R. Melzak and J. Wall, *The Puzzle of Pain,* Penguin, New York, 1973.
26. E. Lindemann (1944), Symptomatology and Management of Acute Grief, in *Death and Dying: Challenge and Change,* R. Fulton, E. Markusen, G. Owen, and J. L. Scheiber (1978), Addison, Redding.
27. R. Kastenbaum and R. Aisenberg, *The Psychology of Death,* Springer, New York, 1972.
28. J. D. Morgan, Living our Dying, in *Thanatology: A Liberals Arts Approach,* M. A. Morgan and J. D. Morgan (eds.), King's College, London, 1987.

CHAPTER 3

An Expanded Meaning of Caring in Palliative Care

Mary Ann Morgan

There are many definitions for the words care and caring. Nonetheless, many professionals agree that caring for others, in the professional context, involves taking responsibility for well being by providing for, attending to, or performing necessary personal services [1, 2]. This chapter examines the manner in which palliative/hospice care fostered an understanding of the meaning of caring in the professional relationship and explores how professionals need to change their traditional views about caring.

SHORT HISTORICAL REVIEW

Allopathy, a system of medical practice which makes use of all measures that have proven to be valuable in the treatment of disease [3], is the model of care which is universally accepted. It is important to notice that the emphasis in allopathic medical practice is on investigation, diagnosis, cure, or the prolongation of life [4]. This model of care holds a prominent place in the health system. However, the consequences of the universal acceptance of this paradigm have included, on the one hand, increased successes with curing diseases and prolonging life with the development of sophisticated technology and, on the other hand, large bureaucratic structures, an emphasis on disease rather than on the individual, increased competition for limited financial resources, specialization, and movement of control and decision making away from the patient and family to professionals [1, 2]. For these and other reasons, an alternate model of care emerged to accommodate the needs of individuals who did not fit into the allopathic orientation. This is the hospice/palliative model.

To palliate means to ease without curing [3]. Palliative care is a model of care which is directed at easing distress rather than curing disease. Because quantity of life is no longer an issue for individuals with a terminal illness, palliative care emphasizes the quality of life which remains. In medieval times, a hospice was a way station for travellers [5]. If one examines the meaning of the words "hospitable," "hostel," "host," "hostess," and "hospital," one concludes that these words convey the idea of care for travellers on a journey. They are rooted in the Latin word "hospitium" which means hospitality or lodging and "hospes" which means host, stranger, or guest [3]. The word hospice shares the same root and it is this understanding which underlies the philosophy of the contemporary hospice. However, the journey is not a business or vacation trip but is the trip which begins with conception and ends (at least in the biological sense) with death. Every human being engages in that journey although each person is at a different point on the road. Care on this journey refers to the attention given to the traveller who is approaching the end of his/her voyage.

Years ago, Sylvia Lack outlined the requirements of hospice which included care given in different environments by a multidisciplinary team which is headed by a physician; symptom control; the patient and family constituting the unit of care; bereavement follow-up; and a commitment to caring [6, p. 43]. These requirements, outlined in 1983, continue to be relevant in the field today. Mount and Saunders, both hospice pioneers, would agree with Lack but each would probably refine some of these elements for specific implementations of palliative care delivery [7, 8]. The rest of this chapter addresses how each component of palliative care reflects a commitment to caring in a "delivery of services" paradigm and demonstrates how the meaning of caring in the professional relationship needs to be augmented to empower both the professional and the patient.

In its initial phase of development, it was reasonable to assume that a commitment to caring in hospice involved an orientation to caring which differed from the allopathic model of a commitment to curing. Palliative care developed and flourished because research demonstrated that dying individuals were not receiving the kind of care they needed or desired [9, p. 33]. At that time, this understanding of caring was adequate. But professional care-givers who work in traditional models of health care are also committed to caring. Therefore, how did caring in the palliative care setting differ from caring in traditional health care settings?

The following synopsis demonstrates how each of the components of palliative care facilitates an understanding of caring in a "service delivery" model. An analysis of caring utilizing the allopathic model would result in similar conclusions. But hospice philosophy emphasizes caring. And it is said that what is acknowledged as being important for the dying teaches the living what is important for everybody.

PALLIATIVE CARE AND CARING

One could infer from Lack's components of hospice care that the presence of a multidisciplinary team necessitates that professionals with diverse expertise are required to address the complex needs of the person who is dying [6]. These needs can be physical, psychological, emotional, social, financial, and/or spiritual [7, 8, 10]. Ideally, any member of the team can access the expertise of another member to help a patient or family. This is traditional caring behavior because it demands that professionals assess the diverse needs of the patient and arrange for necessary appropriate interventions [1].

Usually the palliative care team is physician-directed. Besides providing leadership, the physician uses his/her knowledge, information, and expertise to manage the multiple symptoms which are frequently associated with terminal cancer. Maslow recognized that physical needs must be relatively well cared for before other needs in the motivation hierarchy could be addressed [11]. Starting with the physical and progressing to the different levels of the motivation hierarchy, palliative care team members recognize and treat the whole person. If the team works well, the patient and family experience support and understanding. Again, there can be no doubt that relief of pain and competent control of the symptoms which frequently accompany terminal disease is caring professional behavior which correlates positively with a "delivery of services" model.

Recognition of the person rather than the disease is an integral part of any hospice set-up. In specifying that the patient and family are the unit of care, palliative care team members recognize that an individual is part of a larger social network. In free standing or hospital based palliative care units, visiting hours are usually unlimited; children, grandchildren, babies, toddlers, and friends are welcomed; husbands and wives are allowed to spend the night together in private surroundings; pets are permitted in hospital rooms for a visit. Hospice staff members encourage interaction among family members, relatives, and friends as they attempt to facilitate resolution and closure of personal, familial, professional, interpersonal, and other unfinished business prior to death. Different aspects of caring are self evident in these situations. The patient and family are recognized as important members of the team, are allowed to address their own issues, are given support in each of their realities, and are encouraged to interact with each other. Palliative care professionals ensure that they create an environment which induces, enhances, and facilitates quality of life.

Bereavement follow-up further indicates the importance of a commitment to care. Ideally, after death, hospice workers visit or stay in touch with survivors until they integrate the death into their personal lives and establish a restructured way of living without the deceased person. Sometimes the support is minimal; at other times it is more intense and lasts for an extended period of time. Because the allopathic medical model emphasizes diagnosis and treatment of disease rather than the person and is oriented to curing or prolonging life, financial and human resources preclude bereavement follow-up. Bereavement care is important in hospice even though financial and human resources are limited [12]. Again, caring is obvious in this situation. Supporting survivors after the death of a significant other by telephoning, visiting, sending newsletters, organizing support groups and memorial services helps to facilitate adaptive healthy grieving with eventual reintegration into the world. Caring behavior is evident in this "delivery of service" model of care.

CARING

As one reviews the literature, one begins to understand what professionals believe caring for another really means. As has already been demonstrated, caring involves appropriate "doing" (delivery of service) to help others. Many professionals agree. Cockburn [13], Downie [14], Hadlock [15], Hoy [16], Kavanaugh [17], Millett [18], Poss [19], Stedeford [20], and Tigges [21] are hospice professionals from different disciplines who support this conventional "delivery of services" model of caring. But professionals who define caring only in this manner, limit their understanding of caring.

Close scrutiny of caring behavior in this chapter reveals that it is the professional who does something for another while the patient and/or family receives the care. Even when the "doing" is well grounded in an assessment of or interaction with a patient or family member, the subtleties of this dynamic merit examination. "Delivery of service creates a false dichotomy between the deliverers and the recipients—we find one rank of people 'service deliverers' who have been trained and hired to treat the rest" [1]. This model of care fosters attitudes of passivity and dependency among the recipients and encourages health care professionals to maintain the status quo. Perhaps it is time for professionals to re-examine their values, beliefs and philosophies which are inherent in the accepted model of caring for others.

AN EXPANDED MODEL OF CARING

Marcel, the existential philosopher, believes that individuals must be personally involved and touched by the events and circumstances which they are required to address. "The person who is at my disposal is the one who is capable of being with me with the whole of himself when I am in need" [22, p. 40]. Bringing oneself as person to the professional interaction represents a new way of caring in that relationship. He encourages people to bring themselves to their relationships and states that "there are some people who reveal themselves as "present" when we are in pain or need to confide in someone, while there are other people who do not give us this feeling, however great is their goodwill" [22, pp. 39-40]. Marcel teaches the importance of being present to oneself and others, but one questions whether an individual is naturally capable of being present in a relationship or whether one develops this ability.

The extent to which professionals are willing to bring themselves, as persons not as professionals, to their professional interactions determines how comfortable they will be in transforming their interventions into caring practice. Mount (personal communication, June 5, 1985) stated that "hate is malignant but love can also be malignant." This idea is unnerving but thought provoking. Professional caregivers might be uncomfortable with the latter part of this statement. How could love, in any relationship, ever be malignant? If professionals define their roles only in terms of what they do and the services they deliver, they may be engaging in unhealthy relationships (malignant love), and they have limited their possibilities in caring for their patients.

Models of caring relationships, such as parent-child and spousal, assist in this discussion about the meaning of caring. When a five year old struggles to tie shoelaces, the caring parent is the individual who allows the child to experience the struggles and rewards the child's tying of shoelaces. Parents know that the laces will likely become untied within a short time, but nevertheless, they encourage and support the child's behavior. Some parents have such a strong need to protect their children that they step in and accomplish the task for the child. But the parent who supports the child in his/her attempts to tie shoelaces demonstrates caring behavior which facilitates normal growth and development, enhances the child's self-esteem, and recognizes the need of the child to participate in this learning process.

Unquestionably, the parent who ties the shoelaces for the child produces a safer environment in the short-term but one questions whether the needs of the parent or the needs of the child are being addressed in this situation. When a parent allows the child to struggle with the shoe laces, he/she empowers the youngster. When the parent accomplishes the task for the child, he/she manipulates the power in the relationship and fails to allow the child to grow in a safe healthy environment.

A further component merits consideration. The parent who "does" more likely experiences positive feedback from observers while the parent who stands back and allows the child to struggle is not as likely to experience these plaudits. Consequently, the parent who ties the shoelaces feels good about what she/he is doing and receives positive reinforcement. The other parent knows that she/he is doing the correct thing, may not feel comfortable about watching the child's struggle, and is not likely to receive positive feedback from observers. Sometimes, caring means standing back and allowing an individual to struggle. However, simply standing back and allowing the struggle to take place is limiting unless the individual brings him/herself as person to the situation.

Professionals may indicate that their professional behavior is more complex than the simple example just presented. But these common illustrations of simple caring behaviors can help place some accepted assumptions about professional behavior in perspective and help elucidate an existential meaning of caring in the professional relationship.

Health care professionals need to re-examine their strong desire to help others by "doing." Standing by and allowing a patient or family to struggle is difficult, sometimes more difficult than doing, but can demonstrate caring. Professionals who enumerate the numerous services they deliver as they care for patients empower themselves. They receive positive feedback from patients, other professionals, and performance evaluations. But the professional care-giver, who is willing to use the power in the therapeutic relationship to make a patient a functioning team member, encourages patients to live fully until they die, recognizes that achievement is important for individuals, enhances self-esteem, and demonstrates caring behavior in the professional relationship.

The spousal relationship elucidates a further meaning of caring. It is generally agreed that good relationships just don't happen: They demand a great deal of work if they are to survive and regrettably, even with work, many do not endure. Salient elements of an intimate relationship are love, respect, consideration, negotiation, and even confrontation. Peck claims that any deep relationship involves—*indeed requires* (emphasis mine)—turmoil [23, p. 248]. In any relationship, some elements are more easily accepted than others. Perhaps this is one reason why professionals prefer to consider the positive aspects of love, respect, consideration and place little emphasis on turmoil in their professional interactions. Those involved in intimate relationships recognize that turmoil is a difficult but necessary element of growth, development, and respect in the relationship. The salient point is simple; any relationship that survives demands that people work on the relationship and experience both the positives and negatives of the partnership. Obviously, this involves communication. Peck claims that the overall purpose of human communication is—or should be—reconciliation which ultimately serves to remove the walls and barriers of misunderstanding that unduly separate human beings from one another [23, p. 257].

This is important in the professional caring relationship. Seemingly there are times when a professional believes that it is better to stress and search for some positives rather than focus on difficult and turbulent issues. Yet confronting tumultuous concerns inevitably leads to a stronger relationship.

This is particularly relevant in palliative care where quality of life is a predominant theme because living fully until one dies can naively lead professionals to believe that they are responsible for creating an environment which emphasizes only the positive. However, the entire spectrum of human experience involves all aspects of living. In their daily lives, human beings are happy, sad, joyful, angry, lonely, depressed, and exhilarated. Professionals need to examine whether a commitment to quality of life allows for the full experiencing of the entire spectrum of human existence.

And, is this commitment to quality of life appropriate only for the patient and family or is it an ideal philosophy which applies to all human beings? An understanding of caring is limited if quality of life is important only for the patient and family because, in this situation, the professional holds all the power in the relationship. When quality of life is important both for the patient and the professional, the therapeutic relationship encourages mutuality and frees both parties to engage in a relationship as persons and as equals. Essentially, when individuals interact as persons rather than professionals, they create an environment of mutual respect and concern.

Mutuality in a therapeutic relationship means that the professional brings him/herself as person to the situation and allows the patient to do the same [24]. Obviously, the professional brings the expertise of his/her discipline but mutuality is not possible unless the professional enters the interaction first as person who acknowledges and alters the power which is covertly inherent in the professional relationship. This is threatening because it equalizes the power and changes the expectations of the participants in that relationship. Frequently, people who are dying need to give as much as they need to receive. Kiley writes that "what is essential does not take place in each of the participants or in a neutral world which includes the two and all other things; but it takes place between them in the most precise sense, as it were, in a dimension which is accessible only to them both" [25, p. 68]. Mutuality ensures that each party will give, take, receive, and exchange during an interaction. Operationalizing mutuality means that the professional enters the therapeutic relationship as a person who recognizes his/her own needs and the patient's need to be him/herself. But this is not easy.

One consequence of allopathic medical practice is objectification of the person [26, p. 23; 1]. Cassell agrees when he writes that contemporary doctors tend to treat the patient and the disease separately [27, p. C3]. In accepting a philosophy which stresses quality of existence for everyone, the caregiver introduces an existential component into the therapeutic interchange. The consequent mutuality changes the power balance in the relationship, results in mutual exchange, and transforms "delivery of service" into caring practice. In this situation, both the patient and the professional have an equal opportunity to experience a full quality of life.

CONCLUSION

There have been many changes and developments in hospice care since its inception in the Western world over two decades ago. This chapter has explored some new possibilities about the meaning of caring in the professional relationship. Originally a commitment to caring was a reaction to the commitment to curing in allopathic medical practice. But today, professionals need to re-examine the basic values inherent in a "delivery of service" model. Further, when professionals bring themselves as persons to their patients, they alter the power structure in the professional relationship and empower both themselves and their patients.

The professional who values quality existence for everyone is more likely to engage in truly caring professional behaviors.

These broader understandings about caring are consistent with the philosophy of palliative/hospice care. But they challenge professionals to continue to develop, re-examine basic values, and move forward. Hospice/palliative care started because it challenged traditional allopathy. It has matured over the past twenty years and should continue to teach us about the important things in life.

REFERENCES

1. R. Fried, *Empowerment Versus Delivery of Services,* New Hampshire Department of Education, 1980.
2. J. Lord and D. M. Farlow, A Study of Personal Empowerment and Implications for Health Promotion, *Health Promotion,* Fall, pp. 2-8, 1990.
3. P. B. Gove (ed.), *Webster's Third New International Dictionary of the English Language,* G & C Merriam, Springfield, Massachusetts, 1966.
4. E. J. Cassel, Dying in a Technological Society, in *Death and Dying: Challenge and Change,* R. Fulton, E. Markusen, G. Owen, and J. L. Schieber (eds.), Addison-Wesley, Reading, Massachusetts, pp. 121-126, 1978.
5. W. E. Phipps, The Origin of Hospice/Hospitals, *Death Studies, 12,* pp. 91-99, 1988.
6. S. A. Lack, The Hospice Concept—The Adult with Advanced Cancer, in *Hospice Care: Principles and Practice,* C. A. Corr and D. M. Corr (eds.), Springer, New York, pp. 42-52, 1983.
7. B. M. Mount, *Palliative Care of the Terminally Ill,* Royal College Lecture, British Columbia, Vancouver, Jaunary 27, 1978.
8. C. Saunders, St. Christopher's Hospice, in *Death: Current Perspectives,* E. S. Shneidman (ed.), Mayfield, Palo Alto, California, pp. 356-361, 1980.
9. I. Ajemian and B. Mount, The McGill University Palliative Care Service, in *The Hospice: Development and Administration,* G. W. Davidson (ed.), Hemisphere, Washington, D.C., pp. 32-49, 1985.
10. D. A. E. Shepherd, Principles and Practice of Palliative Care, *CMA Journal, 116,* pp. 522-526, 1977.
11. A. H. Maslow, *Motivation and Personality,* Harper & Row, New York, 1970.
12. D. O'Toole, Hospice Bereavement Services in the United States: Fact or Fancy, in *Bereavement: Helping the Survivors,* M. A. Morgan (ed.), King's College, London, Ontario, pp. 183-202, 1988.
13. M. Cockburn, Nursing Care of Dying Persons and Their Families, in *Hospice Care: Principles and Practice,* C. A. Corr and D. M. Corr (eds.), Springer, New York, pp. 119-134, 1983.
14. P. A. Downie, The Place of Physiotherapy in Hospice Care, in *Hospice Care: Principles and Practice,* C. A. Corr and D. M. Corr (eds.), Springer, New York, pp. 148-158, 1983.
15. D. C. Hadlock, Physicians Role in Hospice Care, in *Hospice Care: Principles and Practice,* C. A. Corr and D. M. Corr (eds.), Springer, New York, pp. 99-118, 1983.
16. T. Hoy, Hospice Chaplaincy in the Caregiving Team, in *Hospice Care: Principles and Practice,* C. A. Corr and D. M. Corr (eds.), Springer, New York, pp. 177-196, 1983.

17. E. Kavanaugh, Volunteers in Hospice, in *Hospice Care: Principles and Practice*, C. A. Corr and D. M. Corr (eds.), Springer, New York, pp. 209-222, 1983.

18. N. Millett, Hospice: A New Horizon for Social Work, in *Hospice Care: Principles and Practice*, C. A. Corr and D. M. Corr (eds.), Springer, New York, pp. 135-147, 1983.

19. S. Poss, *Toward Death with Dignity: Caring for Dying People*, Allen & Unwin, London, 1981.

20. A. Stedeford, Psychotherapy of the Dying Person, in *Hospice Care: Principles and Practice*, C. A. Corr and D. M. Corr (eds.), Springer, New York, pp. 197-208, 1983.

21. K. N. Tigges, Occupational Therapy in Hospice, in *Hospice Care: Principles and Practice*, C. A. Corr and D. M. Corr (eds.), Springer, New York, pp. 160-176, 1983.

22. G. Marcel, *The Philosophy of Existentialism*, Citadel, New York, 1967.

23. M. S. Peck, *The Different Drum: Community Making and Peace*, Simon and Schuster, New York, 1987.

24. M. C. Curran and J. C. Kobos, Therapeutic Engagement with a Dying Person: Stimulus for Therapist Training and Growth, *Psychotherapy: Theory, Research, and Practice, 17*, pp. 343-351, 1980.

25. W. P. Kiley, *Human Possibilities: A Dialectic in Contemporary Thinking*, Philosophical Library, New York, 1963.

26. G. Marcel, *The Existential Background of Human Dignity*, Harvard University Press, Cambridge, 1963.

27. E. J. Cassel, *London Free Press*, p. C3, September 18, 1986.

CHAPTER 4

The Right to Die and the Need to Grieve

E. W. Keyserlingk

The sub-title of this chapter is: *How can we say goodbye, if we won't let them go, if we won't let them die?* When I tried that out on one of my medical students, she thought it sounded like a title of a song by Dolly Parton! Be that as it may, the meaning of that sub-title will become clearer and even persuasive in the remarks which follow.

The patients of interest in this chapter are not the terminally ill in the usual sense of the term, that is, those who are dying and will die, often relatively soon, no matter what we do for them.

Those of us involved in bereavement issues and palliative care tend to focus most of our care and concern on those patients and their families and friends. Bereavement has been considered mainly in the context of the terminally ill patient, the patient who is dying, the patient who has died, the family and friends left behind. But there are some patients whose condition is horrendous and irreversible, whose prognosis is hopeless, who are totally or almost totally dependent on intensive medical support. Many if not most would have died in earlier times. But thanks to medical technology they are not terminally ill, not dying. And we won't let them die.

In some (and I underscore "some") of these cases the fact that the patient in question has been resuscitated and continues to be supported is not in my view testimony to our heroism, humanity and commitment. It testifies rather to our technical prowess, our cockeyed priorities and our sometimes great reluctance to tell patients and their families the truth.

By way of example, I refer specifically and especially to what is usually called in medical parlance the patient in a persistent vegetative state, the "PVS" patient, as a result of massive neurological damage and deterioration. Recent and very

31

public examples of such patients were Karen Ann Quinlan and Nancy Cruzan. Incidentally, "PVS" is a terribly insensitive term, one that should never be used with families of such patients. I use it here with apologies only because it has become the standard term for this condition. In clinical terms it involves massive and irreversible brain destruction resulting in irreversible coma. Patients with this condition are not medically or legally dead since they continue to have sufficient lower brain function to maintain unassisted respiration and circulation. Clinical and legal death requires the irreversible cessation of all brain functions [1].

The following applies to some other conditions as well, but one should avoid generalization in such matters. Therefore, concentration will be more or less exclusively on the PVS patient. The concern and focus will not be only on the interests and rights of those patients themselves but on their families, their friends and their health care providers, and what their experience with such a patient does to their grieving.

In other forums on other occasions I have claimed orally and in writing that such patients have a right to be allowed to die, to not be resuscitated should they arrest, and to have life-sustaining medical interventions stopped, including tube feeding, and that in some cases we, their community, family and health care providers have a duty to let that happen. I have so argued on the grounds that although they may well be feeling no pain or discomfort they remain persons, and therefore continue to have interests and rights. They retain the right not to be medically assaulted by no longer useful and justified treatment which violates their dignity and humanity, whether or not they feel discomfort.

Some are prepared to forego resuscitating PVS patients who arrest, and to stop other therapeutic and life prolonging interventions which have become therapeutically useless, but only if such patients have clearly expressed such a wish in advance in a living will or to a family member or friend. But that is equivalent to requiring people to ask physicians and hospitals in advance to please practice good and humane medicine. Why should people have to ask for that as if it is an exception to the rule? Why not make the practice of good medicine in this regard the rule [2]?

Since such patients cannot any longer express a wish, they rely on our sense of proportion, reality and humanity to carry out our duty by acknowledging the limits of aggressive medicine and doing the truly heroic thing by letting them go. Here is a different or at least additional focus. Not only are the interests and rights of those patients violated—but also the grieving processes of their family, friends and health care providers. I add this last group advisedly, since the grieving needs of health care professionals who care for these patients are too often ignored.

In brief because we don't let them go, we can't say goodbye. What follows are only some tentative reflections exploring the subject of grieving by family and friends for the patient who is no longer accessible to us, and never again will be, but is not dying and may linger on for months and years.

I know of a woman who became irreversibly comatose in 1943 and died last year. She was a twenty-two year old in 1943 and an elderly woman when she died after some fifty years of being unaware of her surroundings, in a fetal position, totally dependant on medical feeding, and routinely provided with antibiotics to heal infections and pneumonia. Most bereavement and palliative care literature and reflection has linked grieving with death and dying. But this other class of patient, an expanding one thanks to our growing skills in resuscitation and life support, has not yet attracted much attention from the bereavement community or bereavement literature.

Let me try to apply to this context, to those patients, and their families, friends and health care providers, some of the current findings and shared experience about grief when a family member is dying or has died. With families and friends of the irreversibly comatose patient there is almost always a short circuiting, an interruption, a blockage, a marking time, a needless and often unacknowledged prolongation in the grief process—in many cases with tragic results. Aspects of the concept of disenfranchised grief could help us to understand and better cope with grief in this context [3].

The exact label for the grief experienced in this context has so far escaped me. One of my students suggests "agriefus interruptus." Other candidates for the right label might be, "chronic or arrested anticipatory grief," or, "medically prolonged grief," or "grief aggravated and distorted by medicine."

In the meantime the already familiar concept and reality of "anticipatory grief" for dying patients appears to be a very useful one for these cases [4]. The notion and elements of anticipatory grief have been much analyzed and debated in recent years. I say "debated" because some continue to deny that such an animal exists [5]. Personally I have no such doubts. I have seen it and it is alive and well.

A first finding about anticipatory grief worth noting and applying here is that because grieving actually begins well before a dying loved one actually dies, there is the opportunity for preventive or therapeutic interventions before the death, which can sometimes facilitate grief work and a more positive post-death bereavement for the survivor-to-be. Turning now to our case— the irreversibly comatose husband, wife, child or friend. "Anticipatory" grief is in fact to some degree a misnomer [6]. Grieving, will have already begun in the face of real past and present losses, the loss of accessibility to the comatose husband, the loss of her husband's company and comfort, (he is not the person he was), the loss of dreams, of lifestyle, of a future that won't be realized, the progressive debilitation and continuing dependence, the wife being already forced to attend social functions alone, children having to accommodate to a missing father at their big moments. But since he is not dying because the staff or the family, or both, won't allow him to, there can't be the normal facilitating of the grieving process, the normal comforting with a view to assisting the post-death grief.

Up to a point the anticipatory grief model does apply not only in cases of fatal diagnosis, but also in these non-fatal cases of deep and irreversible coma. Up to a point so does the model of post death bereavement.

The difference is that though in cases of PVS the medical condition is often acknowledged to be irreversible, and the loss is in fact almost as substantial as death, for all intents and purposes as tragic and total a loss as death, yet that husband's or wife's or child's or friend's living physical presence is still there in the bed, and could be for many years, the blood is circulating, and air is pumping, whether artificially or not, despite the irreversible loss of higher brain function.

Almost every aspect of the losses involved in the death of a loved one are already present here, not just anticipated, but we have no language for what loved ones are experiencing—no legitimating concepts, no existing rituals. No outward grief for an impending or realized death is yet appropriate in such cases, because death isn't acknowledged, isn't allowed to happen. Given that the patient is stalled somewhere between life and death everyone is understandably awkward and uncertain. Friends are inclined to encourage with false hopes—"Don't give up—I heard of someone who recovered . . . ," disregarding or not knowing the evidence that the patient's massive neurological destruction makes recovery of awareness and function impossible.

In some cases, the intensity and tragedy and neverendingness of the protracted watching by the bedside, with no chance to get on with life has taken a terrible and unnecessary toll on the emotional and physical health of the mother, spouse or father, and indirectly on the rest of the family, especially the other children. Some will be torn apart by the conviction that their loved one could never have wanted this and that a terrible violence is being done. Such a one was Mrs. Quinlan, who wrote her thoughts and poems about the futility of it all in the long hours she spent waiting at the bedside while the doctors refused to stop the respirator and the courts deliberated.

Some other parents and spouses adopt an attitude of fierce determination to protect their comatose son, daughter, wife or husband from what they perceive to be the threatening doctor or nurse ready to pull the plug at any moment. I know of such a case in one of our hospitals, in which the family took shifts guarding the door all day and night for many months. They are not necessarily being paranoid, cruel and heartless, but are hanging on to a groundless hope of recovery, in some cases unwittingly planted by a doctor or nurse unwilling to tell them the truth at a much earlier point.

With these patients many of the small comforts and important opportunities for staff and family members to serve them are not available. Because they are generally institutionalized they are therefore doubly inaccessible in strange antiseptic surroundings far from home. Family and friends cannot feed them, that most basic and fundamental of caring and loving gestures. They are fed mechanically and impersonally by means of tubes. There are then no or few ways to mitigate the distress, to allow family and friends to serve, to care. These patients are very different from, for instance, the long term care chronic or dying patient. At least those in the latter category who are accessible or conscious can express needs and often appreciation as well. One can encourage and help them. They can often still enjoy some basic pleasures, a short walk, a book, music, a cup of tea, the presence of loved ones. They may still feel life is worth living, and so can the caregivers.

How did these patients get into this state? Why are they sometimes wrongfully resuscitated and/or not allowed to die? What practices and attitudes could we adopt in order to better respect their rights and the needs of their grievers?

At least four related factors appear to contribute to the problem:

1. Health care providers still sometimes put too much reliance on life saving interventions such as CPR (cardiopulmonary resuscitation) in the event of arrest, and are still too reluctant to give DNR (Do Not Resuscitate) orders when appropriate and recognize the limits of life support. CPR was originally intended and used to restore and extend life for patients who have a cardiac arrest as a result of an acute incident such as a drug overdose, a complication of a procedure or anaesthesia, or an acute myocardial infarction. Physicians sometimes have not done their homework as to its short range and long range effectiveness given a variety of patient conditions and prospects. CPR and some forms of life support have become too routine despite the fact that it is becoming increasingly clear that for many conditions CPR will be of no long range benefit, and in fact may well leave the patient worse off. It is a desperate technique that works relatively infrequently and in many types of patients virtually never [7].

2. Some physicians and families almost routinely equate the cessation of life support or the non-resuscitation of patients when it is biologically possible, with killing or active euthanasia. But to make such an equation in disregard of the circumstances such as prospects of recovery can be simplistic and erroneous, both morally and legally. Some feel that having begun some form of life support such as a respirator or medical nourishment, they are morally and legally obliged to continue until biological death, as if there is a morally significant difference between not starting and discontinuing. In fact, it may have been justified to begin life support in view of the patient's condition and available information at that time, but it may have become unjustified now in view of that patient's present condition and prospects.

3. Sometimes in the guise of a distorted respect for the autonomy of patients and family, and/or a reluctance to give the family the bad news, to tell them the truth, they are offered a choice when there is no choice, two or more options when there is only one in the patient's interests. All too often the family of a presently irreversibly comatose patient will be asked whether they would like CPR to be used if the patient arrests, or whether they want the respirator to continue, when in fact the medical staff know or should know that it will be of no benefit, it may even leave the patient in still worse shape. To the staff's surprise the family says yes, continue. But it should not be a surprise. It is hardly surprising that a family,

when offered a choice, one of which is to prolong the life of a loved one, will latch on to any apparent reason for hope, and that it will interpret the offer of this choice as meaning there must be hope—otherwise why would the doctors offer them a choice?

4. Sometimes a family simply won't listen to the bad news, despite full disclosure, and insists that life support continue, or if the patient arrests that he or she be resuscitated. Some health care teams are too inclined to do whatever the family wants, on the grounds that, after all, the patient is probably beyond pain and discomfort, so why not in effect, make the family the patient. If the family is comforted by needlessly supporting or resuscitating that patient, so be it, is the misconceived rationale here. Such a view ignores the fact that to do so is a violation of the dignity of such patients, and of their right not to be medically assaulted.

What can we do to ease the problem?

1. Health care providers and patient families should become aware or be made aware that in a number of circumstances the law does not consider the cessation of life support (such as respirators or tube feeding), or not resuscitating a patient, to be a form of killing or euthanasia. If a competent patient refuses such interventions (now or in advance), or if they are no longer therapeutically useful on quality of life or patient prospect grounds, then their cessation or non-provision are not legally the cause of the patient's death, not killing or euthanasia. The cause of death is the patient's condition, not the medical "omission." Patients have a right to refuse medical interventions, including life-prolonging ones. If they are unable to express a wish, their families or legal guardians have the right and the duty to decide for them in their best interests. Sometimes their best interests will require stopping life supporting and life saving interventions including tube feeding, because it has become therapeutically useless and to continue would be a form of medical assault. When justified, such decisions have nothing whatever in common with killing.

2. We must tell the truth to families—if the prospects are poor or non-existent, then we must say so—sensitively of course, but also directly and clearly. To protect them (or ourselves) from the truth is not only a form of paternalism, but denies patients and families the opportunity to make informed decisions and preparations, and can lead to the sort of aborted, arrested bereavement we have been discussing. Much experience and many surveys attest to the fact that we (all of us) are still not good at doing that. Honesty and directness are easier to take if accompanied by the sincerely meant assurance that though aggressive and life-prolonging measures have to stop, caring and palliative measures will continue. In such cases we are changing the approach, not deserting the patient.

3. Don't offer choices when there are none. First of all, it is dishonest to ask the families of such patients if they want their loved one to be resuscitated or prolonged when the patient's condition and prospects make those no longer realistic options in the patient's interest. Secondly, the very fact that the family is being offered resuscitation and life prolongation will be taken to mean that there

must be hope whether meant that way or not. The family may then be inclined to choose that option since not to do so seems to be contributing to the death of their loved one.

4. Don't let families tie our hands, when what they want is clearly not in the patient's and their best interests. They do have rights to decide, but only within the scope of what is best for patient. Our laws provide that surrogate decisions can be made, but always in the patient's best interests. They cannot insist on clearly futile treatment. When it is ambiguous and there are options and it is legitimate to go on or stop, then of course the decision is the family's or other legal representative's to make. It is not doing the family any favour to go on supporting their loved one when it has become meaningless. They will become the victims of that decision along with the patient. We may have to say no to them for the patient's good and theirs. If they continue to disagree despite careful and sensitive explanations over a period of time, then one side or the other can of course apply for authorization to continue or to stop. Clearly such recourse should always be a last resort in view of its potential for divisiveness.

Finally, some cautions and disclaimers: I am not suggesting that there is, or should be, any magical short cut whereby we can always protect loved ones from grief. On the contrary, why would we want to do that. I am in fact proposing the opposite. In these cases of irreversible and prolonged coma, we should try to unblock what is obstructing a healthy process of grief, make it likelier that "healthy" grief can begin and evolve—allowing loved ones get on with their lives.

Let's not dump all the blame, all the responsibility in this matter on health care professionals, especially doctors and nurses. This is a community problem. Doctors and nurses often do extremely well—most are honest and empathetic, with no illusions about available technology. Sometimes family members don't want to let go of their loved one and can make protecting their family member almost a full time profession. That is neither surprising nor blameworthy; if we want doctors and nurses to persuade families to let go and be prepared to let go themselves, they will need more support and approval of such a policy by the larger community.

I am not proposing that we casually "let everyone go." We should be very careful about generalizing. I have deliberately argued my case in the narrow context of one type of disorder. Those same reasons may well apply to some other serious medical conditions but certainly not to all.

This analysis is in no sense meant to make a case against "high tech" medicine, CPR, ICU, etc. These and other interventions comprise a very important array of techniques for saving life and improving health. I have tried only to make a case against their use when inappropriate.

REFERENCES

1. Law Reform Commission of Canada, *Criteria for the Determination of Death*, Report to Parliament No. 15, Ottawa, 1981.

2. E. W. Keyserlingk, The Right to Natural Death, *Humane Medicine, 1,* pp. 37-40, 1985.
3. K. Doka, *Disenfranchised Grief: Recognizing Hidden Sorrow,* Lexington Books, Lexington, 1989.
4. T. A. Rando (ed.), *Loss and Anticipatory Grief,* Lexington Books, Lexington, 1986.
5. C. M. Parkes and R. W. Weiss, *Recovery from Bereavement,* Basic Books, New York, 1983.
6. T. A. Rando, Anticipatory Grief: The Term is Misnomer, but the Phenomenon Exists, *Journal of Palliative Care, 4,* pp. 70-73, 1988.
7. L. J. Blackhall, *Must We Always Use CPR?, 317:*20, pp. 1281-1285, 1987.
8. E. W. Keyserlingk, *Sanctity of Life or Quality of Life in the Context of Ethics, Medicine and Law,* Law Reform Commission of Canada, Ottawa, 1979.

CHAPTER 5

Grieving: The Pain and the Promise

Deanna Edwards

When you think of the word "grieving," what words come to your mind? Sadness, sorrow, fear, tears, loss, growth, love, pain, hurt. . . . If you work in hospice or you work with dying patients or with the elderly, as I do, so often people ask, "Isn't your work depressing?" What does that say to you? It's really a persons way of saying "I'm afraid, I'm really afraid of what you do, so your work must be depressing."

I was on a radio talk show with a very wide listening audience and the radio announcer asked me: "What kinds of songs do you write Deanna?" I said, "In our country, because we live in a death, age, and pain denying society most of our patients, people who are grieving, those who have handicapped children, and the elderly have no musical voice. There is a tremendous void in musical literature in our country addressing these topics." I told the announcer, "I write about those feelings that are not commercial. The commercial feelings are falling in love, 'sleeping around,' and falling out of love feelings. The purpose of a song is to 'express what I feel.' So I write about feelings that very much need to be addressed that aren't selling very well." He again asked, "What kinds of songs do you write?" I answered, "Songs for the sick, the dying, and the elderly." He looked appalled and said, "Do people really listen to this kind of morbid and depressing music?" I found a perfect opportunity to teach and I said "Only people who are afraid use words like 'morbid' and 'depressing'." He changed the subject very quickly.

Music is not just entertainment, it is both a powerful therapy and teaching tool. Music can help to mend broken bodies as well as broken hearts. It also helps us to teach about difficult subjects in a gentle and non-threatening way. Music defuses the tremendous explosive effect that grief can have in the sense that I can be safe when I am singing or listening to music and you can be safe when you are participating in a music experience. However we should never use music to exploit human emotions. If I am singing for a group of people who have experienced tragic losses I explain the power of music and tell them they are free to leave for awhile if they hear a song that is too overwhelming for them to listen to in that moment. They are always free to come back and join the group when they are ready to do so. Music can put us in touch with our deepest feelings. It transcends the physical and touches the soul. This is why music is one of the most important tools we can use in grief counseling.

We can use music in many ways and there is a great deal of research that needs to be done. In the United States over a hundred universities offer what we call a "Registered Music Therapy" degree. The field is constantly growing and expanding. As I share music with you, I hope you will be able to think of new ways to apply music in your chosen field in the helping professions.

Two years ago I was asked by my publisher to write a book about grieving. They told me I had only ten days to write it because they wanted it in time for a booksellers conference. The first book I wrote took me seventeen years, so at first it seemed an impossible task. Then I began to look through my files and I discovered wonderful letters and poems that have been shared with me over the years. It was from people like you, your strength, your energy, your insight and your wisdom that the book happened. During my research I made what was to me a profound discovery. I began to associate the word **grieving** with the word **loving**.

Wanda Hilton, a dear friend of mine, came to my home one day. She had suffered a great deal. Her young son had been killed in a sledding accident. She had a severely handicapped daughter, and her husband was terminally ill with cancer. She herself was to die within a year after giving me a very special gift. She handed me some poems she had written and said "When my little son died I discovered that grief is a very powerful creative force and that if we create something beautiful when we're hurting we can use what we have created to help others. If you could take these poems and use them to help someone else it would mean so much to me." One of the poems was entitled, *If One More Day*. It changed my life and I hope it can change yours too.

If One More Day

I did not hold you warmly,
Close within my arms enough.
I did not cup your sweet child face
And look deeply in your eyes enough.
I did not smooth your soft and ruffled hair enough,
Or listen to your precious words
Or hear your tumbling laughter.

I did not look upon you
In your quiet sleep enough

Or kneel and pray out gratitude enough
As I beheld you sleeping thus.
I was not soft, patient, kind,
Indulgent half enough
In my administrations to you.
I do not carry the exact impress of you
Indelibly enough upon me
And in me and through me.
Oh, to have you back just one more day.

My eyes would never leave you.
I would memorize you with every sense
And repeat you with tender
And delicate precision.
I would store up unforgettable impressions
On my very soul
To mitigate this primal loss
If you were here **just one more day!**[1]

There is so much power in this poem because it taught me that we don't have to wait until loss comes to live life with passion. I can memorize you with every sense and repeat you with tender and delicate precision, as I do with my family and close friends. Because of such creative expressions I can live each day as if it were the last day of my life. So the word I have come to associate closely with **grieving** is the word **loving**. Perhaps the most significant line I ever wrote in a song is a very simple one:

If we could take the sorrow from every loss that comes along, we'd have to take the loving out of life.

Is there anyone here who would be willing to make that trade so we would never have to hurt again? Would we forfeit our capacity to love in order to avoid pain? We couldn't do that, so love and grief go together. Sorrow speaks only from the depth and the clarity of our love. The thought is expressed in the song, **Love Is All That Matters**, from my new album, **Share Love's Light.**

Love Is All That Matters

Some search long for wisdom,
Others search for gold.
While some reach out for power
Some just want a hand to hold.

---

[1] Used by permission, © 1989 *Grieving: The Pain and the Promise,* Deanna Edwards, Covenant, Inc. American Fork, Utah, p. 64.

When joy is found in giving
And wealth is found in friends
You'll know LOVE IS ALL THAT MATTERS
In the end.

Chorus

Love is all that matters
And love is all I need,
Just a song to break the silence
And a time to plant the seed.
When we've travelled
Life's long highway
And we look around the bend
We'll know LOVE IS ALL THAT MATTERS
In the end.

Love can fill the hunger;
Love can show the way.
It gives a heart a reason
For living life today.
It takes us on the journey
And brings us home again
For LOVE IS ALL THAT MATTERS
In the end.[2]

The idea for a song was born in a convent in St. Louis, Moussuri. I was co-presenting there with a trauma chaplain who works at Cook County Hospital in Chicago. Having gone through the recent deaths of my beloved sister, and a close friend, I was struggling with my owns sense of loss. He wisely pointed out some unresolved grief as we were preparing for the seminar. Later that evening I entered a beautiful cathedral on the grounds. I asked God how he could use me when I felt so broken inside. I thought of a wonderful saying I had heard years before.

People are like stained glass windows. They sparkle and shine when the sun
is out but when darkness falls and adversity comes their only true beauty is
revealed if there is a light from within. (author unknown.)

I began to think that if there is a light within us perhaps the only way for the light to get out is through the cracks in our hearts and that God can use us, even in our brokenness, to help and to heal others. As Earl Grollman has said: "We are all

[2] Used by permission. © 1990 from the album, *Share Love's Light*, Deanna Edwards, Rock Canyon Music Publishers, 777 E. Walnut, Provo, Utah 84604.

searching for those missing puzzle pieces of our lives." That's one of the reasons many of us are doing what we do, not only to learn how to help those we serve but to help ourselves. So this song means that we must allow those little cracks inside us to be used as windows, so the light can come out and shine for other people who need to see our light.

Broken Windows

There is pain in me that you cannot see.
I can hide all my tears with a smile.
In my darkest night I can see your light.
Let me walk by your side for awhile

Chorus

Let the light of love shine through!
Let the light of love shine through.
Through the broken windows in our wounded hearts
Let the light of love shine through!

Love is worth the price
That we have to pay
But we can't make the journey alone.
Let me care for you as you care for me
For the promise and pain are as one.

A few years ago I was invited to teach at a little country church in Tracy, Minnesota. As I was about to begin the program, the pastor of the church showed me a small clipping he had cut from the want ad section of the *Tracy Headlight Herald* newspaper. It said simply: "Wanted: One Family to eat Christmas dinner with. I will furnish the turkey." It was placed there by an elderly man who lived alone in the community. It broke my heart that someone would have to place a want ad to be loved so I wrote a song with a special chorus . . .

Wanted: one family to share my Christmas day.
Wanted: one friend to take the loneliness away.
I'm not asking much of you.
I'll only stay an hour or two.
I'll even bring the turkey if you call.
It's been a long and lonely day
Since I have watched a child at play
And children are the greatest gifts of all.

The song was recorded on an album called *Two Little Shoes.* My niece, who was only eight years old, asked me to go back to Minnesota and find this old man so she could write to him. I called the pastor and told him I could return for a repeat performance at the little church, providing this elderly man would attend so I could meet him. He was standing on the top of the stone steps of the church when I arrived. His name was Joe Smarzik. I told him I had written a song for him and he said, "No one has ever written a song for me before." The tears slipped down his cheeks as I sang. When I finished I asked him, "Joe, why did you place that want ad in the paper?" He replied, "Because people are too busy."

I thought of a wonderful "sermon in a sentence" I had heard one day in the form of a question. "Is there a difference between loving someone and paying attention to them?" So we decided to pay attention to Joe. When KSL radio in Salt Lake City began to play the song before Christmas I was invited to come in for an interview. "Is it OK if we give his address out over the air?" I asked—then told the audience his address. Within a few weeks we received an article from the *Tracy Headlight Hearld* with a picture of Joe, bringing the mail in buckets because he couldn't carry it all. Five hundred cards and letters poured into his mail box, banana bread and cookies and pictures from little grade school children. Many of their letters said, "You can come to our house for Christmas dinner and you won't even have to bring the turkey." After the story made the front page of the *Minneapolis Star,* Joe received a letter from the President of the United States. President Regan had enclosed a copy of a picture of him and his wife, Nancy. It was so exciting to receive a phone call from Joe last year.

> "Joe where are you?" I asked.
> "Greenriver, Wyoming," he replied.
> "What are you doing that far from home." I wanted to know.
> He said, "There is a family here who wrote to me and now they are cooking me a turkey dinner. I received so many letters and cards from Utah I did not have time to answer them all. So I'm coming to Utah to say 'thank you' in person for all the love I received."

It may not have seemed so unusual except that Joe was eighty-four years old, had a heart condition, and jumped into a 1976 pickup truck and drove 2700 miles round trip to say "thanks." I hurriedly arranged for radio, television, and newspaper interviews and Joe ended up on the front page of the *Desert News.* In the article he said, "You are all invited to my house this Christmas and I will furnish the turkey."

The beautiful thing about this story is that people respond to love. From broken hearts come great lights. It was Teilhart de Chardin who said, "Someday, after mastering the winds, and the waves of the tides of gravity, we shall harness, for God, the energies of love—and then, for the second time in the history of the world, man will have created fire." Maybe, that is what we are trying to do— harness the energies of love. We are looking for ways to comfort, to heal. There is no greater mission in my mind than to reach out and comfort those who are hurting, and we always find ourselves healed in the process, as Joe was. As he received all those cards and letters he found himself wanting to give back. I guess that's what grief does for us. It makes us want to give back to those who have reached out to us.

Whenever I am in Canada I tell my audiences that in America people never die and they never cry. Before I can explain I often hear several people whisper, "Then we're moving to America!" Instead of "dying" people pass on, pass away, expire, expirate, terminate, depart, decease, kick the bucket, jump in the chariot when it swings low, give up the ghost and go onto their eternal rest. If you are a native American you go to the "happy hunting grounds." Nobody dies. My son and I were visiting England. I decided if nobody dies there maybe we could move to England! As we were wandering through a small cemetery in Stroud I noticed on many of the head stones the words, "He(or she) **Fell Asleep.**" I wondered how a little kid feels, after going through such a cemetery, when Mom says, "Honey, it's time to go to sleep!" The child may say, "No Way! I know what happens when you go to sleep!" So they have trouble dying in England too. It must be a universal tendency to avoid the word, "death." We also have difficulty with tears. When someone is describing another person who is crying it is not uncommon to hear an American say, "You should have seen Martha. She just broke down, lost control, fell apart and went to pieces!" It's not easy for us to look upon tears as a gift of trust, a gift of love.

There was a time, because of this cultural denial, when I was afraid too. I had no education about the subject in the schools I attended or the communities in which I lived. In my family we never talked about death. When I reached the age of twenty and was preparing to be married, I invited my father, who was divorced from my mother when I was three years old, to come to my wedding. Dad said, "Honey I am very sick, but I will expect you to visit me after the honeymoon."

Shortly after our honeymoon I went to see my father. He was being cared for by some friends in a little white farm house. As I walked into the room and my father turned to greet me, I suddenly saw how emaciated and jaundiced he was. I needed no physician or nurse to tell me my father was dying. As soon as I became aware of his impending death I experienced what I call "verbal isolation," I began to play the game, "I'll pretend that I don't know you know if you'll pretend that you don't know I know." During the long summer my father was sick we talked about very superficial things . . . what was going on at school and how the weather was. So the summer passed and the passion I felt was lost in my fear so we never talked about our feelings. When October came, and the leaves were beginning to turn to gold on the trees, he did something very beautiful. He pulled my head down to his chest and whispered in my ear, "Deanna, I love you." "I love you too, Dad," I said, noticing that we had never shared our love with quite that awareness before. It seemed to erase all those games we had played, but it did not erase my fear.

My second denial was what I call "emotional isolation." I didn't cry when my father died. Using my faith as a reason to avoid the grief work I thought, "I have so much faith that I don't have to cry." Of course, at that time I did not know grief was hard work and a necessary part of the recovery process.

My third denial was "physical isolation." I did not go to the hospital in my father's final hours, nor did I attend his funeral service. Afraid that I would retain a negative memory picture if I saw my father in a casket I told everyone I didn't feel well. It wasn't until nine years later that I began to realize I had a problem.

A friend invited me to become a volunteer at a local hospital when we were living in central Illinois. A nurse and I started a music program there, singing to patients. After I sang the song, "You've Got a Friend," in the room of a cancer patient, she looked at me and said, "How did you know that I am dying?" I suddenly saw my father's face in her face. She needed a friend, someone to talk to, but I found myself unable to help her. I began to realize that unless I faced my own fears and feelings about death I could not help others. The nurse I worked with invited me to go with her to Carbondale, Illinois, where Dr. Elisabeth Kübler-Ross was giving a lecture. That was the beginning of a very special journey, a journey that would help me to overcome my fears. She invited us to participate with her in a five day retreat. I met a wonderful counselor there named Dick Obershaw, founder of the Burnsville Grief Counseling Clinic in Burnsville, Minnesota. I wish every community had a Dick Obershaw and a grief counseling clinic. When he began to question me about my father's death I felt very uncomfortable. I told him I didn't know much about it because I wasn't there. When he asked me why I wasn't there I was irritated as first, and finally I was able to say, "Because I was afraid."

He suggested **four principles** that helped me work through my own pain and enabled me to help many others.

He suggested that I go back to my father's bedside and in a letter, journal, role-playing setting or in a support group, share with my father all the things I wished I had said before he died. That's when I learned that grief work can be done in retrospect. There are things we can do long after a loss has occurred, that can help us. "Verbal freedom" can be a good beginning!

The first word that came to my mind was, "thank you." "Thank you for all the things you gave me that money cannot buy; my unshakable faith in people, my belief in their goodness, my optimism." While others complained about snow my father would say, "Look how gently the arms of the trees are holding the snow." I thanked him for teaching me that it's better to have a dream that never comes true than never to dream at all, because the last gift he gave me was a story he had written which he hoped would be made into a movie. I thanked him for teaching me to love waterfalls and wildflowers and chided him for cultivating my love for donuts! I thanked him, most of all, for cultivating my love for music. It has been a great gift in my life. He taught me all the old songs he knew and loved and I am passing them on to my children and the people I teach. To a man who felt he had failed his family what would those words have meant to him? I couldn't help writing a song after the conference to express some of my gratitude for my father.

Where Have All the Dreamers Gone?

He never had a dime to spare.
His suit was faded grey.
The only things he cared to own
Were those he gave away.
We used to drive in Dad's old car
And talk of things to be,
And I still recall a question
My Daddy asked of me.

Chorus

Where have all the dreamers gone?
When did hope get lost?
Sometimes we have to take a risk
And never count the cost.
And though our dreams may not come true
As our curtain starts to fall,
I'd rather have a broken dream
Than never dream at all.

The years have passed, and Dad's old car
Has finally turned to rust.
His poems that lay unfinished
Have crumbled into dust.
But I have a dream to change the world
And sing love's legacy.
My daddy was a dreamer
And he gave this dream to me.[3]

The second thing Dick suggested was to give myself emotional freedom. Sometimes we look at freedom from the outside in instead of from the inside out. We appreciate a democratic way of life, the ability to travel, the freedom to write what we want to write, the freedom of speech. All of these are very important, cherished freedoms. But sometimes we overlook what it means to be free inside. I'm not sure I truly understood that until I visited Berlin last summer. I had gone to East Berlin with my son a few years earlier. He is a gifted linguist and speaks fluent German, so we spoke with and felt the pain of people who wanted to be free, but were separated from freedom by a giant wall that cast a dark shadow over their country. Then the Berlin wall fell, something I thought I would never see in my lifetime. As we watched a world away a picture on television caught my heart. A

---

[3] Used by permission. © 1988 from the album, *Music Brings My Heart Back Home*, Deanna Edwards, Rock Canyon Music Publishers, Provo, Utah.

Where Have All the Dreamers Gone?

Arranged by
Greg Hansen

Words and Music by
Deanna Edwards

man, with tears streaming down his face, his daughter cradled in his arms, was running into the open arms of freedom through a hole in that wall. I thought—I have to see this myself and be an eyewitness to history! So I went to Berlin and was met at the train station by a wonderful taxi driver named Richard. Richard was an older man with a faded green jacket and a very wise heart! In him I found a tour guide, a financial advisor and a friend. He took me to some of the sections of the wall that were still standing. I don't know where he found the metal hammer and chisel but he put them in my hands. As I hit the wall harder and harder it hurt and I realized how difficult it would be to break off pieces of it. As Richard watched me quietly he made an observation that I will never forget. He said, "It's not the walls we build around our cities that represent the greatest danger. It's the walls we build around our hearts. To these we must apply the mortal blows that we may know the greater freedom from within."

Freedom from within! I began to wonder what it means to live the freedom of the heart, and decided to make it my life-long quest to find out. Is it the freedom to laugh, to cry and to be who you really are? John Powell said, "I'm afraid to tell you who I really am because you may not like who I am and I'm all I have." Sometimes we grow up with a family, growing old together yet never growing to know each other. So I went back to my hotel and wrote a poem.

The Wall

I stood at the wall with hammer and chisel poised
And threw my might against the metal in my hand.
It would take far greater strength than mine
To loosen bits of concrete from this giant barricade.
It stood, a monument to shame, man's inhumanity to man,
Stripped of it's power and it's name.
I wondered where the blood was shed
Of those who gave their lives
To cross it and to conquer it.
Freedom was dearer far than slavery to them
And we, the benefactors of the price they had to pay.
Rainbow colors crossed it's face.
Some, daring to challenge the arrogance
Of unrighteous dominion, had written in words
 Never to fade from human consciousness . . .
We Have the Right To Be Free.
And now those vital words were being chipped away,
Soon to be scattered far and wide,
The cry of every human soul inscribed in seven words
Upon the ancient page of history!
The tragedy and triumph, in tiny bits of stone . . .
Tragedy that it was ever built—
Triumph that it fell before a power

Greater than its own!
Could this same structure rise again
If those who held aloft the flame
Of freedom were not vigilant?
I saw him standing near the wall
With aging face and graying hair.
An audience he found in me.
I listened to him quietly.
"The greater danger lies,
Not in the walls we build around our cities
But in the walls we build around our hearts!
To these we must apply the mortal blows
That we may know the greater freedom from within!"
I wish I had asked him to explain
The further meaning of this truth.
He had lived around these walls for years
And knew the close proximity of freedom and of tyranny.
Was it freedom to lift every man to God,
Regardless of his race or creed?
Freedom to affirm the right to be,
The legacy of all humanity?
I knew t'was my own mortal task
To learn to know the greatest art . . .
To come to know the power of love—
To Live the Freedom of the Heart![4]

As I begin this life-long quest, I am only now learning what it means to be free of heart. A part of that freedom can be defined in the freedom to laugh, to cry and to be who we really are.

When I think of the power of laughter and the power of tears, several of my mentors come to mind. One is Father Rick Arkfeld, a Catholic priest who lives in Nebraska. One day he called me on the phone and said, "Deanna, I want you to come to my parish because we are going to have a big celebration. We need three ingredients; music, laughter, and tears. You can bring those with you!"

"Just what are we celebrating, Father?" I asked.

"I've just been told by my physician that I have lung cancer and may not have long to live," he said.

After a shocked silence I exclaimed, "Father, have you lost your mind? I love you and I don't want you to die! Why are you celebrating this diagnosis?"

He was quiet for a moment and then said, "Can't you understand? This is my opportunity to teach people to die with dignity and grace and with a sense of humor. Are you going to help me or not?"

[4] Reprinted by permission, Deanna Edwards, Rock Canyon Music Publishers, Provo, Utah. © 1990.

"I'm coming, Father!" I exclaimed with no hesitation. "You can teach me too!"

Six hundred people from the parish and surrounding communities came to celebrate life and to talk about death. Father Rick addressed the audience and gave each one a sense that death is just another window in our lives, another chapter. We don't have to be perpetually sad and we can learn to talk about it. I provided the added dimension of singing about it. Father put us at ease with some of his "grave news" stories. I'd like to share one of them with you.

A priest was giving a sermon on preparation for death. At the end of the talk he summarized loudly: "One day, every man, woman, and child in this parish will die." A man in the second pew began to laugh so Father repeated solemnly: "One day, every man, woman, and child in this parish will die." The priest then asked the man in his congregation why he was still laughing. Grinning broadly, the man replied: "I'm not from your parish!"

Father already has his head stone picked out. On one side is a serious theological message, "I will be standing, waiting and watching, at the bank of the river of death to take you home." When you walk around the other side of the headstone the epitaph reads, "I told you I was sick!"

"It will be great to know that in a hundred years people will laugh when they walk by this. You only die once. Let it be you and your personality!" said Father Rick.

"The best way to prepare for death is to live life! Sell your farm, spend your money and go live with your kids. If you don't, they will spend the rest of their lives fighting with each other! There are some people who die when they are age twenty-seven and fall over when they are eighty-three. They share common characteristics . . . they don't like birthdays, noise and dirt, and what they buy owns them. The don't like kids. But someday we'll have to break things, spill the milk and go to heaven because only people who are like little kids will get there!"

As Father concluded his speech he spoke the most profound words of all: **"Fear does not come from God. Courage does."**

Father Rick has been too busy to die in the last several years and we've had some wonderful experiences together doing workshops and travelling through Nebraska. But I was with Father Rick two weeks ago and I noticed that he can't carry my suitcase into the parish house as he used to because he is becoming weaker. But his sparkle and his inner courage have never diminished.

Equally as important as laughter is the ability to cry. I have four sons so I have had to teach them that great men can cry. When children are very small we start to program them: "You were such a brave boy when you got that penicillin shot that you didn't even cry." "I am so proud of you that you didn't cry when you cut your head and had to have stitches." We praise children for not crying and often scold them when they do. One little boy of seven was told at the funeral service of his father, "Don't cry, son. You're the man of the family now." Can you imagine growing up being told all the time how wise and brave you are when you withhold feelings and lock them inside? Is it any wonder we have problems with tears when we get older? If I could give three gifts to those I love they would appear in this song I wrote for my children . . .

Music, Laughter and Tears

"The toys are all broken you opened last year
And your coat isn't new like before.
Your puzzle is missing some pieces, I fear,
And your train set won't run anymore.
Your teddy is missing his black button nose
And you're tired of the old games we play,
But I have something special to give you, my son.
Don't forget what I'm giving today.

I want to give something that never grows old,
Sweet moments to warm you when
Life is turning cold.
What gifts can I give you
To last through the years?
I'll give you music, laughter and tears![5]

I had a wonderful experience at a workshop in the midwest. There were three ladies sitting in the second row and they all began to cry at once. The lady in the middle had only one tissue so she graciously tore this in three pieces and handed a piece to the ladies on each side of her. Finally one of the ladies said, "I'm going for the toilet paper!" We had a wonderful time passing this paper around because we were freeing our hearts, tearing down those wall we had built so solidly.

I remember once when my youngest son, Eric, fell from his favorite pear tree. A branch betrayed him and he fell to the ground with big cuts and abrasions on his tummy. We took him to the doctor and the doctor said, "Eric, you're such a big, brave boy I'll bet you didn't cry when you fell from that tree and you're going to be so brave you're not going to cry when I fix up these cuts on your tummy, are you?"

Very defiantly, our four year old looked into the doctor's eyes and exclaimed, **"I did too cry when I fell from that pear tree."** Then he added, "I cried **a lot!**"

Later I told Eric I was proud of him for defending his right to cry and that someday when he grew up he would be able to cry with the people he loved. There was a little girl, Jennifer, a four-year-old who was watching a sad movie with her mother. When the tears began to run down Jennifer's cheeks she caught her

---

[5] Reprinted by permission, Epoch Universal Publications, Phoenix, Arizona © 1978 from the album, *Music, Laughter and Tears,* Deanna Edwards.

mother's glance and quickly said, "I'm not crying, Mommy. I just drank too much water and now it's coming out of my eyes!" He mother quickly said, "That's OK, honey. That's the way God gave us to get the hurt out." Another little boy who was crying said, "I'm not crying, Mom. I just have nervous eyes."

I have a wonderful friend, Dr. Walter O'Connel, who said this: "The experience of natural lows is essential to happiness. Sharing tears about unwanted endings, unrealized ideals, and insufficient time and energy is practice for your own self growth. Again, no blame, shame, guilt or inferiority complexes over the tears of human compassion. Tears are gifts. They are not symptoms."

What would it be like if you could never cry again? I had never thought about it until I received the following letter:

Dear Mrs. Edwards,

I heard you speak at Kettering Memorial Hospital in Ohio. In February, 1965, I was a senior in highschool. After school I was in the first car stopped at a red light and another car going the opposite direction, ran the light and hit my car head on. I was thrown through the windshield five times. That evening I had my brain operated on. The next year my shoulder, the next year my eye. The eye doctor said that my condition was worsening and there was nothing he could do. He referred me to an internationally known physician. Glass had scraped my eyes and punctured my pupils. There was muscle and nerve damage. There is no natural moisture when I blink so I cannot cry. I get choked and my face gets all screwed up but there are no tears. I have prayed and pleaded that I may cry. Before the doctor operated the first time I asked if I would be able to cry. Very compassionately Dr. Bullock replied, "Oh, Trina I hope so!" [6]

I recently received another letter from Trina. A new surgical procedure has enabled her to cry for the first time since 1965 and she wanted me to be the first to know! So I celebrate the gift of tears with Trina and I celebrate tears with you because it is a part of our humanness—the "emotional freedom" that Dick advised me to give myself.

The third suggestion Dick advised was to "do for significant others what you failed to do for your father." This works beautifully. Now I try to give this gift to my family, my friends and all the people I teach. After suggesting this idea in one of my workshops I received a letter from a woman who wrote, "You know, when my grandpa was in the nursing home I always used to take him to see the Christmas lights during the holiday season. But one Christmas I was too busy shopping and wrapping presents and cooking, so I didn't take Grandpa out. Shortly after Christmas he died. I felt this tremendous guilt for a long time. Now I

---

[6] Used by permission. © 1989 *Grieving: The Pain and the Promise,* Covenant, Inc. American Fork, Utah, pp. 88-89.

know that I can go to the nursing home every year and take someone else's grandma or grandpa to see the Christmas lights."

Sometimes it is hard for us to give this help to the people closest to us, even when we have been involved in this work for many years. We can lose objectivity when it is our own loved one who is suffering. I remember when my father-in-law was diagnosed with stomach cancer. This time there were no games. I had tried out the strategy of avoidance and found it not to be effective. So I let him know that I knew that he knew. I offered to talk with him at any time about his feelings, even in the middle of the night. When he was dying I flew in an all-night race against time, from the East coast to the West coast, so I could be there for him. He died two hours before my arrival, but I involved myself all the way. I had learned the meaning of "grief work," the work we do to reclaim control that has been taken from us. We cannot control the event that has happened, but we can control our response to that event. I went to the funeral home, helped pick out the casket and helped with arrangements for the funeral. But when my brother-in-law asked me to sing at the funeral service I had second thoughts. "I'll fall apart and break down," I told him. We are programmed to fail at our own grief work, so we often turn over some very significant tasks to other people when we could perhaps do them best ourselves.

"Who do you think Dad would rather have sing than you?" Glen asked me.

That was a different story. I could not think of anyone who would be better qualified to take my place. So I consented to sing. Shortly before the funeral service I began to wonder what I should sing but there seemed to be no songs that really captured who my father-in-law was. So I wrote one for him and was amazed when I got up to sing how much strength I had. I could stay on my feet, I could perform, even through my tears.

You're Going Home

Oh, Dad, you gave us so much we can be thankful for.
By your faith you've shown us all that love is an open door.
You lit so many candles that we all could feel the glow
And now it's hard, so very hard, to let you go.

Going home, going home, to the arms of love.
You've seen his face, you have a place
Now you're with God above.
And with all His warmth around you
You will never be alone.
The pain is gone, and life goes on,
You're going home![7]

---

[7] Used by permission. © 1988 from the album, *Music Brings My Heart Back Home,* Deanna Edwards, Rock Canyon Music Publishers, Provo, Utah.

I have found within myself what Martin Gray calls, "The Fragile Miracle hidden within us all." I hope all of you will read his book, *For Those I Loved.* It is wonderful and very sad. I cried for days after reading his book. Martin was a child street guerrilla fighter in the Warsaw, Poland ghettos during World War II. Eventually his entire family was taken to a concentration camp where they were put to death. Part of Martin's job in that camp was to take bodies from the gas chambers and carry them to graves of yellow sand. He escaped in a trainload of Jewish clothing and joined the partisans in the forest, continuing in the war effort. After the war was over he moved to America where he made a fortune selling antiques. He met a beautiful Dutch girl named Dina. Dina and Martin found a lovely stone farm house in the south of France, in the small village of Tanneron. He delivered his four children, two daughters and two sons, because he wanted to "feel" their lives in those first moments of existence. One day, as they were having lunch, they smelled smoke. The area had been known for forest fires when the weather was very dry, and it had not rained in Tanneron for a long time. Even though they had been told by local peasants to stay in their homes at such a time the children were frightened. Dina said she would take the children down to the village of Mandelieu, on the shores of the Mediterranean. Martin decided to rescue a bedridden neighbor and meet them later. As Dina drove down the winding mountain road, smoke from the fire obscured her vision and her car went off the road. She and all four children perished in that fire. Though he was terribly devastated, Martin decided to plant beside a dead tree, a tree of life. He wrote a book which became an international bestseller, *For Those I Loved.*

I went to the South of France two years ago to research the life of this great man. Though Martin was in Canada at the time of my visit, I was able to climb the winding roads to the stone farm house. Down a ravine the old rusty car, burned out by flames of long ago, slept silently on the hillside. I peered through the gates of the farm house in time to see Johnathan, a beautiful little boy, his blond hair shining in the sun, running down the grassy slope. He stopped long enough to ask me what toys children play with in America. Martin has remarried and lives in the same farmhouse with his wife and three children, Barbara, Larissa and Jonathan. With my own eyes I could see the fragile miracle of his life, knowing that the miracle to create and to survive lives within us all.

Little did I dream then that another painful experience lay ahead. My sister Miriam was born twenty-one months before me. She was the exact image of Elizabeth Taylor. It's not easy to grow up with Elizabeth Taylor. As a young girl my favorite hobby was oil painting. Whenever, I came in with a canvas full of wet oil paint my sister would nervously say, "Deanna, don't get too close to me!" as she stood there in her white angora sweaters. I never meant to leave rainbows of fresh paint on her sweaters but they seemed to appear as I would walk by her. Being so close in age we purposely tried to be different. When she became very fastidious about her room mine turned upside down. It looked like my garage looks today. I've been cleaning it for years and it's not done yet. When my sister became shy and introverted I became outgoing and open. When my sister became very glamorous I became very plain. But the one thing we always shared was our music and we became a singing sister team when we were very small. At the ages of five and seven we joined a children's radio program and my mother didn't know it until she heard us singing on the radio. My sister was diagnosed with diabetes at the age of sixteen and that was very painful for me. I had many wonderful years with my sister because of the man who discovered insulin, and to see his eternal flame burning in London, Ontario until a cure is found . . . you don't know what that did to my heart.

You would never know my sister had diabetes. She lived an active and viable life and we were very, very much together all of our lives. A year ago, the day I completed recording sessions for my new album, "Share Love's Light," I returned home. My husband gathered me in his arms and said, "Honey, Miriam died this morning of congestive heart failure." All of a sudden my world just crumbled. My husband and older sons were very supportive but were more spectators to my grief. It was my thirteen year old son, Eric, who hurled himself into my arms and began to cry with me. He said, "I'm crying because I didn't get to know Aunt Miriam as well as you did." But I knew what he was really saying to me; "Mom, I'm going to jump into this pain with you because I don't want you to be alone." That was a great gift for me, one I will never forget. On the new album I had just recorded a song that seemed very appropriate for my sister and I sang it at her service. I want to share this for all of you who have lost a very special brother or sister that you miss very much. This is an unusual song about the old house I used to live in. Maybe you could be thinking about the house you used to live in with all the hurts, joys and the great memories of love that old houses contain.

The House I Used to Live In

The house I used to live in
Is fading now with age,
Like a treasured book from yesterday,
A story on each page.
The weeds have taken over
Where flowers used to grow.
The paint is cracked and peeling
And the fence is bending low.

Chorus

But the house I used to live in
Has magic on its face
And the memories it holds for me
No mansion could replace,
And so I walk with reverent step
As I visit it today

> Where the little child I used to be
> Once more goes out to play.
>
> The words of love once spoken
> Within those silent walls
> Have drifted into distant dreams
> That still my heart recalls.
> Grey cobwebs cross the windows
> From which we used to peek
> And refuse hides that little yard
> Where we played hide and seek.[8]

When someone said to me, "Deanna, how could you possibly sing at the funeral service of your own sister?" I said, "How could I possibly not? She would have killed me if I hadn't!" I found the experience to be both moving and growth-promoting.

What I learned from this experience was that I had the power to do my own grief work. Roy Nichols, in a wonderful article in my book, *Grieving: The Pain and the Promise,* summarized the surrogate suffering syndrome in this way [1]:

> The surrogate sufferer is one who would attempt to suffer in the place of the sufferer in the hope of reducing the suffering of the sufferer. A pervasive pattern in caregiving it encompasses our attempts to shield persons subject to pain from painful or otherwise difficult experiences. An attempt to run interference on pain it is truly a well intentioned strategy for caregiving. Tragically, however, the intention is seldom realized, perhaps never. Can one cry the tears for another? Do the grief work for another? Solve the problems for another? The surrogate sufferer syndrome is rooted in feelings of helplessness. If we take the approach that conveys— 'this is so tragic, this should never have happened to you, this is more than you should have to bare, you can't handle this, let me take care of this for you'... an air of victimization and despair is cast over the entire experience. Those who are grieving should be permitted and encouraged to stay on their feet—to engage in the decision making process, to demonstrate that even when life is painful they can still function, cope, perform and live on.

I decided to apply Roy's principles in my own grief counseling. A graphic example of this illustrates what I am trying to say.

A few years ago a tragedy happened in our state. A beautiful sixteen year old girl and her ten month old son were brutally murdered by a young man who did not want to claim that he was the father of the child. The baby was thrown into a

---

[8] Used by permission, © 1989 from the album, *Share Love's Light,* Deanna Edwards, Rock Canyon Music Publishers, Provo, Utah.

river and was found five days later by a fisherman. His body was taken to a funeral home to await the discovery of his mother's body so they could be buried together. A petite, dark haired Greek grandmother wanted to see the body of her grandson. The funeral director, who in this case was functioning as the surrogate sufferer, said, "No, you can't look at the body. You'll have nightmares. You can't handle this. For your own sake, don't make this request."

People are like computers. What we put into a computer will be reflected back to us. If we tell someone they're going to have nightmares what happens? They're going to have nightmares anyway because the imagination is always worse than the reality. Another of our problems is our preoccupation with physical appearance. When we are growing older we use "Lady Clairol" and "Rose Milk Skin Cream" because we fear changes, afraid that age or injury will make us believe that we are not beautiful anymore. So when there is disfiguration of the body in death, this fear becomes very much intensified.

I was asked to meet with the family at the funeral home the following day so I called Roy Nichols and asked for his advice, knowing that it was a very sensitive case. Roy told me that there were three conditions that must be present when we are working with such families.

1. There should be a desire on the part of the family member to see the body or an invitation extended to see their loved one.
2. Many options should be given to the grieving person. "Do you want to see all of the body or part of the body? Do you want me to cover the body so you can see or hold a hand? Do you want me to look first and tell you what I see and then you can make that decision? Do you want to open the casket or do you want me to? Do you want to be alone or do you want me to be with you? Do you want to enter the room first or would you like me to?
3. Once given the options they should be given **Time** to consider them. "You don't have to make the decision right now. I can meet you here in a few hours or we can meet at the funeral home tomorrow morning. Or you can call me and we can speak further about the options available to you."

The next day I met Maria and her husband, Roger, at the funeral home. I asked, "Maria, do you want to see Christopher's body?"

Immediately she said, "Yes, that is why I am here."

Her husband, Roger, had not expressed a desire to see the body so I focused my attention on Maria. "Do you want to see all of the body or part of the body?" I went through all of the options previously mentioned and then asked Maria if she needed more time. She told me that she had more than enough time and that she considered it her right to see her grandson. She did not want the funeral director present and asked if I would accompany her. Most people who are grieving do not want to do their grief work in the presence of surrogate sufferers because they believe that their rights are being threatened and that the surrogate sufferer does not believe in their strength and their ability to handle the situation.

I will never forget, as we went into this little room and she uncovered Christopher very slowly. Sons are very important to the Greeks. When Christopher was born, Maria had been in the delivery room. When the physician lifted him up Maria exclaimed, "There's his little chuchuna! It's a boy!" As she gently uncovered the body, Maria said softly, "Ah, he's still well-hung! That's our boy!!" She suddenly asked if I would go and ask Roger to join her.

I walked into the waiting room and found Roger and asked if he would like to join Maria. He said, "Of course I would like to be with her—but no one had invited me." Sometimes men are not as assertive and they need to be openly included in the grief process. He and Maria spent fifteen minutes alone with the body of their grandson. When they emerged from the room they both said, almost simultaneously, "That's not as bad as we had thought it would be."

It was obviously a healing experience for them and their recovery was better because of it. Most persons, when given time to consider options, will choose to fight rather than flee. You can let them know that they are pioneers in their own grief processes. We cannot do this work for them.

Dick's fourth suggestion was to create something beautiful with grief. As I contemplated what I could create for my father, I realize that the one thing he did not have was a musical voice. I could not remember ever hearing a song written from the point of view of a dying patient. So, in a matter of minutes, I wrote a song that would send me on a musical mission that would last a lifetime. It was eventually used on an NBC News Special, "On Death and Dying," based on a book written by Elisabeth Kübler-Ross. It was sponsored by the United Catholic Conference. The production manager of the special, Joan Paul, heard the song and asked me if I needed help finding a publisher for the song. She sent it to the Franciscan Communication Center in Los Angeles and they published the song in my first album, **Peacebird**. The song has since been recorded on the album, **Music Brings My Heart Back Home**. It has been used for state and national hospice groups and in films produced by the American Journal of Nursing. It is entitled, **Teach Me to Die**.

Teach Me to Die

"Sunlight filters through my window
Falling from the sky.
Time slips a silent stranger,
Softly passing by.
Life goes on in busy circles
Leaving me behind.
Memories, like portraits,
Fill the attic of my mind.

I know it isn't easy
Seeing me this way,

It hurts to watch me
Lying here day after day.
Trade your fear of parting
For the faith that knows no pain.
Don't be afraid to say goodbye.
I know we'll meet again!

Chorus

Teach me to die. Hold on to my hand.
I have so many questions,
Things I don't understand.
Teach me to die.Give all you can give.
If you'll teach me of dying
I will teach you to live.[9]

What a wonderful bargain is revealed in the last line of the song. If you'll walk with me through the final moments of my life . . . if you'll have the courage to laugh with me and the freedom to cry with me . . . if you will give me information about what is happening to me, I will teach you to live and love as you never have before! Love is a process of giving and receiving, both for the patient as well as the caregiver. Our dying patients are our mentors and teachers, and we are their students. I often use this song with dying patients and they are so grateful for a musical voice when they hear this song, if they are ready to receive it. If I am not sure the patient is ready to hear the song I may give them a tape consisting of several different songs and ask them to tell me which songs are most meaningful to them. If they pick this song, they are usually ready to share their feelings in a deep and meaningful way.

After seeing how effective this song was in working with patients I decided to try music as a tool in grief counseling. My first song about grief was inspired by a wonderful book, *Eric,* by Doris Lund. In this fine example of creative grief, Doris Lund shared the journey of her son through leukaemia and told of his great courage and his sense of humor. Shortly before his death, he was lying in a hospital in New York. He looked up from his hospital bed and saw the anguish on his mother's face, pain which you would expect to see on the face of a mother whose child is dying. He said something very simple but very profound. "Mom, **Walk in the world for me.**" What he was really saying was, "Mother, I don't want my death to diminish your life. I want you to live better and love better because I was there." I thought what a wonderful idea to use for a song that would give people hope for more life and more love in the future.

---

[9] © 1987 from the album *Music Brings My Heart Back Home,* Deanna Edwards, Rock Canyon Music Publisher, Provo, Utah.

Teach Me to Die

Arranged by
Greg Hansen

Words and Music by
Deanna Edwards

Thoughtfully ♩ = 76

Sun - light fil - ters through my win - dow
I know that it is - n't eas - y

Fall - ing from the sky.
See - ing me this way,

Time slips like a si - lent stran - ger
It hurts to watch me Ly - ing

Soft - ly pass - ing by.
here day af - ter day.

Walk in the World For Me

The time has come now
For me to say goodbye.
No sad farewells
Will we share.
For you will live within me
And I will live in you.
No words can say
How much we care.

We've walked together
On the dusty roads of life,
But kept our eyes upon a star.
We've laughed at the little things
And cried along the way.
I've come to know
The friend you are.

Walk in the world for me!
Sing a happy melody!
And keep my memory
Not far away.
May you find
That life will bring
All the best of everything!
Take special care of you
For me today![10]

So often when we are in the presence of someone who is dying or a person who is grieving we feel helpless and impotent, as if nothing we say or do could possibly make a difference. I have felt that many times in the face of great loss. Then I read a statement, written by Sam Keene, that made a great difference in my life. "Eventually we discover that we can never take each other's loneliness, fill the void in the bottom of the heart, make the world safe, or take away the shadow of death. In the end, the best we can do is to hold each other in this luminous darkness and if, through our struggles, we finally come to be close to each other, **That is enough!**"

After reading this profound statement I wrote a song I would like to close with entitled, "That's Enough."

---

[10]Used by permission, © 1986, from the album, *Listen With Your Heart*, Deanna Edwards, Rock Canyon Music Publishers, Provo, Utah, 84604.

That's Enough

Arranged by
Greg Hansen

Words and Music by
Deanna Edwards

That's Enough

I can't remove your loneliness
Or heal your broken heart.
Can't take away the shadows
That make your night so dark,
But I can stay beside you
When life is getting tough
If we come close together,
That's enough.

I don't have all the answers
And I don't know what to say.
I can't bring you the sunshine
Or take the rain away,
But I can always hold you
When the storm is getting rough
If we come close together,
That's enough.

I had to learn so many things
And fail so many times
Before the day I finally realized
If we could take the sorrow
From every loss that comes along
We Would Have to Take the Loving out of Life!

I can't remove the dangers
From a world so full of fears.
I can't make living safer
Or take away your tears,
But I can always love you
With a love that you can trust
If we come close together that's enough![11]

REFERENCE

1. D. Edwards, *Grieving: The Pain and the Promise,* Covenent, Ogden, 1990.

[11]Used by permission, from the album, *Music Brings My Heart Back Home,* Deanna Edwards, Rock Canyon Music Publishers, Provo, Utah.

CHAPTER 6

Pathways Through Grief:
A Model of the Process

Karen Martin and Sandra Elder

INTRODUCTION

For eight years we have been trying to understand what happens to people when they experience loss and grief. We read the literature; we talked to each other; but most of all we listened to the bereaved—those who had lived through and learned from the universal human condition of coping with grief. The result is a model of the grieving process we call "Pathways Through Grief." This chapter is about that model. It begins by discussing the issues that were a blueprint for developing the model. Next is an explanation of our design process and the actual contents of the model. We end by discussing how we have used Pathways in counselling and educational settings.

DEVELOPING THE MODEL

Grief is . . .

By grief we mean the emotional, physical, intellectual, behavioral, and spiritual process of adjusting to the loss of someone or something of personal value. Grief arises from an awareness that the world that is and the world that "should be" are different. Since this "should be world" is a unique construction of each person, the reactions to losing it can be unique. It is like a journey with many choices along the way, some healing and some harming. The choices that are made reflect the uniqueness of each griever. We wanted our model to allow for this uniqueness.

Grief is Triggered by Losing Someone or Something of Personal Value

Bowlby's work on attachment and loss provided the foundation for our under-standing of grief [1]. He reminded us that attachment comes before grief. Worden pointed out that the degrees of strength, security, and ambivalence of that attach-ment affect the reaction to its loss [2]. Therefore, we believed that our model should somehow include the beginnings as well as the endings of relationships. Since attachment provides people with a sense of meaning, when that relationship disintegrates so does its meaning [3]. Part of grieving is the reaction to that lost meaning. Part of healing is developing new relationships, not only with others but with oneself. We wanted our model to reflect this too.

Grief Affects the Total Person Within the Context of Their Present and Past Life

When we saw people travelling through the grief process, we saw them strug-gling with the assumptions and expectations they had of themselves, others and their world. This assumptive world contained everything they believed to be true. It came from previous life experiences and information from inside their heads and hearts, from their relationships with others and from their culture and society. These got challenged or invalidated when a loss occurred, leaving people strug-gling with the need to redefine their world [4]. They were continually matching the present experience with what they once believed. Their goal was to once again feel oriented, recognize what was happening around and in them, and plan their behavior accordingly [5]. Their whole selves could be involved in this grief work.

The more personally significant the loss, the more people experience grief in all parts of themselves. While the emotional, physical, and behavioral manifesta-tions of grief are quite well-known and accepted, we found that references to the spiritual issues gave us some important clues about what needed to be included in a comprehensive model of grief. Events are experienced as a crisis when they touch the vital center of a person [6]. The significant loss or death of someone special often throws people into existential and spiritual crisis. This may be manifested by: feelings of worthlessness, loss of purpose and meaning, and a sense of non-being [6]; a massive revision . . . in their understanding of what the world is about [7]; and a questioning of the philosophies by which they have lived [8]. To come to terms with the crisis, people often embark upon a search for some meaning for their loss [7, 9, 10] and for their lives [11]. We strongly believed that the search for meaning was a central issue because: "it is a fundamental proposi-tion that human experience is imbued with the pursuit, construction, and the alteration of meaning" [12]. We decided that our model had to indicate that the search for meaning is an integral part of the healing process.

Grief Occurs Throughout Our Lives and Is a Process, Not an Event

We decided to go beyond grief related to just death and look at people's reactions to life transitions. There are very few times in people's lives when they are not involved in some type of change. Some changes are minor while others cause tremendous upheaval. With each change, there is a choice to be made: acknowledge it or ignore it. Past losses affect new ones. There is no real beginning or end to this. It really is a process. We wanted to design a model that represented this continuous recycling.

Grief Has No End Point

Our professional, personal, and research experience told us that there is no end point for grief. Our conclusions are supported by others [2, 10, 13, 14]. SIDS families and clients in counseling have told us that there are still elements of grief in their daily lives, even as long as twenty-five years after the loss. Although these people are functioning members of families and society, they still occasionally feel intense despair over their loss, especially on anniversaries and missed milestone events. Such events may trigger a return to the earlier pain although with less depth to the feelings. We knew that our model needed to reflect this continual recycling rather than a straight progression toward acceptance as an end point. Many of the existing models that tried to describe the grief process, especially the one developed by Kübler-Ross [15], were linear and, therefore, they implied that grief had a beginning and an end. We agreed with Wambach's statement [16, p. 209]:

> That the grief process is thought to be a simple, linear, and unidirectional is probably the result of research techniques that assume such a process.

Linear models suggest that there is only one way to grieve and that one must progress from one stage to the other. There is no allowance for returning to a stage without feeling like it is a set-back. Since our discussions with the bereaved told us that they returned many times to the same place in the process, we wanted our model to reflect this cycling and recycling, the returning to some central spot. This could not be accomplished with a linear image.

Grief Changes Over Time

We also examined the identification of phases or stages of the grief process. According to Bowlby, when separated from significant others people exhibit similar categories of responses: protest, despair and eventually detachment [1]. Building upon Bowlby's work, Lamers described the thoughts and feelings that went with each phase and added a final phase: recovery [17]. These phases were then incorporated into a wave-like image that represented the passage of time. It began with a loss event, went through protest, despair, and detachment, and ended with recovery. We liked this model. We began to use it in bereavement support groups, individual counseling sessions, and educational presentations.

Initially people said it was very helpful. The wave-like image reflected the way grief felt. The ability to visualize the process gave them some sense of direction in the midst of what felt like confusion. It allowed for a return to the first phase. Eventually, however, people started to reveal that they were troubled by the leap from the detachment phase to recovery. From their point of view, there was something missing. They wanted to know how one made such a big leap and if the term recovery was really appropriate. We decided that recovery was an unsuitable term since we believed that [18, p. 139]:

> No one who has ever suffered a loss is ever again the same: [they] are either further enlightened in harmony, or [they] are imprisoned in the darkness of [their] own bitterness, resentment and self-pity.

Our model needed to go beyond recovery and look at how people were changed by grief, either constructively or destructively. Using these issues as our blue print we set about working on the design and contents.

MODEL DESIGN

Designing the physical structure for the model was both the most difficult and exciting part of its development. Because the Lamers' model was initially so powerful we used it as our beginning point (revisions shared and approved of by Lamers). A new image began to take shape as we listened to the bereaved and bereavement counselors and as we examined both the academic and literary writings about grief. C. S. Lewis' *A Grief Observed* [19] and the following passage from Moss were particularly inspirational [20, p. 179]:

> The sense that the mourner is going down to the grave, that he is placing himself beside the dead one, is the first step of the grief work cycle. . . . The second step of the grief work cycle is a 'coming up' from the depths of 'the grave.' In this stage the mourner must gradually begin to form his ties again with the living and with life.

The Lamers' model already reflected the first step, the downward or inward journey. What was missing was the second step—the coming up or moving outward from the self to form attachments to others, to rejoin life. That's what the bereaved had been asking us—How do we rejoin life? When we drew one circle on top of the other, intuitively we knew we had it! The model now looked like a figure eight or, when turned on its side, the symbol for infinity. There was no beginning or end to the process, no entry or exit. This reflected the continual process of dealing with attachments and losses throughout life. Once we had the image, we set to work researching and exploring the phases in the top circle. Our conversations with the bereaved proved most useful in defining the three phases of the top part of the model.

Then we worked on the ordering of the phases. Initially we believed that people always began the grief process by going down into the bottom circle. They would first withdraw into themselves and then they would move upwards and outwards. But our counseling sessions and research with SIDS parents has revealed that some people choose to begin in the top half of the model. They may look to others first or they may explore their loss cognitively rather than emotionally. This expanded the model to allow considerable flexibility and took away the "right way to grieve" image that we had first unknowingly implied. To reflect this new awareness, we added double-headed arrows between the phases. This reflected the back and forth movements that the bereaved had so eloquently described to us.

One even larger question troubled us for a long time—how do people get out of one circle and into the other? What is it that propels them? After much discussion and further questioning of the bereaved and the literature, we realized that the definition people give to the transition, that is the meaning they assign to it, makes the difference. There are two types of definitions of meaning. The first occurs when the loss is newly experienced and the person asks: Why did this happen? What does it mean to me? The more meaning the loss has, the greater the depth of grief. The second definition may occur when some time has passed and the person is able to ask: What now? How will I go on? If the experience is ever to be a positive one, the person must eventually define the loss as a challenge and a change that can be managed. It is the re-definition of the event that propels people from one circle to the other.

The last and most recent addition to the model is the outer circle of people. Prior learning and experience with loss and the support and comments of other people all play a significant role in the grief process. People do not grieve in isolation from others. To reflect this we added the outer circle of people. We decided to call it the Circle of Influence because it represents all the influences, positive and negative, past and present, of other people upon the grieving process. It also represents the relational context in which the loss occurs. (See Figure 1 for Pathways model.)

MODEL CONTENT

Circle of Influence

This Circle of Influence has been designed to reflect many different issues. At first glance, one notices that the figures are varying in size and tone. This reflects the different degrees of influence and the time frame of that influence. People

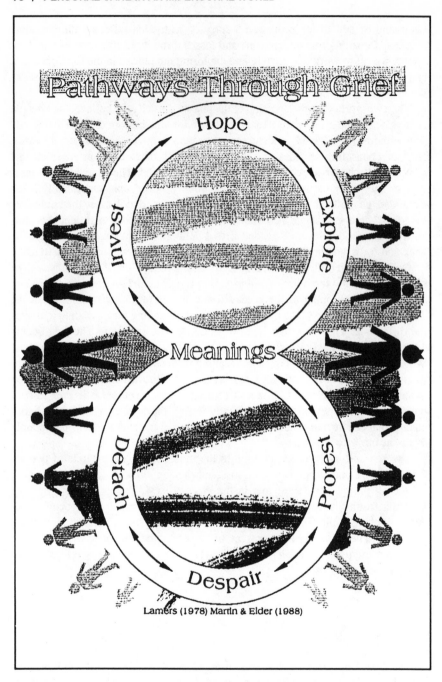

Figure 1. Pathways through Grief Model.

learn how to express their grief and disappointments early in life, often before they experience a major loss. This is represented by the small and shadowy figures. The larger and darker figures can represent those who are currently influencing grief reactions. This may include family, friends, co-workers, medical and counseling professionals, clergy and the general public's attitudes towards death and the grief experience. It is important that the bereaved understand the potential power of this influence and that they have a choice as to how they will let others affect their need to grieve.

The figures are in both genders because people are socialized as males and females in terms of how much emotion they are allowed to show and what coping strategies they may employ when they are distressed. They are also influenced by their ethnic and religious upbringing. Because these strategies are learned so early in life, the bereaved often do not understand their own grieving behavior and needs. By examining family influences and understanding the reasons behind their grief strategies, people can be helped to learn new and more effective coping styles.

The wave-like brush strokes that connect some figures and not others is meant to represent the existence of a support network. Some people will have a very close-knit and supportive group of people who will help them through their crisis while others will have a scattered and unconnected collection of individuals to whom they may turn. The bigger the safety net, the more supported the bereaved may feel. By helping clients to identify their needs while they are grieving, the counselor can help them build up their safety net to meet those needs.

The Circle of Influence is also meant to remind us that any loss occurs within a given relational context. The darker figures can also represent important relationships, which if lost would trigger strong reactions. The shadowy figures are less significant and, therefore, the grief will likely be less intense. This imagery will help the bereaved to understand that they alone have the right to decide how deeply they will need to grieve their loss.

The Pathways

It is very difficult to describe a continuous process without implying that there is a beginning and an ending. But we have to start somewhere. Although we are choosing to start with the inward path represented by the bottom circle, please remember that some people will begin their journey by going outward first.

INWARD JOURNEY

Protest

Even if a loss is anticipated the immediate response is to deny that it has really happened. People are not able or willing to conceive of this loss as actually happening to them. They cannot take in all the news at once since they cannot know for some time how the loss will affect them. So at first people may feel numb or like they are in a fog as they struggle to make the bad news go away. The predominate feature is the inability and unwillingness to accept that the loss has occurred. Once the person realizes that the event has really happened, very intense responses begin to occur.

Despair

The numbing effect of the protest phase eventually wears off and then the real pain of grief is felt. Every human emotion may be experienced in varying degrees of intensity. Behavior seems without purpose and it is difficult to concentrate on anything that is not related to the loss object. The predominance of strong emotions and the struggle to find the deceased make this an extremely difficult phase to be in. These intense feelings, thoughts, and behaviours cannot persist forever and people seem to eventually need to withdraw completely from others and to isolate themselves for a time. This withdrawal signals a shift to the next phase.

Detach

This phase is characterized by apathy and disinterest. People almost become petrified with grief. For some, there is a noticeable withdrawal and disinterest in life and new relationships, partly perhaps to protect themselves from the pain of new grief. Although this is not conscious, the reasoning seems to be: no more involvement means no more grief. Others involve themselves in frantic busy work to avoid any deep attachments and to avoid feelings. In a sense, the bereaved at this stage are in an emotional cocoon. Simos says their grief has drained them of all energy and there is none left for the real world [21]. To use a household analogy, their circuits are overloaded and they need to shut down emotionally for awhile. They need time to step aside in order to see what they have lost and what they still have. If this time is used constructively to recoup energy and to care for oneself, it can be a time of healing. If, however, people use this time only to hide from themselves and others, likely the inward path will be travelled again and again. The complete range of psychological defence mechanisms can be utilized to protect them from the too painful realization that their life has changed. These defenses may succeed in preventing anxiety from becoming too disorganizing, but they are also likely to delay the relearning process necessary for healing and growth [22]. There will be no movement up and outwards. This is chronic or unresolved grief.

OUTWARD JOURNEY

Explore

Explore is the opposite of Protest. It involves a more active examination of the loss. The predominate activity of the bereaved in this phase is the cognitive examination of the relationship they have lost. People may begin to develop an appreciation of how much the relationship enhanced their lives [23] and to look at it more realistically than they could before. They may be more open to reading, going for counseling, or joining a support group than at any previous stage. As the bereaved explore their emotions and their loss with others they begin to re-establish their shattered lives and find some order and direction.

Not all people begin their journey of grief by going inward and downward first. Some, more particularly men, begin by first analyzing and exploring the lost relationship. They intellectualize their grief rather than connecting at an emotional level. Research has shown that men use more cognitive strategies to deal with their grief. They may use self-control and positive re-appraisal [24]; active problem solving [25] and solitary expression, thought blocking, reason, reflection, and diversionary activities [26]. It is important to remember that women may use these strategies as well. All of these strategies help the griever to look at the loss without feeling emotional pain.

Hope

Hope is the opposite of despair. If the bereaved started their healing by going inward and downward first, by the time they reach this phase, they have begun to incorporate the loss into their lives. Life takes on new meaning and begins to have a direction and purpose again. Thoughts focus more on the future than on the past. There is more peace. Although the bereaved will talk about their loss, the deep sense of pain will be missing. It will likely be replaced by a renewed sense of appreciation for life and relationships. The positive and resolved memories of what they have lost can enhance new relationships with themselves, others, and life in general.

If the journey has been outward and upward first, the Hope phase seems to have some of the elements of peace but it may not be as grounded in a sense of peace. People may talk about the great plans they have for the future but there may be a certain hollowness to it. There will likely be a connection to what has been lost since the future may revolve around the past. Attempts to replace what has been lost may take precedence over dealing with the feelings.

Invest

This phase occurs when people begin to take the opportunity to begin again to experience joy in their lives. They are no longer the "walking wounded." They are involved with life and with relationships. If they began their journey by first going inward, this will feel like the end of their grief but experience will tell them that there are many possible triggers that can remind them of their loss and propel them down and back into their pain. If they began their journey by going outward first, they may discover that they cannot fully invest themselves in a new relationship because they have not yet released the old one. Premature investing, that is, making commitments to another before resolving a previous relationship, may mean the new relationship is doomed to failure. This realization may propel them downwards.

It is here too that attachment begins. With each new attachment comes the reality that every relationship we will ever have with any person, object, place, or idea will eventually end. The transition experience teaches people that grief is the price they must pay for caring. The healthy bereaved know this and often live their lives more fully, appreciating the transient nature of relationships. Those who have not adequately dealt with old losses may fear new ones. They may over-invest or under-invest in new relationships. Either choice may lead to the very thing they dreaded—another ending.

Meanings

When individuals experience major life transitions they have a need to make sense of them. How people define events determines whether or not grief will begin and what path will be chosen. Their definitions are affected by their past experiences with such events, their emotional socialization and current health, their gender and personality style, their spiritual and cultural beliefs, the nature of both the relationship and the event itself.

The first confrontation with meaning occurs when the bereaved become aware that a change has begun. Making sense of it the first time often involves asking important questions such as: Why did this happen? What was my role in it happening? At this point, the griever has a choice—look inward and deal with the emotional reaction to the event or move outward and deal with it in a less emotional fashion. The choice is a reflection of their usual coping style.

People will change the focus of their journey, that is from inward to outward or from outward to inward, only by redefining the meaning of the transition. Once they are able to make this shift in focus they enter into a whole new kind of grief work. The major questions are different: What do I do now? How will I deal with this change in my life? They reflect the knowledge that life is a series of transitions and that if we are to be fully alive we must learn to accept change and be open to it.

When people grieve they are mourning not only their obvious loss but also the loss of their world view. In order to deal with the discrepancy between their ideal and real world, they must redefine their goals, identity, and world view. Not everyone is able to accomplish this. Perhaps this is the difference between those who build their lives around their losses and those who are able to let go and move on. Our role as counselors and educators is to help people understand this process and to make the best use of their choice points.

USING THE MODEL

We have been using Pathways through Grief in counseling sessions, bereavement support groups, and educational presentations about grief. This model seems to help those who are experiencing major life transitions to understand and manage personal change in their lives. Seldom, if ever, does an individual move neatly from one phase to another. The model shows them that there is a pathway through the confusion. It seems to be reassuring for them to know that what they are experiencing is not uncommon, that it will pass, and that they can determine how it will pass. As one woman who was dealing with marital separation wrote: "The model is a concrete sign that what you are experiencing is fluid and that you won't lodge forever where you are."

The model acts as a catalyst for helping the bereaved to understand what is happening to them. An eleven year old boy whose mother died said that the model gave him the language that he does not have to describe what is happening inside him. Adolescents involved in Dr. Robert Stevenson's death education class say the model is like a road map that shows them where they are, where they are going, and where they have been.

Three other observations from clients have been helpful. The fact that we did not number the phases of grief seems to help people realize that there is no correct order to the process. Their grief will be as unique as their relationship. Having the arrows pointed in both directions allows for movement in both directions and also implies that there is no right way to grieve. The second observation is that the grief process often seems to feel like a roller coaster ride over which the bereaved have no control. This contributes to their feelings of craziness and powerlessness. If they can see the whole process laid out before them then they are less afraid to experience it fully. Lastly, knowing that this model was developed as a direct result of talking to others who are grieving helps the bereaved realize that they are not the only ones who are thinking, feeling, and behaving this way. If they have not been exposed to others who are grieving, they may not know that others share their experience. This model then can be used for those who have no access to bereavement support programs. It helps them feel like a part of a community of shared pain and growth.

Knowing when to present this model is sometimes a guessing game. Timing is a very important factor in counseling the bereaved. An understanding of their learning styles and how they have handled other transitions is important when trying to decide when to show them the model. Clients are given several copies of the model between counseling sessions to help them to both chart their journey through grief and to see their movement. Using the model creates a feeling of control over their grief. It also invites them to learn more about the grief process and themselves. Giving them work to do on their own further reinforces the belief that they still possess the skills to resolve issues. The model can be used as a tool to empower the bereaved at a time when they are feeling the most powerless.

The model has also been used as an educational tool to teach professionals (public health nurses, teachers, school counsellors, psychologists, social workers, clergy, and funeral directors) and community volunteers. It has also been used in presentations to whole communities in grief, senior citizen groups, parents with handicapped children and to members of support groups for those with chronic health conditions. Those who attended these presentations responded to the design itself since the similarity to the symbol for infinity seems to make so much sense to them. It helps them to see that we must all deal with losses and attachments as we go through life. They are able to see that the process involves many choice points and that each griever will go through it making their own choices. This helps them to see that they need to allow for uniqueness rather than following the linear model which implies that there is only one way to grieve. As each phase is described, suggestions about helping strategies are given. This information, however, is given with the reminder that helping a person who is grieving is like dancing with them. Helpers should never see themselves as leading; the bereaved should be allowed to determine the pace, the degree of closeness, and what steps will be taken next.

The other important observation is that the model reminds people that we each make our own meanings out of an event and that each person lives within a different relational context. This has proven helpful for those who thought that all members of a family would share a similar response to a loss. They can see the difficulties that might be experienced when one member is in the bottom of the model while another is in the top. The most important feedback has been about the usefulness of meanings as the centre point for the whole process. Much can be learned by asking one basic question: What does this loss mean to you? Asked a number of times while the person is dealing with their loss, the counselor can get a good idea of the client's changing perspective on the experience.

CONCLUSION

The Pathways model, like the experience it depicts, is more process than product. It is a beginning, not an end. We are presenting it in its present form in hopes that it will provide a conceptual framework on which we can all build. That way the model can be improved as we improve our understanding of the process it endeavors to illuminate. For that to happen, the model needs to be continually tested against the reality of research, experience, observation, and contemplation. The more it is used, the more useful it will be become.

REFERENCES

1. J. Bowlby, *Attachment and Loss, Volume III, Loss: Sadness and Depression,* Penguin Books, London, 1980.
2. J. W. Worden, *Grief Counselling and Grief Therapy: A Handbook for the Mental Health Practitioner,* Springer Publishing, New York, 1982.
3. J. Benoliel, Loss and Adaptation: Circumstances, Contingencies, and Consequences, *Death Studies, 9,* pp. 217-233, 1985.
4. K. Lewin, Field Theory and Experiment in Social Psychology: Concepts and Methods, *American Journal of Sociology, 44,* pp. 868-897, 1939.
5. C. Parkes, Bereavement as a Psychosocial Transition: Processes of Adaptation to Change, *Journal of Social Issues, 44*:3, pp. 53-65, 1988.
6. S. L. Dixon and R. G. Sands, Identity and the Experience of Crisis, *Social Casework, 64*:4, p. 227, 1983.
7. J. Cornwell, B. Nurcombe, and L. Stevens, Family Response to Loss of a Child by Sudden Infant Death Syndrome, *Medical Journal of Australia, 1,* p. 658, 1977.
8. J. DeFrain and L. Ernst, *Coping with Sudden Infant Death,* Lexington Books, Lexington, Massachusetts, 1982.
9. Y. Craig, The Bereavement of Parents and Their Search for Meaning, *British Journal of Social Work, 7*:1, pp. 41-54, 1977.
10. D. R. Lehman, C. B. Wortman, and A. F. Williams, Long-Term Effects of Losing a Spouse or Child in a Motor Vehicle Crash, *Journal of Personality and Social Psychology, 52*:1, pp. 218-231, 1987.
11. R. J. Knapp, *Beyond Endurance: When a Child Dies,* Schocken Books, New York, 1986.
12. M. J. Mahoney, Psychotherapy and Human Change Processes, in *Cognition and Psychotherapy,* M. J. Mahoney and A. Freeman (eds.), Plenum Press, New York, p. 7, 1985.
13. L. Videka-Sherman, Coping with the Death of a Child: A Study Over Time, *American Journal of Orthopsychiatry, 42*:4, pp. 688-698, 1982.
14. D. V. Hardt, An Investigation of the Stages of Bereavement, *Omega, 9*:3, pp. 279-285, 1978.
15. E. Kübler-Ross, *On Death and Dying,* Macmillan, New York, 1969.
16. J. A. Wambach, The Grief Process as a Social Construct, *Omega, 16*:209, 1986.
17. W. Lamers, Helping the Child to Grieve, in *Proceedings of the Conference "Helping Children Cope with Death,"* G. H. Patterson (ed.), King's College, London, Ontario, pp. 105-119, 1985.
18. D. O'Toole, *Growing Through Grief: A K-12 Curriculum to Help Young People through All Kinds of Loss,* Mountain Rainbow Publications, Burnsville, p. 139, 1989.
19. C. S. Lewis, *A Grief Observed,* Walker and Company, New York, 1961.
20. S. Moss, The Grief Work Cycle in Judaism, in *Perspectives on Bereavement,* I. Gerber, A. Weiner, A. H. Kutscher, D. Battin, A. Arkin, and A. Goldberg (eds.), Arno Press, New York, p. 171, 1979.
21. B. G. Simos, *A Time to Grieve,* Family Service Association, New York, 1979.
22. C. Parkes, Bereavement as a Psychosocial Transition: Processes of Adaptation to Change, *Journal of Social Issues, 44*:3, p. 57, 1988.

23. G. Swartz-Borden, Grief Work: Prevention and Intervention, *Social Casework, 67*:8, p. 504, 1986.
24. N. Feeley and L. N. Gottlieb, Parents' Coping and Communication Following their Infant's Death, *Omega, 19*:1, pp. 51-67, 1988.
25. R. A. Williams and S. M. Nicolaisen, Sudden Infant Death Syndrome: Parents' Perceptions and Response to the Loss of their Infant, *Research in Nursing and Health, 5*, pp. 55-61, 1982.
26. J. A. Cook, Dad's Double Binds: Rethinking Father's Bereavement from a Men's Studies Perspective, *Journal of Contemporary Ethnography, 17*:3, pp. 285-308, 1988.

CHAPTER 7

The 1990's Loss Process
and Vulnerable Personalities

Nan Giblin and Sr. Frances Ryan

INTRODUCTION

This chapter is based on four assumptions:

1. Adults of the 1990's would have experienced a previous major loss;
2. That major loss would most likely have occurred in early childhood;
3. Adults of the 1990's probably will have more vulnerable personalities;
4. Therefore, grief therapy dealing with complicated mourning [1] rather than grief counseling [2] will be needed.

Regarding major loss, recent estimates indicate that "almost half of the children born in the 1980s will experience a parental divorce, and for those whose mothers remarry, about half will experience another family disruption before they reach the age of sixteen" [3, p.797]. The majority of divorces occur within the first seven years of marriage, thus happening within the period of personality development of the child [4]. In the 1990s, the drug culture and the impact of AIDS have led to premature deaths of parents and siblings. The remaining parent, very often, has little emotional reserves to parent the child. Thus, as the child grows, fragile personality structures give rise to a growing number of *dual diagnosis* in adults and implications for complicated grieving [5].

NATURE OF VULNERABLE PERSONALITIES

Vulnerable personalities are defined as those persons having narcissistic or borderline characteristics. Margaret Mahler gives us insight into the origins of vulnerable personality structures [6]. She gives us a model of separation-individuation necessary for the birth of the psychological self. The phases include the autistic phase within the first eight weeks of the child's life. The child is aware only of physiological sensations of pleasure or displeasure and strives for homeostasis.

The symbiotic phase illustrates the omnipotent fusion with the representation of the mother and is characterized by *echo phenomenon* in the mutual cueing dialogue between the mother and child. The height of this stage is at four to five months. Later, there begins the hatching process for the symbiotic membrane and the differentiation stage begins. The child then has a capacity to move from the symbiotic union to examination of the environment and back.

In the early practicing phase, there is a rapid differentiation of the child's body from the mother. Because the child is bonded with the mother, the child returns for *refuelling* needing the presence of the mother. The child develops ambitendency, the precursor to ambivalence. In the rapprochement phase, the child, now possessing object-constancy at the end of the second year, fears, not so much losing the mother as losing her love. Splitting to "all-good" and idealization versus "all-bad" and devaluation, combined with aggressive, libidinal drives is common in this stage. In the third year, the child arrives at ego differentiation and the sense of the psychological self by seeing the self as distinct, knowing one's gender and having object constancy with mother and father [6]. There is an integration of good and bad with a better tolerance of narcissistic disappointment. This usually occurs in the third year of life.

Masterson points out that Real Self emerges from the dual symbiotic mother-child bond [7, 8]. The characteristics that come from the emergence of the Real Self are spontaneity, alertness and aliveness of affect, self-entitlement, self-activation, assertion, support. The Real Self expects acknowledgement of self activation and maintenance, is able to soothe painful affects, has a continuity of self, is committed and is creative. Kohut defines self as a developing, shifting picture or symbol of an individual encompassing both the unconscious and the conscious [9, p.21].

When there is family pathology and poor self-objects with little mirroring, idealization, and twinship [9-10], narcissistic and borderline personality structures form. Kernberg, Kohut, and Masterson [7-11] differ as to the etiology and fixation that mark narcissistic and borderline personalities, though the rapprochement subphase seems to be central to the disturbances with the borderline personality whereas the Early Practicing phase is important for fixation on narcissistic disorders . . . Kohut defines narcissism as healthy self-expression [12, p. 305] but narcissistic disorders tend not only to be described as "self-absorbtion, but indicate poor differentiation, with a tendency to include the world in the self or to lose the self in the world" [13, p.109]. Affect for vulnerable personalities having narcissistic or borderline personality structures usually includes a need for love, boredom, anger, disgust, estrangement, and emptiness [14-17].

The Narcissistic personality is characterized by a lack of empathy and sees the world as an extension of self. The Narcissistic personality has difficulty attaching with another as different form self, thus, manipulation tends to characterize the relationship.

The Borderline personality is characterized by a pervasive pattern of instability of mood, interpersonal relationships and self-image, manifest in early adulthood with at least *five* of the following *eight* characteristics:

1. a pattern of unstable and intense interpersonal relationships characterized by either over-idealization or devaluation;
2. impulsiveness in at least two areas that are potentially self-damaging e.g. spending, sex, substance abuse, shoplifting, reckless driving, or binge eating;
3. affective instability: marked shifts from mood to depression, irritability or anxiety, usually a few hours rather than a few days;
4. inappropriate intense anger or lack of self control of anger;
5. recurrent suicidal threats, gestures or behaviour;
6. identity disturbance with uncertainty in at least two areas: self-image, sexual orientation, career choice, friends, preferred values;
7. chronic feelings of emptiness or boredom; and
8. frantic efforts to avoid real or imagined abandonment.

(DSM., 1987)

CONCLUSION

Because of societal pressures and changing family systems, adults of the 1990's will usually have experienced a major loss, particularly in childhood and there will be increasing numbers having the characteristics of vulnerable personalities.

TREATMENT IMPLICATIONS

According to Worden, grief counseling is appropriate for people who are grieving normally and grief therapy is appropriate for those who are grieving abnormally or have a propensity to grieve abnormally due to predisposing factors such as multiple losses in a short period of time, a history of mental illness and hospitalizations, a strained relationship with the deceased, or a sudden and/or tragic death [2]. If the above hypotheses are true, an increased number of vulnerable personalities will be seen by therapists in the future due to the increased numbers of children who will experience the circumstances in early childhood which will dispose them to a fragile personality matrix. Further, this means that the treatment method of assisting grieving adults, grief counseling, will be increasingly replaced by grief therapy, a much more intensive and time-consuming therapy.

The primary difference between normal and abnormal grief is one of duration and intensity [2]. Of course, there is no exact line which separates normal from abnormal grief, rather the two appear on a continuum with severe pathology at one end and a normal expression of emotions and behavior at the other. The intensity and extended duration of abnormal grief necessitate that grief therapy must not only include all of the therapeutic behaviors of grief counseling such as establishing the relationship, reviewing the circumstances of the loss, experiencing the emotions of loss, and reorganization, but must also include a searching for abnormal patterns in the past of the client and gently confronting the client to accept the reality of the loss.

What is needed in the counseling framework, is exploring the past of the client to find abnormal patterns of feeling, thinking or behavior according to the growing knowledge-base of the vulnerable personality. Such an added dimension in the exploration phase is far more time-consuming than the grief counseling process which is often helpful for the client who is grieving normally.

Thus the implications for grief therapy in the 1990s are:

1. More grief therapy will be needed in lieu of grief counseling.
2. Longer term therapy will be needed for grieving vulnerable personalities as contradistinguished from normal personalities.
3. More hospitalization of grieving people will probably be required because of the fragile nature of the vulnerable personality in light of multiple losses.
4. Continued training in vulnerable personalities' dynamics in the symptoms and treatment of grieving will be necessary.

TREATMENT OUTLINE FOR GRIEF COUNSELING AND GRIEF THERAPY

A suggested counseling framework for vulnerable personalities would include sessions one to three, *building rapport,* by telling stories, the use of encouragement, and normalizing grief. In these sessions, *assessment* is on-going, particularly the tasks of mourning, where the persons are in the stages of loss, the use of inventories, substance abuse assessment, health profile, use of referrals and resources available to grieving individuals. Sessions four to one year in therapy include *grief counseling* following normal grieving processes (Table 1) and supportive therapy.

The sessions in the second and third years are *grief therapy and issues in abnormal grief.* Using any psychodynamic theory, the therapist would insist on the reality of the loss; continue to search and treat maladaptive patterns, giving in the Therapeutic Alliance corrective, reparenting messages and affective

Table 1. Treatment Outline for Grief Counseling and Grief Therapy

SESSIONS 1-3: **BUILD RAPPORT:** Telling Story; Encouragement; Normalizing Grief
ASSESSMENT: Tasks of Mourning, Stages of Loss, Inventories, Substance Use, General Health, Referrals/Resources

SESSIONS 4-1 Yr: **GRIEF COUNSELING:** Normal Grieving, Supportive Therapy

Stages (Parkes)	Needs	Examples	Counseling Techniques
DENIAL/NUMBING "I can't believe it happened."	PHYSICAL: Needs to talk, do things.	Food, plan funeral, child care, exercise	Acceptance, reassurance, normalizing
YEARNING/SEARCHING "I want it to be like it was before." "I see them everywhere."	EMOTIONAL: Needs to act it out over and over again, accept the loss, dream saying goodbye.	Photos, art, journals, videos, talking, visit old places, travel, review of relationship	Did you ever feel like this before? What was that like? What do you miss? What don't you miss?
DEPRESSION "How can I go on?"	EMOTIONAL/INTELLECTUAL: Needs to find meaning, create something, get outside self.	Social involvement, join groups, read books	Plan, do something every day. Draw me a picture of how you feel; of your dream.
REORGANIZATION "I never thought I would again."	INTELLECTUAL: Find interests, new friends, new goals.	Vocational planning, plans for moving, new relationships, prepare for termination	How did it go this week? Referrals to support change.

SESSIONS 2-3 Yr: **GRIEF THERAPY/ABNORMAL GRIEF:** Grief Counseling + Insist on Reality of Loss; Search for Maladaptive Patterns; Use Any Psychodynamic Theory

RECURRING THEMES: Loneliness, Sadness, Anger, Guilt, Meaningless

Source: © Nan J. Giblin, Chicago, Illinois.

91

experiences that support the vulnerable personalities [8]. Recurring themes that are met with throughout the therapy are often Loneliness, Sadness, Anger, Guilt, and Meaninglessness.

Case Study

Alice was a twenty-five year old female who entered treatment with the presenting problem that her boyfriend tried to run over her with his car when both of them were drunk. The client wanted the therapist to talk to the boyfriend about the inappropriateness of his behavior which also included physically and emotionally abusing her on a regular basis. Alice engaged in splitting; her father was "a terrible man" and her mother was "a wonderful women" and her boyfriend vacillated between being all-good and all-bad.

Alice's art work revealed this theme of splitting, as most of her pictures had lines drawn down the middle of the page from top to bottom. These lines were usually panes of windows which separated calm scenes from pictures of mass destruction by means of fire and nuclear blasts.

Alice related that her mother had been seriously "disturbed" and that she committed suicide when Alice was seven years old. However, Alice was not told about the loss until a girlfriend inadvertently told her about the suicide. Learning about the mother's cause of death did not occur until Alice was twelve years old.

As a teenager, Alice engaged in many types of acting-out behaviors including drug abuse and promiscuity which led to her having several abortions before the age of twenty years old. Alice, at twenty, was diagnosed "a borderline personality" and given little hope for relief of her overt symptoms of anxiety, depression, and the inability to form relationships with others.

Treatment of Alice began with the traditional first step in grief counseling, establishing the relationship and using that relationship to facilitate the grieving process. Since, Alice's problems were most likely rooted in childhood losses, particularly the emotional withdrawal and subsequent suicide of the mother, exploration of this loss and searching for patterns of behaviour which arose from this loss, were explored in great detail.

Mild confrontation was used to help the client engage in fewer splitting processes. The client returned to her hometown and talked to friends of her mother who brought Alice to a realistic view concerning her innocence with regard to her mother's mental problems and suicide.

Alice was able to partially resolve her anger at her father related to her mother's death and to subsequently begin a better relationship with him and other surviving members. This grief therapy which lasted approximately two years ended when the client moved to another town for work advancement, leaving her boyfriend whom she "no longer needed."

CONCLUSION

This case study illustrated that vulnerable personalities can be helped through the use of grief therapy if the therapist is willing to build a strong relationship, and to explore patterns related to childhood losses. Gently confronting the splitting processes, reality alterations, denial, devaluation, and working through the projective identifications of the client can be therapeutic for vulnerable personalities.

REFERENCES

1. T. Rando, *Grief, Dying and Death,* Research, Champaign, 1984.
2. J. Worden, *Grief Counselling and Grief Therapy: A Handbook for the Mental Health Practitioner,* Springer, New York, 1982.
3. V. Keith and B. Finlay, The Impact of Parental Divorce on Children's Educational Attainment, Marital Timing, and Likelihood of Divorce, *Journal of Marriage and the Family, 50,* 1988.
4. F. Ryan, *Ego Identification of the Preschool Child in the Divorced Single Parent Family,* University of Michigan, Ann Arbor, 1983.
5. L. Grinspoon, "Dual Diagnosis," *The Harvard Mental Health Letter,* Harvard, Boston, 1991.
6. M. Mahler, F. Pine, and A. Bergamn, *The Psychological Birth of the Human Infant,* Basic, New York, 1975.
7. J. Masterson, *The Narcissistic and Borderline Disorders,* Brunner/Mazel, New York, 1981.
8. J. Masterson, *The Real Self: A Developmental, Self and Object Relations Approach,* Brunner/Mazel, New York, 1981.
9. H. Kohut, *The Analysyis of the Self,* International Universities, New York, 1971.
10. H. Kohut, *The Restoration of the Self,* International Universities, New York, 1977.
11. O. Kernberg, *Borderline Conditions and Pathological Narcissism,* Jason Aronson, New York, 1975.
12. B. Shrive and M. Kunkel, Self Psychology, Shame and Adolescent Suicide: Theoretical and Practical Considerations, *Journal of Counselling Development, 69,* 1991.
13. T. Carrilio, Testing a Theory of the Borderline-Narcessistic Personality, *Social Work,* March, 1981.
14. P. Martocollis and L. Horwitz, *The Inner Void: Borderline and Narcissistic Disorders,* Unpublished: Menninger Foundation Conference, Smith, Kline & French, Philadelphia, 1980.
15. R. Blanck and G. Blanck, The Development Approach to the Borderline and Narcissistic Conditions, Unpublished paper: Loyola University of Chicago School of Social Work, p. 21, 1980.
16. W. Goldstein, *An Introduction to the Borderline Conditions,* Jason Aronson, Northvale, New Jersey, 1985.
17. M. Horowitz, C. Marmar, J. Krupnick, N. Wilner, N. Kaltreider, and R. Wallerstein, *Personality Styles and Brief Psychotherapy,* Basic Books, New York, 1984.

CHAPTER 8

Sexual Responses to the Stimulus of Death

Patricia MacElveen-Hoehn

> From where they stood he was overcome by the emotion that always beset him during the last minutes before an execution, a mixture of melancholy and carnal excitement. It was not obscene. It was caused by a sudden awareness of his own evanescence. Touched by the shadow of death, his flesh responded with a feverish lust for life. Had he remembered this, he would not have suggested that they wait here, for now the lust for life concentrated on the girl by his side [1, p. 351].

We have remarkably little understanding about the range of sexual responses to death. The purpose of this chapter is to bring to light the need for a more comprehensive exploration of the relationship between sexual behavior and the stimulus of death. An effort is made to appreciate the wide spectrum of situations in which that relationship occurs. In my practice I often see clients who are dealing with issues around terminal illness, death and bereavement. I have been struck by the variation of sexual behaviors in response to the exposure to the death stimulus.

Of particular note is the observation that some people experience an unusually deep and compelling desire for intercourse as an immediate and often one-time response to death. This includes reaction to one's own mortality or to that of a loved one. For some people incidents of a sexual response to death engendered much guilt and shame as they acted on impulses they did not understand. Sometimes other individuals were shocked and offended by what they thought was another's insensitive and egocentric desire for sexual pleasure around the time of tragic loss. Such sexual feelings and the related behavioral responses are often unexpected by the person and misunderstood by others during a period of need and vulnerability.

The sexual revolution of the past few decades and the emergence of research on sexuality has created the opportunities for many contexts of sexual concerns to be addressed. For example: chronic and terminal illness, and physical and mental disabilities are being recognized as challenges to peoples' sexuality rather than as permanent obstacles to this important aspect of selfhood and relationships. Sexuality has become a legitimate quality of life issue in the illness-care system.

To begin this discussion the general aims of sexual behavior will be addressed briefly. Review of the literature will be focused first on the inhibition of sexual activity and experience in response to death. Then connections between sex and death will be reviewed: the existential linking of sex and the fear of death; orgasm and death; observations in the illness-care setting, and necrophilia. Following the methodology, the case findings will be presented to illustrate a range of sexual responses: to the threat of death to the self; in bereavement; in wartime. Shadow aspects of death as an aphrodisiac are noted. In the discussion and conclusion section, a beginning continuum of sexual responses to death is offered and possible explanations for understanding these responses are explored.

AIMS OF SEXUAL BEHAVIOUR

According to Katchadourian and Lunde the sexual relationship satisfies many human needs besides reproduction, the attainment of pleasure and the reduction of "sexual tension" [2, p. 3-5]. Sex is used to obtain love, express affection and as a defense against loneliness. Sexuality is important to self-esteem; the concept of self, and moral and spiritual identity. Sexual behavior can be used as a means for economic and other gains and can be involved in many ways that satisfy a wide spectrum of human needs and desires.

An intimate relationship characterized by empathy, safety and acceptance may or may not include sexual activity. Having an intimate other or confidant relates significantly to high morale, a sense of well-being and support during difficult periods of life, even during one's dying or bereavement [3, 4]. People who are widowed, terminally ill or who have lost their most important relationship suffer from major losses and deprivation that constitute serious stressors [5, 6]. These studies suggest that such people may be at risk for physical and mental distress, premature death and suicide. According to Leviton, individuals who commit suicide have the lowest satisfaction in meeting their intimacy and/or sexual needs, indicating again the association between close relationships and the maintenance of health and well being [5].

INHIBITION OF SEXUAL ACTIVITY IN
RESPONSE TO DEATH

A common assumption (and experience) is that following a death there is often a lack of interest in sexual interaction or intimacy. The dynamics of the inhibition of libido and sexual activity associated with the stimulus of death are not clearly understood. These behaviors are parallel to that seen in depression which is part of the grieving process, however, depression is not usually and initial response to a death. Perhaps the immediate sexual inhibition is a function of the emotional and psychic numbness that often follows the trauma of the loss when people find it difficult to feel anything. When sexual activity is rejected along with other pleasures, the underlying dynamic may be connected with acute guilt requiring punishment, or at least the forfeiture of joy and other positive feelings.

Withdrawal of sexual activity may accompany separation as a function of anticipatory grief in preparation for death. This may be true for the dying person as well as a spouse or partner. There are numerous other reasons why people end their sexual relationship in the face of a terminal illness that are unrelated to the fear of death, and these are described elsewhere [7].

Many men experience temporary impotence or withdrawal from sexual activity for prolonged periods during mourning [8, 9]. This can be a normal part of the painful process of disengaging from the attachment to the lost person. Other times, withdrawal from usual expressions of affection, as well as sexual activity, occurs in men who cannot articulate their grief but do it in this more silent way.

Many women report no sexual interest or desire during the first six weeks after the death of their husbands. For some women this withdrawal lasted as long as a year [10]. Donnelly found many women for whom "sex, or any connotation of pleasure, was abhorrent," following the loss of a child [11, p. 64]. Requests for sex from their husbands caused great conflict for couples whose grieving patterns were not congruent. This incongruence in bereavement is a common, often painful experience for many couples.

An Existential View of Sex and the Fear of Death

In the development of his existential psychotherapeutic paradigm, Irving Yalom identified the four most significant concerns that are the sources of existential conflicts that each person confronts in life [12]. These are: death, freedom, isolation, and meaninglessness. Death, of course, is the ultimate concern; its inevitability and the cessation of being. Life and death are inseparable and as such, death "exerts a vast influence upon experience and conduct." In addition, Yalom stated that ". . . death is a primordial source of anxiety . . ." Thus, our ever-constant task is that of coping with the profound fears and anxieties about the loss of self, the pain of dying and the unknowns of what happens after death to ourselves and the people we love. Even young children struggle with powerful fears of death.

In order to manage this fear of finitude, Yalom believes we mount various defenses against a consciousness of death that may become maladaptive [12]. Defenses originally based on denial evolve into displacement, sublimation, and conversion to keep the terrifying anxiety out of awareness. He articulated two fundamental defenses against death which he called: "Personal Specialness" and

"The Ultimate Rescuer" [12, p. 117]. Specialness is the irrational belief that others are subject to the laws of life and death, "but not me." Compulsive heroism, aggression and control, workaholism and narcissism are some of the individuating expressions of "Specialness." People use them as protection against the ubiquitous fears of their mortality. The "Ultimate Rescuer" is predicated on the belief in an all-powerful force or figure, ever-present, caring and protecting. While sometimes seen as capable of anger, the Ultimate Rescuer may be placated through rituals or other means. This entity may be a loved one, a supernatural being, a human leader or a higher cause. Extreme dependence on this defense can lead to a restricting fusion with the Ultimate Rescuer and a great resistance to taking risks, growing and changing or engaging in the uncertainties of fully living life. Loneliness and vulnerability of being so different (i.e., special), or contrastingly, the loss of autonomy in the fusion of the self with another, are the costs of these defenses. Being stuck in the extreme of either defense produces neurotic maladaptation. Either of these opposite defenses may push the individual more toward the promise of comfort to be found in the other direction. Yalom noted that the anxiety of individuation is a sense of profound aloneness that is relieved temporarily for some people by sexual intercourse. They seek in sexual union the protection and solace of physical oneness with another. For some the sex act, symbolic of procreation, is the antithesis of death, the human's thrust into the future in the face of finality and non-being.

Yalom cited the case of a man who sought therapy because while his wife was dying and after her death, he reached a frightening level of sexual preoccupation and compulsivity [12, p. 145-146]. He was seeing pornographic films, visiting singles' bars and masturbating several times a day. On the night of his wife's funeral he went to a prostitute. The sex itself was not satisfying being devoid of joy or other positive feelings. The women were not encountered as other human beings but more as a means to some end which wasn't really working. The behavior was unacceptable to the client, distressing and out of his control, which were the reasons for which he sought help. During ensuing therapy, his dreams clearly demonstrated that his wife's terminal condition caused him to struggle with the possibility of his own death. Yalom provided other case examples where sex was used to alleviate the pain of existential anxiety and fear of death in counterphobic and neurotic behavior patterns. These elaborate sexual responses are defined as pathological and might be reflective of the level of illness in the client population of his practice.

Thus we see that certain life experiences penetrate the defenses against the fear of death and profound anxiety surfaces temporarily, only to be buried rapidly again. Being confronted directly with death, or its possibility, whether for self or a loved one, is often such an experience.

Grief itself can feel overwhelmingly intolerable. Peretz described individuals who are unable to endure the excruciating loneliness of grief, who seek refuge in a flurry of sexual activity [13]. They try to avoid these feelings by quickly seeking a replacement for the loved one who has died. They may attach almost immediately to one person, have a series of relationships, or have sex with a number of people in a relatively short period of time. Exposure to the loved one's death can also raise the issue of the undeniable mortality for the survivor. Perhaps some of these people are in touch with a profound existential loneliness; others with their terror of death. The sexual behavior to which Peretz refers may represent an effort to find protection from unbearable pain or fear in the fusion with another. In Yalom's paradigm sexual fusion can serve as a refuge from both existential isolation and death anxiety even if that refuge is only transitory.

Orgasm and Death

Keleman connected sex and death through the common force of excitement [14, p. 27]. For him dying is also associated with unformedness, unconnectedness and unknowingness. He related these issues to the surrender of orgasm, "la petite mort"—the little death. "The orgiastic state produces feelings of dying, raises fears of dying . . ." [14, p. 119]. He proposed that sexual intercourse provides practice for dying—the orgasm simulating the letting go of life with its concomitant intensity and exhilaration.

Sexual Behavior in Illness-Care Settings

The illness-care setting provides a ready stage for the enactment of the sex and death drama. Leviton described a young woman receiving test results from her physician indicating Hodgkin's Disease [5, p. 161]. She experienced and "overwhelming desire to be held—to be loved and caressed." She had hoped that her physician "might possibly understand" her reactions from cues she gave him. Instead he fled from her room; her sexual or intimacy needs left unaddressed, and importantly, probably misunderstood.

When a kidney transplant is not possible dialysis treatments are a literal life line for people with end-stage renal disease. Reichsman and Levy reported overt masturbation among many male patients during the early months of dialysis [15, p. 37]. The authors define this sexual behavior as a response to the anxiety and stress of dialysis. An alternative explanation is also available. The move from more conservative treatments to dialysis is an undeniable message that kidney function has become inadequate to sustain life. Without technological intervention the person will die. Perhaps these men were using masturbation during initiation into dialysis to cope with the awareness of how close to death they really were.

When patients have severe myocardial infarctions, medical priorities focus on the support of cardiac function and the preservation of life. Consideration of sexual issues is not essential to these efforts. Casem and Hacket found that many of these men expressed concern about impotence while still in the coronary care unit [16]. "Three percent of the patients acted out sexually toward the nurses.

Themes related to sexual prowess and function were found in these patients' conversations. Once the threat of death was no longer present, the patients' behavior in many instances became sexually provocative" [17, p. 29]. In referring to this study, Woods speculated that a shift away from death towards quality of life issues might account for sexual behavior that is testing the patient's sexual image. That is, the response to his flirtatious behavior from opposite sex staff (the nurses) might provide validation for the patient that he is still regarded as a sexual person.

On the other hand, I would question whether the observed sexual behavior may have been a strategy to reduce the anxiety from the patients' brush with death rather than a consequence of being past the threat of death and on to quality of life issues. Further, death is not a stranger in a coronary care unit. Indeed, it is an arena in which physicians pit their skills and powers against death. Surviving patients are not unaware of this struggle or that physicians sometimes lose the battle and that nearby patients die. The staff themselves sometimes use sexual behavior or conversations with sexual connotations in intensive care settings probably to bind their own death anxiety.

In medical schools the stories are legend about what happens in the anatomy labs. Despite instruction to treat cadavers with respect in deference to their humanity, medical students are known to use sexual behavior and humor as counterphobic coping mechanisms to deal with the anxiety of working with corpses [18, 19].

Jaffe observed that sexuality and death, the alpha and the omega, are conflicting forces with amplify already present anxiety [20]. She described connections between sex and death that are important for care providers. She stated: "Confronting death generates more anguish and fear than any other area of human behavior" [20, p. 110]. Persons who are terminally ill and their spouses often get caught in double binds. Sex being the forward-moving life force may feel inappropriate as a well person is trying to disengage from a spouse who is dying. Instead, the well person may turn to another for sex, "as an antidote to loss and death;" sexual and emotional support being withdrawn from the spouse who is dying. At the same time, the dying spouse may want more sexual contact to counter his or her own anxiety about death as deterioration progresses.

Orfirer affirmed that a mature sexual relationship can offer comfort and reassurance through warmth, closeness, love and tenderness for the bereaved person [8, p. 161-162] . This is in spite of the stereotype that withdrawal is the usual response for the grieving person and further, that wanting sexual pleasure at such time is inappropriate. He suggested that it is the pleasurable intensity of sexual activity that makes the use of sex a strong defense to avoid mourning by denying that a loss has occurred. Sexual engagement provides a false reassurance (even if only temporarily) that the bereaved person is not alone or abandoned. He illustrated these issues in his report of a physician who visited a friend who was the wife of his patient. The father of his patient had died a week before. The wife privately expressed her embarrassment and concerns to the physician about her husband's request for intercourse at this time. She was reassured by the physician's support for her husband's need for comfort through sexual activity. She accepted her husband's sexual needs as normal rather than as a "gross insensitivity," worthy only of her refusal. She was then able to respond to his needs because of the information and validation from a respected authority figure and friend.

Sexual acting out by adolescent girls on residential treatment units pose difficult challenges to the staff [21]. For these girls the normal mourning associated with the tasks of separation and individuation is amplified during a period of psychic vulnerability. Initially there is the series of losses predicated on the need for separation from home and family and any current death of a loved one. Then there are the separations from staff to whom they get attached due to the usual vacations, attrition and rotations. Female patients often respond to these losses by trying to establish a sexual relationship with a male patient or therapist. The authors rejected an explanation that sexual acting out following a loss represents a "pathological masking of grief" [21, p. 4]. They used a psychoanalytic approach and the first stage of Bowlby's mourning process to understand the girls' immediate reaction to grief. Disturbed adolescent girls believe they are dependent on important external relationships for survival of the self. They desperately try to replace the loss of such a relationship by sexually acting out. This activity is seen as both regressive (intense wish for reunion with the pre-oedipal mother) and progressive (attempt at a passionate relationship with a boy to ward off the terror of those merger fantasies). The sexual acting out was also believed to relieve the "painful sadness and longing for love" [21, p. 12]. The authors described one patient's fluctuation "between clinging avariciously" to the ward manager and "abruptly refusing to have anything to do with her." This is reminiscent of the oscillation between Yalom's fusion with the powerful protector and separation to individuation and specialness [12].

Thus, in the face of the threatened loss of self (psychic death?) the disturbed adolescent girl chooses efforts at sexual activity to insure her survival even though it is not in the best interests of her growth and development.

Necrophilia

An extreme association between sex and death is necrophilia, i.e., sexual intercourse with a female corpse described by Krafft-Ebbing in 1906. He determined that only a man in a psychotic state would be able to surmount normal human repugnance to be able to experience sexual pleasure with a dead body [22, p. 611]. Little treatment of this topic was found outside the work by Karpman on sexual offenders [23]. Paraphrasing Brill, Karpman states: "Destruction of the dam of shame, disgust and morality in necrophilia requires more psychic labor than in the construction of any other perversion" [23, p. 128]. Necrophilia is usually thought be quite rare although Brill believed it was "more frequent than recognized" [23, p. 128]. Corpses are obtained from graves or used in mortuaries. At times the body is also mutilated. The necrophiliac is said to derive pleasure from the defenselessness for the corpse and its inability to reject or demean. East suggests that necrophilia is used by some sadists as a way to avoid committing murder [23, p. 126]. Because necrophilia is associated exclusively with psychoses it is beyond the purview of this discussion. In a sense however, the fact does remain that the necrophiliac derives sexual arousal and pleasure by penetrating death.

Closely related to sex with a dead body is sex with a live woman who looks dead [24, p. 358]. Prostitutes providing this option simulate corpses by using "powder or wax on their skin to look lifeless, dress in a shroud and even lie in a coffin" [24, p. 347]. The fantasy of the dead body as sex object is thus acted out. Here we see men consciously using the most powerful symbol of death, the corpse, as an aphrodisiac.

Summary of the Literature

A search of the psychosocial and medical literature revealed a limited number of references linking sexual activity as a response to death. Descriptions of sexual response in bereavement included a reduction of libido and sexual inhibition for some persons. Yalom's existential paradigm provided a conceptualization of sexual activity as a defense against fundamental death anxiety [12]. The few observations of sexual behavior in response to life threatening illness were discussed. Availability of a mature sexual relationship was identified as a source of comfort and solace for the bereaved spouse or partner.

What has not been found is a phenomenon where there is an immediate, powerfully intense urge for sexual intercourse in response to death or the threat of death. This sexual response may occur easily within an established relationship when one is available. When not available the response may be manifest as a one-time sexual encounter which does not seem to alter the previously platonic or casual relationship. Description of this phenomenon is included in the case material which follows.

Methodology

Clinical data from a number of cases have been gathered over a fifteen-year period from my own practice. In more recent times, nursing colleagues, physicians, psychotherapists and hospice workers have shared their clinical observations and experiences of sexual responses to death. (In almost all instances they had not understood these phenomena and usually had not discussed them with anyone.) These cases are used to illustrate a range of situations in which sexual activity in response to death has been observed.

Reports sometimes emerged spontaneously from a client's discussions about experiences related to exposure to a life threatening situation, being close to someone who is terminally ill or the death of a loved one. In later times the data surfaced from bereaved clients in response to my descriptions of the wide spectrum of normal behaviors associated with the grieving process. This list includes physical, cognitive, emotional, social, spiritual, and sexual manifestations of grief. These domains are characterized by statements about the variety of experiences people have during bereavement.

Specifically, about sexual behavior I usually say, "Some people may notice a lack of interest for a while. Some men may be temporarily impotent but this usually goes away by itself. Some people find they have a greater need for sex following a death. It is not uncommon for members of a couple to have different levels of desire than usual or for their sexual needs to be very different from each other during bereavement."

Some details in the case examples have been changed to protect the anonymity of the people involved.

Findings

The threat of loss of one's being can often evoke sexual behavior in surprising and unexpected ways. The following brief sketches illustrate the many circumstances within which we see sexual responses to death.

Threat of Death to One's Self

Case 1

A young psychiatric nurse described the frightening event when her usually healthy husband collapsed from what was later diagnosed as an acute electrolyte imbalance. He was transported to the hospital by ambulance during which his condition continued to deteriorate at a rapid rate: muscles feeling weaker, ability to move more difficult, and his energy level ebbing dramatically. En route to the hospital, his wife sat beside him, neither one knowing what was happening to him and both being very frightened for his life. She was stunned by his efforts to fondle her breast and to engage in other behavior which were clearly sexual signals. She reported being unable to make sense of what he was doing. The strangeness of this behavior was lost in the subsequent emergency admission and the procedures which were able to reverse his life-threatening condition. She was very puzzled by his sexual response but they never spoke of it.

Case 2

A sixty-one year old professor who had been permanently disabled by a major heart attack for several years was experiencing progressive cardiac myopathy (weakening of the heart muscle) resulting in increasing deterioration of his condition. He was referred to a heart transplant team to be worked up as a possible transplant patient. The possibility of being on a heartplant transplant list represented a possible reprieve from death to him and he desperately wanted even the hope of that fantasy. The testing took several days in the hospital after which he waited agonizingly at home to see if he would be accepted into the transplant program. When he received the news that he was rejected, he reported having what was probably "the most driving and profound feeling of pure lust" he had ever experienced, even though at this point he had been impotent for some time. He describes it as seeming to come from the deepest part of himself and he did not speak of it to his wife who had given him the bad news. She had suggested that they lie down and she held him in her arms for a long time as they cried together.

Case 3

Ms. D had been accosted on her way home from having had dinner with a friend. She had been grabbed from behind and a knife was held to her throat. She was afraid the man would kill her but she tried to resist as he pulled her toward an alley. Miraculously a door opened and the two men who emerged saw her plight and ran to help her. The assailant released her and fled. The police never caught the man. The rescuers saw her home safely. She was in a state of shock for some time and found herself telling her story repeatedly to her friends. Ms. D. reported that in the next ten days she slept with seven different men. She had been romantically involved in the past with two of them. The other five had been men with whom she had varying degrees of platonic friendships. She was quite startled as she thought about her behavior which followed the attack where she thought she might be killed.

Case 4

Mrs. Y was a thirty-five year old woman who had been plagued with severe vaginal bleeding for almost a year before the fibroid in the center of her uterus had finally been identified through vaginal ultrasound. A medication was required for twenty-five days prior to the surgery during which there was a marked decrease in sexual activity for fear of stimulating the bleeding. She and her husband are both professionals, well informed consumers with access to the finest health care providers. They knew the operation although highly specialized was in the hands of an expert and was a fairly low risk procedure. In spite of that information, two weeks before the operation Mrs. Y and her husband began sharing their mutual fears about the possibility of her death from the surgery or paralysis from some mishap with the spinal anaesthesia. They shared much intimacy and tenderness as they experienced what might possibly be their last days together. In the shower on the day before admission to the hospital she found herself planning all their activities for the time they had left. She decided that they would go to bed early to have some special time to make love in case it was their last time. She smiled to herself because she and her husband were aware of the sex and death connection and she knew that her urge for making love was an effort to bind her death anxiety.

Case 5

Mrs. G, a woman in her sixties who had breast cancer with numerous metastases, was in the hospital during the final stage of her illness. Her daughter, Jane came from another city and was with her mother most of that last week. Mrs. G. drifted in and out of coma. When she was conscious she was so weak she was barely able to speak, however, she masturbated almost constantly. Jane and the nurse were all aware of the obvious masturbatory behavior although no one spoke of it. The nurses were mystified and were unable to provide any explanation to Jane or support her during this distressing experience. Jane was left with the disturbing memory of spending hours watching her mother masturbate as she was dying.

Hospice nurses report sexual behavior by some dying patients. Both men and women have been observed masturbating in the days when they are close to death. Dying men sometimes express concern about whether they will ever have another erection; some men do have erections. Some men's conversations are full of sexual topics and innuendo and some are wanting to touch the nurses in intimate ways. These sexual behaviors are hardly the norm among dying patients but they do occur. Hospice bereavement visitors (mostly women) have reported that occasionally widowers have made passes at them or wanted to talk about their sexual feelings. These events were fielded by the bereavement visitors individually usually from an assumption that the men were lonely and missed their partner with whom they had shared many years.

Threat of Death to a Loved One

Being close to a loved one whose life is, or seems to be, in imminent danger or who is ill and getting close to death has also been associated with a strong sexual response. It is not known whether the loss of a loved one is the primary stimulus for sexual response or whether such emotional proximity to death engenders fears about the person's own fragile mortality.

Case 6

Mrs. R had been with her in-laws for two weeks while her husband remained on the critical list still in a coma from an automobile accident. During this time the family had a young man staying with them, a Mr. T. He and Mrs. R went to see a physician because of Mr. T's sudden and sever difficulty in swallowing and inability to speak. He was eventually diagnosed as having globus hystericus (swallowing problems of an emotional origin). His symptoms were later relieved when the story emerged about how he and Mrs. R had unexpectedly found themselves in bed together. Mr. T's problems were the result of his acute guilt over having had sex with Mrs. R, whose husband was between life and death. Mr. T and Mrs. R were both chagrined about their "shameful behavior" which was incompatible with their sense of who they were. Mrs. R could hardly believe that she had made love to a man who was practically a stranger in the home of her in-laws while her husband might be dying at the hospital.

Case 7

Mrs. W was a forty-one-year-old professional woman whose six-year-old son had been very ill. She had endured the period of diagnostic work-up fearing that he might have leukaemia or some other life-threatening blood disease. She was home with him for three weeks. The testing eventually ruled out a serious illness in favor of a "strange virus" which ran a self-limited course. Mrs. W commented that she had "never been hornier in her life," than in those weeks of her son's illness. At first she wondered if she had cabin fever from spending so much time at home. Later, she wondered if her unusual libido was because she thought her son might die.

Case 8

Mr. L was a twenty-eight-year-old man whose wife, the mother of their year-old daughter was gravely ill. In spite of desperate, experimental protocols, his wife's leukemia worsened and the night before she died, he stayed with her until very late. At about 1 a.m., a friend called to check on the patient's condition and to give the husband some support. The friend told him to stop by on his way home even though it was late. He did, and ended up in bed with her. His wife died the next day. He felt very guilty and wanted to talk about it. He had been faithful to his wife throughout the year of her illness when she had been too sick to feel like making love. He hated himself for not being able to wait at least one more day until after she had died. He believed she would probably have accepted his impulse and would have loved him anyway. It was his own inability to understand this event and to forgive himself that distressed him greatly.

Case 9

Mrs. C was a forty-five-year-old woman who had come 3000 miles for treatment for her precious teenaged daughter, Mary who had aplastic anemia. When I first saw Mrs. C her daughter had received a bone marrow transplant from one sibling, and the two others had come to donate blood platelets, hoping to support a recovery. In spite of everything that had been done, complications set in and no new white cells were produced. The fact that Mary was dying became evident. Her father had come with her and his wife when Mary was admitted for the transplant and returned when her condition was deteriorating so rapidly. In working with Mrs. C, I shared that sometimes people had an increased need for closeness and even sex when someone they loved was dying. Her eyes widened and her mouth fell open as I talked. Then she said, "Oh my, yes! But feeling as I do it would never have entered my mind. We do have a very active sex life. We've been apart for several weeks and I know he often uses sex when he is very worried about something. And that's what he'll probably need to deal with what's happening to Mary."

Sexual Responses to Bereavement

In some situations a request for sex immediately after a death may become the crux of a significant disjunction in a couple's relationship if one person's sexual need is misunderstood. For example, it may be perceived as an indication of a self-centered need for pleasure, insensitivity to the tragedy, or indifference to the needs for the other's grief and distress. In the situations below the couples share a major loss and one or both of the spouses has a great desire for sex. How the other spouse responds to this request can be very important to the relationship.

Case 10

Mrs. B's eighteen-year-old son was killed in an accident. On that night her husband insisted on making love to her. She was still in shock feeling "destroyed" by the devastating news. She was unable to understand his request and feelings as she did, refused him. In a move that was out of character for him he took her forcefully against her will. Following the rape they had no sexual relationship for a period of years. They had never spoken of that night and she had never forgiven him although they had remained together. Ten years later the experience was still vivid in her memory.

Case 11

Mrs. T, a thirty-two-year-old wife and mother received news about the death of a best friend with whom she and her husband had been close for many years. Although it was very early in the morning they went immediately to be with the widow and her six children. They didn't return home until almost midnight, physically and emotionally exhausted. Mrs. T was shocked when her husband reached out to her to make love. Her first thought was, "My God, where could he find the energy for this!" She remembered hearing about how some people use sexual activity to reduce stress and tension. She made a quick choice to respond to him. She decided that it didn't make any difference if she really understood why he wanted to make love on the night of their friend's death. She loved him and he wanted her and that was all that was necessary.

Case 12

Mr. and Mrs. K, were a couple in their late twenties. Their six-month-old baby had strangled on a cord which held a toy to the crib rail. Mrs. K was plagued with acute guilt about not having responded to her baby's cries. Her own mother accused her of being responsible for the baby's death. Mr. K was loving and supportive to his wife in spite of his own shock and pain at the loss of their only child. He was angry at his mother-in-law's condemnation of his wife. He blurted out, "I wonder what my mother-in-law would say if she knew we had sex several times during the days right after the baby's death." His wife was shocked at this disclosure and quickly added, "We were feeling so terrible, we didn't know what else to do except to love each other."

At a Cancer Care Conference in 1976, one topic I addressed was the importance of maintaining family relationships while caring for a terminally ill relative at home. "How do you make love when someone you care about is dying in a nearby room?" was a question I posed to the audience, who were primarily health care providers. Following the presentation, a man whose dark hair was frosted with grey, waited to be the last person to speak to me. He told how his twenty-year-old son had recently been diagnosed with an inoperable brain tumor. He and his wife had chosen to care for their son at home. He thanked me for acknowledging the dilemma of what to do about making love as a legitimate one for couples. He said the discussion made him feel "normal" for having thoughts about sex when his only son was dying.

Among couples who are living together, the opportunities to be held and comforted as well as to make love may be very available. If it feels right to them, they are able to use sexual activity as a way to cope with any source of stress or tensions including anxiety about death. For persons not living with a partner, sexual activity in response to a death may be more visible and noteworthy as in the cases that follow.

Case 13

Ms. V was a fifty-two-year-old single woman who had been having a relationship with a man for several years when he became terminally ill with cancer. She spent much time with him at the hospital and was with him when he died one morning about 2 a.m. Before leaving the hospital, she telephoned a man whom she had known as a former neighbor and casual friend. She told him of J's death and asked if she could stop by his apartment. She was aware on her way to his house that she wanted to have sex with him. After a drink, they went to bed. Following that night, there was no further intimate or sexual contact with him. The relationship remained what it had been before, and their sexual encounter was never mentioned.

Case 14

A thirty-year-old single woman, Ms. Y was in therapy for help to deal with her father's oncoming death. She had been very close to him and was his only child. She was not involved in an intimate relationship at the time. After the funeral a friend of the family invited her to come by his house. She went home with him and they had sex. The next day she felt extremely guilty and thought it was a terrible thing that she had done. She knew she had no interest in seeing him again. He, however, did make two attempts to see her but did not continue after her refusals.

She loved her father very much and was very disturbed by her behavior just after the funeral.

Case 15

A young woman at the Planned Parenthood Clinic was devastated when her pregnancy test turned out positive. She had conceived while at home attending a funeral for her little brother in another part of the state. Although she had been using a diaphragm faithfully it did not occur to her to take it with her at that very sad time. While at home she contacted a high school classmate who invited her to come over. There had never been any romantic interest or even dating in their earlier friendship. They had a cup of coffee and then went to bed together. She was mortified that she had become pregnant under such circumstances and for having wanted sex at the time of her brother's death. The clinic nurse (a former student of mine) was familiar with the concept of wanting intercourse around the time of a death. She was able to counsel the young woman that her behavior was not monstrous or repulsive but a response that many people experience. Normalizing her behavior helped the young woman to be more accepting of her sexual response and to focus on the important decisions she had to make about the pregnancy.

Case 16

Mr. G, a psychotherapist, received the news that the young son of a woman client had drowned in a boating accident earlier that day. He went to her home to express his condolences and to support her. She was beside herself with shock and disbelief. They talked in a quiet room alone. It became clear that she was coming on to him sexually and he felt a great need to get out of the private space they had been sharing and left the house soon after. She continued in therapy with him for some time after the loss of her son. Neither one mentioned what had occurred in her house on the day her son died nor was there any further seductive behavior towards him on her part.

Case 17

Mr. R worked as a trainer and educator in the AIDS field. He mentioned how he no longer attended the services for each person he knew saying, "Too much . . . It's just too much." He was a member of a dwindling group who found themselves going to the funerals or memorial services of mutual friends who had died of HIV. At least one of these men was known to arrange "dates" for immediately after the services. Another was known to stop by a local establishment for anonymous sex on his way home. The others in the group left the funerals and went out to eat together. There was joking and laughing about the explicit arrangements of their buddies for sex following funerals. The behavior was accepted but there was no discussion or understanding of why it was happening.

Case 18

Ms. M, a single woman, returned to her home town for the funeral of her father. She had not been back there for some time and stayed about six weeks. She stated that she called up all her male friends and old boyfriends because she wanted to have sex with them. During those weeks after her father's death she said she just couldn't get enough sex. The behavior was most unusual for her but her sexual needs were so powerful she felt compelled to act on them. She had never before shared with anyone about that experience for fear of what people would think of her.

Case 19

Mr. V talked about how he dated a young nurse who worked in the local hospital. On occasion she would call him late at night and ask him to come over. If he was already in bed he would usually decline. If she insisted that he come, he would then go to her. That instance was usually connected to the death of one of the patients with whom she had formed an emotional attachment. He came to recognize and respond to that special need she had. He said the lovemaking at those times was very passionate but different. He felt she was somewhere by herself, not connected the way they usually were. He didn't mind however and was more than willing to be there for her at those times when it seemed so important to her.

Case 20

A sex therapist reported a strange occurrence with a young woman he had been treating for severe sexual dysfunction. Almost immediately after hearing of her father's death she engaged in a sexual encounter with a friend. The whole event went quite smoothly. Without any thinking, attempts to control, or conscious efforts to make something happen she had surrendered to a satisfying and fulfilling sexual experience. She did not know how or why it had all happened so easily. None of the difficulties common to her usual dysfunction and unsatisfying intercourse were present. The therapist was at a loss to explain her experience or why it did not affect or improve the condition for which she was being treated.

Sex and Death in Wartime

Sexual attitudes and mores often change allowing more freedom for sexual activity in wartime. During the Civil War prostitutes were known to accompany the troops, following the marches and living on the perimeter of the encampments. There are probably many reasons why women willing to provide sex were tolerated or even encouraged to be available to men in the military and many reasons why the men used these women; not the least of which might be the associations of sex and death described herein. Historically, rape and pillage were rewards for conquering soldiers. However, perhaps not all rape in those situations was motivated only by the power and license to do anything accorded the victors of the battle. Perhaps some men were using sex (in this case violent sex) to celebrate their survival of the battle—being alive when so many others were dead, to assuage fundamental fears from their close brush with death, or to ameliorate the sometimes mystical sense of aloneness associated with exposure to death.

Sexual activity was rampant in the 1940s around the camps accumulating the large number of soldiers to be sent overseas in troop ships. The motivation of "make hay while the sun shines for tomorrow we may die," is one explanation for that "lustful" behavior. "Going off to war," means to many soldiers the possibility of being killed; to be in combat is to be surrounded by death. Is it possible that some of those young men were in touch with their terror of dying in battle and were looking for an antidote to that fear? And with whom were they having all this sex? It hardly seems plausible that a complimentary multitude of prostitutes appeared upon the scene. At that time, many young women held the conservative values about sex which prevailed prior to the sexual revolution of the 1960s. And yet a compassionate complicity seemed to occur between the young people participating in that historical wartime moment.

"Why Men Love War," by William Broyles, Jr. a former *Newsweek* editor, is one man's extraordinary personal disclosure about the many exquisitely powerful physical, psychological and spiritual enticements of being a combat soldier [25]. Among a number of allurements the author articulates the love and thrill of killing. Love of the stunning, unforgettable beauty of killing and destruction with white phosphorus. Love of comrades who protect you and share the unspeakable. He provides chilling and haunting accounts of how, "War stops time, intensifies experience to the point of a terrible ecstasy" [25, p. 56]. These are conditions and circumstances which veterans are never able to recreate again in civil life. And for which many of them always carry and unnameable ache and longing.

Broyles acknowledges that sex is never more urgently intense than in war [25, p. 62]. Interestingly, he describes the, "aura, collective power, and almost animal force," of being a soldier rather than being a limited and inadequate individual. He then contrasts that concealment in the image of war to the "agonizing loneliness" of the loss of all that characterizes the soldier as the individual he really is. (In Yalom's terms in the face of death the soldier described here fuses with the powerful protection of the group identity and in turn suffers from the painful loss of his self.) Broyles recognizes that the intensity of sex in war is influenced by the presence of death [25, p. 62]:

> No matter what our weapons on the battlefield, love is finally our only weapon against death. Sex is the weapon of life, the shooting sperm sent like an army of guerrillas to penetrate the egg's defenses—the only victory that really matters. War thrusts you into a well of loneliness, death breathing in your ear. Sex is the grappling hook that pulls you out, ends your isolation, makes you one with life again.

As we see, for Broyles, even conception is glorified as a fierce act of combat violence. Nevertheless, in his essay he portrayed a "death-obsessed lust," being able to see death even more clearly in the gripping experience of intercourse than in killing. And knowing that he "could not get enough [sex] . . . , would keep on coming back again and again." As a journalist Broyles is eloquent in his expression of the unthinkable aspects of his and others' experience of war, sex and death.

Case 21

A forty-five-year-old woman was recalling her time in Vietnam where she had worked in an army camp quite distant from combat. One night the camp was unexpectedly attacked by enemy aircraft. She ran to a foxhole and found herself sharing it with one of the officers. Although she had worked with him they were not friends nor had she any personal interest in him. The attack lasted until dawn. Much to her astonishment, she found herself having repeated intercourse with him all night long, with an incredible level of intensity. The next day they worked together in the office as usual. Neither of them acknowledged the sexual encounter of the previous night. No interest in changing the relationship was expressed by either of them. The experience in the foxhole was an isolated event that seemed totally out of the context of her life and which she was unable to explain.

Case 22

Mr. J was a thirty-eight-year-old male Vietnam veteran, who was giving some accounts of his time in that war. He was a naval communications expert, part of a team that went ashore into North Vietnam during the dark of night. Their mission was to install radio communications and monitoring devices. These tasks required that they work very closely together in pairs. The loss of men was very high; the survivors having lost one buddy after another. They would be at sea for about a week at a time, and then return to the base for a few days for new supplies. While on these leaves, much drinking and partying occurred until the 10 p.m. curfew when each man settled some place for the night, usually with a woman friend or prostitute. Mr. J was invited by a diminutive woman who tended bar, to stay with her in the back of the place where she worked. He spoke poignantly of how he would cling to her the entire night, trying to feel safe and protected in her arms—to get away from the terror of his own death. Neither could speak much of the other's language so there was very little conversation. They had minimal interaction except that each night he was on shore, she held him in her arms all night. He said he was able to separate his grief for his dead friends from the fear of his own death; it was the latter that he was trying to assuage with the woman from the bar.

More recently, in a time of great despair when he contemplated suicide, he again found a woman who was willing to hold him in her arms at night and made little or no demands on him. Although he later developed a relationship with this woman, he recognized that she had initially served the same function in his life as the woman in Vietnam: someone to hold onto and feel safe with when he feared he might lose his life.

Case 23

A crusty old RAF veteran from WWII recounted how less than 15 percent of the men who were part of the RAF crews from that war survived. As the planes returned from their missions the counting of who did and did not make it became a ritual: mournful for those who were lost and joyful for those who made it safely home. There was a tradition among the RAF men called "wenching." It referred to getting as much sex as they could between their missions.

Case 24

An army nurse stationed in Germany was at an American base which had a large military hospital. It also had a "jump school." Parachute jumping is not without its threat of death or serious injury. When a "jump" was scheduled the nurses knew that there would be lots of sex the night before as it had become a predictable phenomenon. They laughed about the need for a good supply of condoms on the eves of jumps but weren't sure how to explain the behavior.

The Shadow Side of the Sexual Response to Death

The conscious link between sex and death where the death stimulus is sought after as an aphrodisiac is a shadow issue. Some men prolong their time in combat in order to stay on that perilous edge which includes that sexual intensity described by Broyles [25]. There are those who use videos which feature death and violence (threat of death?) or "slasher films" to enhance sexual experience. A shadow or pathological element emerges as we follow this line of observations. A horrible step further is the underground "snuff" video of which it said that the torture and killing of the victim (always a woman) is not acted or simulated. In other words the actress actually does die in the making of the video for the pornographic power of watching a real death occur. Where the violence of some sadists and wife batterers fits into this shocking picture is not understood. Some batterers are known to be particularly amorous in the making-up process following a battering episode. Efforts to strangle one's self just short of death have been used to enhance sexual intensity and a few people have died in the process. The information here is useful in extending our awareness of the spectrum of sexual responses to death but it is anecdotal and therefore will not figure in the continuum to be described below.

DISCUSSION AND CONCLUSIONS

A Continuum of Sexual Responses to Death

The stimulus of the presence of death or the threat of death has been demonstrated to have an impact on some people's sexual experience and to evoke a sexual response in some but certainly not all people. The frequency and consistency of these phenomena are not known. Both men and women are affected in varying degrees and for different lengths of time. The case examples presented earlier suggest preliminary work on a continuum of the range of the impact of death on sexual activity and experience (see Table 1).

Points on the Continuum of Sexual Responses to Death

1. Withdrawal from sexual activity or inhibition of interest and libido has been noted. Some men experience impotence. The duration of this response may be very short term around the immediate time of the death, constitute a temporary period or endure for prolonged periods of time, even as long as years. Sexual withdrawal may be paralleled by the inability to experience any measure of joy and pleasure, as well. Prolonged sexual withdrawal may signal serious difficulty in the grieving process or in the response to the anxiety related to a death stimulus.

Table 1. Sexual Responses to the Stimululs of Death

Response	Duration
1. Withdrawal from sexual activity; impotence; inhibition of interest and libido	Prolonged, Temporary, Immediate, or Short-Term
2. Participation in sexual activity; decreased interest and libido	Not known
3. No noticeable change in sexual activity or experience	—
4. Desire for sexual activity as source of solace and comfort	Prolonged, Temporary, Immediate, or Short-Term
5. Powerful, compelling desire for sexual activity; heightened intensity of feeling	Prolonged, Temporary, Immediate, or Short-Term
6. Powerful, compelling desire for sexual activity; no feeling	Not known

2. Participation in sexual activity occurs but with decreased interest and libido. Women more often express this response when they go along with a partner's request even though they have no desire or feeling for sexual activity. Little is known about the duration of this response or its relationship to the management of grief and death anxiety.

3. The presence of death or the threat of death has no noticeable impact on the frequency of sexual activity or the experience of it; the usual pattern remaining intact. In this situation sexual activity is probably not being used to release the tension and bind the anxiety caused by exposure to the death stimulus. Other means of coping are utilized.

4. Sexual activity provides the source for comfort, solace, compassion and tenderness during times of loss or life threatening events. There is often great need to be held in loving arms. The frequency and experience of sexual activity is mainly unchanged. Again, other means of coping are probably being directed at managing grief and death anxiety. The time frame is likely to be as in No. 1, above.

5. Exposure to the death stimulus evokes an incomparably powerful and compelling desire for sexual activity usually beginning around the time of the exposure to the death stimulus. This response may occur only once but may include repeated intercourse with incredibly intense sensations. If a usual partner is not available, former lovers and even casual friends are approached. They seem to understand at some level what is going on and give a compassionate response. Usually it is not mentioned and the relationship remains unchanged by the encounter. In some circumstances such as terminal illness, unavailability of any partner or isolation, masturbation may be used. Besides the one-time event, this response may be temporary lasting for as long as several weeks. Being in combat is to be immersed in an environment of death. In those circumstances this response may endure for most of that time, according to Broyles, without losing its power or incomparable intensity [25]. How this response contributes to the grief process and the binding of death anxiety is not known.

6. The desire for sexual activity is powerfully compelling but devoid of pleasure and satisfaction. The result is a constant search for the next partner and more intercourse. Much time is tied up in the sexual preoccupation and compulsive activity which may become extremely distressing and out of control as with Yalom's client described earlier [12]. The duration for this response is not known. It is clearly unsuccessful in bringing any relief to the urgent feelings driving the behavior and does not aid the grief process or contain death anxiety.

It is not implied here that the universe of alternative sexual responses to death have been identified or that the categories described above are necessarily mutually exclusive. The effort has been to explore one way to organize data from case material that is currently available for our consideration from clinical experience and from the literature.

Towards Understanding Sexual Responses to Death

This section focuses on sexual activity as the response to the death stimulus. So little is known about sexual responses to death that we are still in the process of discovery. Identification of these phenomena is in a starting phase. No initial assumption is held that one explanation exists to illumine all sexual responses to death. For example there may be multiple antecedents any of which might evoke the intense sexual drive and experience described by some people. Many questions are beginning to emerge on that response alone, a few of which are the following: How common is the powerful sexual response to death? How often are individuals who report this experience likely to repeat it in similar circumstances? What aspects of an exposure to death are essential to produce it? What is the function served by this response? What is known about this phenomenon in other cultures? What is the personal meaning of this sexual response to the person experiencing it?

A number of possible explanations for having a sexual response to a death stimulus are inferred from the case material and the literature. For example: The need to manage profound death anxiety is the most significant task with which everyone must struggle according to Yalom's existential paradigm [12]. Fusion with another person through sexual intercourse is one expression of a major defense against such anxiety.

In that same paradigm fusion is also recognized as an effort to ameliorate the deep sense of isolation (another of the four existential tasks). For some people the exposure to death taps into feelings of excruciating aloneness. Achieving physical unity with another can be an attempt to escape that pain. Broyles, too, believed in the power of sex to take one out of feelings of extreme separateness to being "one with life again" [25]. Union can also be emotional, spiritual, mental or physical but not sexual in nature. In our society when people's need is for solace or just to be held, perhaps they get it most easily by asking for sex. This may be especially true for men. An issue here is the comparison between sexual and non-sexual forms of union to achieve oneness with another person pursued in the effort to alleviate death anxiety. The non-sexual forms do not appear in this work because it was primarily aimed at sexual responses.

Feelings of helplessness about mortality may engender a desire to fly in the face of death by engaging in intercourse, the means of procreation: making life at the time life is being taken away or threatened. Love is the weapon of life in the great battle with death, said Broyles, victory being the penetration of the ovum by sperm [25].

In the plant world, certain plants respond to adverse conditions that threaten their survival by coming into bloom prematurely and producing a proliferation of seeds. Perhaps we share with those plants a basic, primitive reaction that might once have helped support our survival as a species by engaging in the procreative act in response to death.

Finally, sex can be a powerful affirmation and celebration of life. Having sex may feel particularly appropriate following a brush with death or having survived when many others didn't, as in wars. Other people feel guilty for having survived. This is a valuable example of how the same exposure to death can elicit very different responses.

Obviously, we need to learn more about these phenomena. Except for the discussion of sexual responses during wartime, the focus here has been at the micro level of analysis. In the section below suggestions for further research open questions at macro levels of analyses.

SUMMARY

My interest in sexual responses to death originated in the clinical setting. Clients who disclosed accounts of their experiences of these phenomena were often distressed, deeply ashamed and feeling very guilty for having acted on sexual drives at a time of tragedy and death. The purpose of this work was to bring attention to these phenomena that they might be explored, thus, increasing our knowledge and understanding of this behavior about which we know so little.

Theoretically, Yalom's existential paradigm was a useful framework from which to consider sexual responses to death [12]. He defined the ultimate challenge in life as the struggle with mortality. Fusion, including sexual intercourse, is identified as an expression of one of the two major defenses against death anxiety. His case examples portrayed sexual responses that were counterphobic and neurotic behavior patterns. A limited number of other accounts linking sex and death were found in the literature and shadow aspects of this connection were presented.

Examples of a wide range of sexual responses associated with the exposure to death, the threat of death or deep awareness of mortality were illustrated from clinical case material and from the literature. A preliminary attempt was made to organize emerging types of responses on a rudimentary continuum. Six responses were identified from withdrawal and impotence to a powerful compelling desire for sexual activity but which was devoid of feeling.

Of particular interest were the observations from clinical practice when the stimulus of death seemed to trigger a powerful urge for intercourse and an almost compulsive behavioral response that often was a one time event. If an established sexual relationship was not available an unexpected sexual encounter occurred with a friend or an acquaintance. Usually, the relationship with these people was not changed by this intense encounter nor was the matter ever discussed.

Several possibilities for beginning to understand sexual responses to death were offered: management of death anxiety, amelioration of isolation, confrontation of death with the procreative act, remnants of a species survival strategy, and the affirmation of life. It seems unlikely that any single explanation will serve all the phenomena.

CLINICAL IMPLICATIONS

Greater awareness of these sexual responses to death is important for several groups of professionals. Psychotherapists frequently work on issues related to old and to recent deaths with individuals, some of whom, may be experiencing distress and guilt about sexual responses to death. Hospice workers, especially, are in daily contact with dying patients and their families and support the survivors in bereavement. Many care providers have frequent contact with person's with life threatening illnesses and terminal conditions. Other health care providers need to know that diagnoses and treatments that are routine for them may feel life threatening for patients and their loved ones thus being potential death stimuli. It would be very useful for care providers to consider their own reactions to these phenomena. How might they feel if a client revealed that she went out looking for someone to have sex with on the night her mother died? How often do care providers themselves have sexual responses to deaths of persons in their care?

SUGGESTIONS FOR FUTURE RESEARCH

Some questions for investigation were raised in the section on the beginning continuum of sexual responses to death. But this is not an easy topic to investigate and will require creative research designs. Some studies do look more feasible: How do medical students manage the death stimulus of dissecting cadavers? What would a survey of the knowledge and attitudes related to the connection between sex and death reveal? What differences might there be among groups in a cross-cultural comparison?

At a macro level of analyses, birth rates might be a conservative indicator of increased sexual activity. What happens to birth rates nine months after major disasters such as the recent San Francisco earthquake? Or the New York City brown-out? Or the Gulf War? Or volcanic eruptions?

As researchers, care providers, and educators, we need to know more about these phenomena in order to increase our knowledge and understanding of this human behavior. Demystifying the sexual response to death will enable us to be more helpful and empowering to ourselves and to those with whom we work.

REFERENCES

1. J. de Hartog, *The Peaceable Kingdom*, Anthenum, New York, 1971.
2. H. A. Katchadourian and D. T. Lunde, *Fundamentals of Human Sexuality*, Holt, Rinehart & Winston, New York, 1975.
3. M. Lowenthal and C. Haven, Interaction and Adaptation: Intimacy as a Critical Variable, *American Sociological Review, 33*:1, pp. 20-30, 1968.
4. M. Lowenthal and Weiss, Intimacy and Crisis in Adulthood, *Counseling Psychologist, 6*, pp. 10-15, 1976.

5. D. Leviton, The Intimacy/Sexual Needs or the Terminally Ill and the Widowed, *Death Education, 1,* pp. 161-180, 1978.
6. C. M. Parkes, *Bereavement,* New York International Universities, 1972.
7. P. MacElveen-Hoehn and R. McCorkle, Understanding Sexuality in Progressive Cancer, *Seminars in Oncology Nursing, 1:*1, pp. 56-62, February 1985.
8. A. P. Orfirer, Loss of Sexual Function in the Male, in *Loss and Grief: Psychological Management in Medical Practice,* B. Schoenberg, et al. (eds.), Columbia University Press, New York, 1970.
9. A. Lawson, *Adultery: An Analysis of Love and Betrayal,* Macmillan, New York, 1988.
10. P. Geghart, Postmarital Coitus among Widows and Divorcees, in *Divorce and After,* P. Bohannan (ed.), Doubleday, New York, 1970.
11. K. F. Donnely, *Recovering from the Loss of a Child,* Macmillan, New York, 1982.
12. I. D. Yalom, *Existential Psychotherapy,* Basic Books, New York, 1980.
13. D. Peretz, Development, Object-Relations, and Loss, in *Loss and Grief: Psychological Management in Medical Practice,* B. Schoenberg, et al. (eds.), Columbia University Press, New York, 1970.
14. S. Keleman, *Living Your Dying,* Macmillan, New York, 1974.
15. F. Reichman and N. Levy, Problems in Adaptation to Maintenance Dialysis, in *Living or Dying: Adaptation to Hemodialysis,* Thomas, Homewood, Illinois, 1974.
16. N. H. Casem and T. P. Hackett, Psychiatric Consultation in a Coronary Care Unit, *Annals of Internal Medicine, 75,* pp. 9-14, July 1971.
17. N. F. Woods, *Human Sexuality in Health & Illness,* Mosby, St. Louis, 1975.
18. S. Bertman, Personal Communication, Seattle, Washington, 1991.
19. M. Rothenberg, Personal Communication, Seattle, Washington, 1990.
20. L. Jaffe, Sexual Problems of the Terminally Ill, in *Home Care: Living with Dying,* E. R. Prichard, et al. (eds.), Columbia University Press, New York, 1979.
21. J. Binder and A. Krohn, Sexual Acting Out as an Abortive Mourning Process in Female Adolescent Inpatients, *The Psychiatric Quarterly, 48,* pp. 1-16, 1974.
22. R. Krafft-Ebbing, *Psychopathia Sexualis,* F. J. Rebman (trans.), 12th German Edition, Brooklyn: Physicians and Surgeons Books (originally published in 1906), 1937.
23. B. Karpman, *The Sexual Offender and His Offenses,* Julian Press, New York, 1954.
24. J. S. De Lora and C. A. B. Warren, *Understanding Sexual Interaction,* Houghton Mifflin, Boston, 1977.
25. W. Broyles, Jr., Why Men Love War, *Esquire,* pp. 55-65, 1984.

ADDITIONAL READING

Kübler-Ross, E., *On Death and Dying,* Macmillan, New York, 1969.

PART II

The Needs of Particular Groups

CHAPTER 9

The Six C's of Christmas and Grief

Richard J. Paul, Joan Burnett,
David Hart, and Susan Brushey

1. CONFLICT

There is a potential conflict between the inside of a person who has unresolved grief and the outside world at Christmas time. Inside you may feel anything but "Merry," you might be feeling lonely, and Christmas carols, trees, lights and churches may bring up feelings which are painful. The outside world can seem commercial, cruel, exploiting, relentless. You may feel like you don't fit in and yet with every one being so "Merry" there may be no place to hide. Children are very vulnerable to this conflict. Their peers may have nothing obviously interfering with their enjoyment, and this presents a striking contrast to the grieving child's Christmas. Young people will notice if no-one will talk about the deceased. The child may assume everyone has forgotten and that he/she may be forgotten too.

It is normal when in grief to feel in conflict with Christmas. Children, and the child in us, may want to feel merry but we feel guilty that we are betraying the memory . . . "I'm not supposed to feel this way."

Christmas may recreate the experiences of grief including any or all of the following.

Denial

The news of a death (actual or impending) almost always catches us by surprise. We usually just aren't ready. The first responses or thoughts may be **NO!; It can't be!; That's impossible! I just saw him/her**. People have often said that they weren't aware that they didn't believe the news until they saw their loved one's body in the open casket for the first time. Part of the denial is numbness— just not feeling. This is our body's way of keeping us from feeling too many emotions at once. It is also natural that these same feelings of denial or suspicion that it is just not true many reoccur.

Anger

Frustration with a situation, with a world we can't control, often generates rage—and this is natural. When a death occurs and you aren't fully prepared for it you my feel anger—at the doctor, the nurse(s), God, relatives, the funeral director, the pastor, yourself, and even the person who died. Anger is not good or bad, it's what we do with it that matters.

Guilt

Regrets come from having things that you needed to say or do that were put off till tomorrow . . . one day too often. Or, on the other hand, if things were said or done and never apologized for, or forgiven, real or imagined, they can also create strong feelings of guilt. Death reminds us, often too late, that tomorrow never comes. Feelings of guilt are also neither good nor bad they just are and they need to be worked, and talked out.

Depression

What's the use? A sense of helplessness, despair or anxiety can set in after a period of time. The way the world was, can never be the same and it was the only world you knew. Life can lose any meaning it had when you lose someone who meant a lot to you. And you may have no desire or energy to do anything about it. You may have felt you had this grief thing handled and some memory will bring it all back. It's common to wonder, "Am I going CRAZY?" Waves of powerlessness can just overwhelm you at a time like this. Children notice the changes a death can bring and they need someone to talk with them about this.

Acceptance

When we can talk and remember and think about the person who died without always feeling any of the above, or without crying, this is reaching a state of acceptance. After we have tended the wounds of the heart and have done the grief work and have learned to live in the presence of absence—then we have accepted or adjusted to the death. One father said, "I haven't gotten over it, I've gotten used to it."

Among all of the feelings of grief, depression is a very possible and normal reaction to the Christmas environment. People might be pushing and pulling you, and you may ask, "How can I look after myself when others are making so many demands on me?" And children can feel overwhelmed with the thought that they may always feel this bad, they need reassurances at this time.

Feelings are neither good nor bad, they just are. And it's OK to grieve and it's OK to laugh. Consider grief with this analogy—when someone dies it is very much like having an injection with an active ingredient called **Grief** and that energy will stay in you, and it will affect your whole being—body, mind and soul—until it is worked out. It doesn't matter how old a child is or the type of feelings he/she has. Whether age one or one-hundred our feelings can still be childlike. A child may be really happy one minute and crying hard the next . . . this is okay . . . this how many children grieve. **Feelings are OK!**

2. CRITICAL TIMES

Christmas can be especially difficult and painful because of the marked conflict between how you feel and how the outside world expects you to feel. The manner in which you handle this conflict makes Christmas a critical time in the process of grief. It is important to know that there are other critical times, i.e.: Easter, weddings, funerals, anniversaries, the season of the year, special places, the anniversary of the death when we will be confronted with our loss and how we are handling it. For the child there are the parent days at school, banquets, club get-togethers, concerts, plays, awards, diplomas, weddings, their first baby. And each, or any, of these critical times can bring on that miniature version of the original grief experience.

Not only do we grieve emotionally, we all grieve **Physically** as well! That is why we hear of people getting sick, having accidents, drinking too much, using drugs, etc. because the unresolved grief can make us sick. The majority of the public and 87 percent of physicians surveyed in the United States believed that grief should be resolved in the range of forty-eight hours to two weeks. However a recent study revealed that the white blood cell count (or our immune system) in our body drops proportionately from 2000 p.p.m. to 400 p.p.m. and the immune system takes roughly **two** years or more to regain the strength held before the death of a significant loved one. Be tolerant of your physical and psychological limits!

3. CONFRONTATION

"I wish I could put the whole world on hold until January 1." For some the choice will be silent avoidance this Christmas. Refusing invitations, staying at home with the blinds drawn—these behaviors only prolong the experience where participating, however painful, moves us through grief. Working through grief has been likened to peeling an onion . . . "It comes off one layer at a time, and there are lots of tears." The pain or discomfort is an indicator that we are working through bereavement.

Some well-meaning people, and some uncomfortable with their own feelings may try to steer you away from your grief saying, "This isn't the time," or "You are grieving too long." You DO have a right to mourn. When we make a commitment to love we also subconsciously make a commitment to grieve if we lose that love. And the amount of pain may be proportional to the amount of love. Well-meaning people can also hinder a child's grief by not allowing them to come to the funeral or to talk about the deceased after.

Talk about the one who dies. A wise person once said, "if you cry when you talk about someone then you haven't talked about them enough." Accept that everyone does grieve differently. Where one person may be laughing about the good times and the funny stories, some one else may be crying. Be non-judgmental! A child on the other hand may not know how to express himself in any way and may need encouragement to draw pictures or to talk about their memories of the person and to know that these memories are their's alone to keep and can never be taken away from them as their loved one had been.

Honesty with others is important but honesty with ourselves is essential. It is more than just OK to cry, laugh, and vent your feelings in a healthy way. We all need to talk so we can hear our own story and get it off our chest. Check first to see if it's OK to talk with another and if it isn't then find the ones who say it is OK.

4. CELEBRATION

The life of the person you love deserves to be acknowledged—yes, even Celebrated! Reminisce, talk about your favorite memories and encourage others to do the same.

Don't enshrine the past or the one who died. He or she was a human being with parts you liked and parts you didn't like and you loved that person as he/she was. There may be special traditions that always included that person and you may be able to carry on if you modify them. Children need to be reminded that they don't have to forget about the person. In fact as long as the memories are kept alive that person will always be in their heart and mind. when they know this children may understand that there is also room in their heart to love others.

New traditions that acknowledge Christmas without the person, i.e., possibly change dinner time, or the place you celebrate, or the people you include, or the gifts, or tree (artificial, real, or palm tree). If creating a new tradition initiates communication among everyone involved, including children, the result will benefit everyone.

5. CONSTRUCTIVE CONCEPTS

Constructive concepts are tried and true ideas for you to consider—there are no doubt many that we haven't included which you will only discover by reading or talking with others who have moved further down the road of grief recovery. We offer the following as some possible tools or stepping stones to help yourself along.

Inititate

It is necessary for each one of us to take responsibility for our needs. Identify what they are. And do what needs to be done to satisfy those needs. Including talking, crying, laughing, hugging, attending groups etc. No-one knows what I'm going through until I tell them. As you care for others so should you care for yourself. The Bible says "Love thy neighbour, and thy God as thy self" (Psalm XXIII). When in grief it is very easy to neglect yourself, to become apathetic, to want others to take care of you. You have to work at taking care of yourself. If you feel that you are burdening others with your story and you hold back, then you are not looking after your need to express yourself. Identify your needs and take responsibility for satisfying them. Encourage others to do the same.

Physical Needs

Remember, you have very definite, physical needs when you are grieving which require your attention in order to stay healthy and grow through your bereavement. 1) Nutrition—Eat small, regular, healthy meals . . . even if you don't feel hungry. 2) Rest—lie down during your regular sleeping periods even if you don't sleep. If your mind is racing , that is because you have a lot to think about, but your body needs to regenerate itself. Avoid sleeping pills unless the situation exceeds several days. Try relaxation exercises, restful music, positive imaging, keep a writing pad by your bed and write out your thoughts. 3) Exercise—Take yourself our for a walk, every day. Or go with someone else. Your body needs to pump blood vigorously, every day. 4) Water—Your white blood cells need moisture. Eight glasses of straight water a day. Avoid alcohol, coffee and tea. A hydrated white blood cell is on your side. 5) Support—Love, touch, talk, contact with other people is essential to our well-being. Try one extra hug a day. Children and pets are happy to return the gesture.

Support Network

Don't make your house a prison, invite someone over for a coffee. And if they can't come try again or try someone else. Don't give up on yourself. Establish with specific people what your needs are and ask if you can call them. If it is difficult, limit the conversation. Then do it again, later. You have people who care about you and want to be helpful if you just tell them how. If for any reason a support network isn't there, or if you don't want to involve your family and friends, try the actual grief support groups in your area. That is what they are there for. Thousands of bereaved people have found comfort through grief support groups that they could find nowhere else.

Diary

For the next two weeks try keeping a diary of your feelings, the highs and the lows. Then after Christmas, read it. You may see that some good things happened and in any case you'll see you've made it through Christmas. Then physically destroy the diary, throw it on the fire. It has served it's purpose, don't keep it. You may surprise yourself that you are actually moving through grief like the 23rd Psalm says, "Yea, though I walk through the valley of the shadow of death. . . ."

Memory Box

For children keeping things that remind them of the one who died that they can take down any time, i.e. Dad's can of shaving cream; it smells like Dad . . . it's not sick or morbid, it's like a teddy or blanky; it's there when they need it and they'll grow out of it if they're allowed to do it. It's like a part of the one who died that they can have just a little longer and when they're ready, they'll get off it. Discuss this with the child.

Grief Work

Grieving is a job, and a hard one. And you have to stick to it if you want to reach acceptance of the death. If you love someone, or something , you are going to grieve if you lose them. It's that simple! You can't just switch love off like a light switch, you've got to work it through. If you have what is called unfinished business with that person it only compounds the problem. The formula we suggest to the families dealing with unfinished business between themselves and someone who dies is as follows. On a blank piece of paper write the titles Amendments, Forgiveness, and Other Significant Statements i.e.:

Amendments (then write below it):

—I'm sorry for . . . (and fill in whatever come to mind and repeat it)
—I'm sorry for . . . (do it again & again until nothing comes out)

Forgiveness (then write below it)

—I'm angry about . . . (fill it in, but add at the end) . . . and I forgive you.
 —or—
—I was hurt when . . . . . . and I forgive you. (repeat it until nothing comes to mind)

Other significant statements (then write whatever else is important to say)

—"I Love You" or "Thanks" (are frequently sentiments that are left unexpressed)

When you have completed the list above, try saying out loud, "Goodbye _____." If you can say goodbye you know you have completed your unfinished business, for now. If not, perhaps you have not been honest with yourself. You may find it useful to repeat this exercise at a later date. I read the entire list out loud at my father's grave, five years after his death, and the relief I felt was incredible. A problem experienced by some people is that they mistakenly believe that the dead (or non-present person) has to physically hear the amendments, forgiveness or other important statements in order to make the resolution of unfinished business complete. We only have control over the change that occurs inside us when we clean up our unfinished business and it is our own quality of life that is improved through this effort.

Agenda

Sometimes all of the complications and responsibilities of life can be overwhelming and cause us to just throw up our hands in despair. Try writing down everything on your mind and rank them in order of importance then make up an agenda for the next few days. Being organized reduces stress. You don't have to follow it precisely but use it a guideline. Delay making major decisions. Let go of what isn't important, it will wait. Remember the important thing is not to get immobilized or to run but rather to walk through grief! Children also need an agenda because they need to be active. Have on hand a list of Christmas/holiday activities they can participate in for when you or they need it.

Reaching Out

There is a saying that, "When you lift your hand to help another, you lift yourself." Grief is a very self-centred emotion. We focus on our pain, our loss, and sometimes lose sight of the fact that others are grieving also. There is a therapeutic benefit in getting out of ourselves for awhile through service to others—it can give new meaning to life. Even while we are dealing with our grief work we all need a rest to help regain our perspective. "The humble person does not think less of themselves . . . they just think of themselves less."

Writing

There is good "home therapy" to be had simply by keeping a daily journal. Writing is a very private, safe way of accessing thoughts and feelings that we store outside of our conscious mind and getting them off our chest. Some people have found that poetry is a creative way to access the deeper feelings of the heart.

Catharsis

Catharsis refers to the cleansing, releasing and vesting of emotional energy through activity. For example: If you go for a walk and you just look at the trees and the scenery, when you get home you will have the physical benefit of the exercise. However, if while you are walking you hold in you mind the unfinished business, the emotion or the grief you will get the physical and psychological value of expending that energy. Catharsis also works through music, painting and other creative and physical expressions.

6. CHRISTMAS GIFT

In the midst of grief at Christmas, there is still a gift to be received. However, it is a spiritual gift, one less tangible than most others but perhaps the most important of all. That gift isn't something we can just go out and pick up at a store when we need it or want it. It's not something that can be bought for any amount of money, used and then disposed of as we are so accustomed to doing in our lives and in our society. This gift requires a lot of preparation just to receive it. The gift in question is an awareness or feeling or intuition of God's Presence in our life. That is precisely what Jesus was born into the world at Christmas to reveal to us. He showed us in physical form God's presence, but also promised to us that we could feel that sense of God's presence in our own hearts, in our feelings and in our intuitions. The Gift of God's presence is the greatest gift and resource available to anyone in times of grief. In order to receive this gift however, two things are critically necessary. The first is understanding and the second is prayer.

When you look in the eyes of others in grief you realize that we are all in this together. All of us have lost loved ones to death. Understanding entails realizing none of us is immune to being separated from the ones we love. It's part of the nature of this world. Even God couldn't make it otherwise.

Our society so much encourages the pursuit of pleasure, encourages us to distract ourselves with one pursuit after another. The reality though is that none of these distractions or pursuits can remove from us the ultimate reality that in this world death is part of our lives. To develop understanding is to stop running from this fact, is to face up to it, and is to then develop a response in the face of it.

The second part of understanding is to recognize the source of our own grief. Our grief derives not so much from the loss of a loved one. Rather our grief is a symptom of our feeling of being alone, of being separate in a big vast universe. Whether you've lost a spouse, child, relative or friend the core feeling in the midst of it is that of aloneness, separateness, smallness etc. When it comes to facing death, we each have to face it inside ourself alone. Death makes us very aware of our ultimate aloneness and separateness in this overwhelmingly immense universe.

This understanding though can lead to wisdom. And that is what spirituality and religion are all about. In the last analysis there is only one way to finally overcome that feeling of aloneness, of separateness and the accompanying grief. If you lose a spouse or lover you may look for another spouse or lover. If you lose a child you may wish to have another child or sink your whole life into your remaining children. Or you may choose to get involved in all sorts of activities, or work etc. to help build a new life. And there is a lot of conventional wisdom about doing these things. Don't do them too quickly, come to terms with your grief but get on with life.

All of that is true. But there is a higher wisdom. And that higher wisdom is this. New lovers, other children or friends will too die some day. And finally, you will have to die. And there is only one ultimate solution for this dilemma and that is a spiritual one.

The only final answer is to develop a love affair, a love relationship with the one who can never leave you—and that one is God. However you understand God to be, God is the ultimate source of all life who is intricately a part of our lives. Our dilemma is that we are not aware of God's presence in our lives.

Without this awareness, however, life is just a beginning at birth, a series of joys and sorrows and then an ending at death. Only God can bring meaning as lasting peace, happiness and relationship in the midst of all this chaos.

To develop that awareness one must learn how to meditate or to pray. And there are many types and methods but all are involved in opening up channels to God who is always with us, tuning in to God's frequency, developing awareness. That awareness or knowledge of God's Presence in our lives is the great gift God wanted to reveal to the world in Christmas. To know God's Presence in our lives is the ONLY source of true lasting peace and happiness and the only ultimate solution to our grief and feelings of aloneness and separation in the midst of this big, lonely universe.

Eventually that sense of Presence develops in such a way that you know yourself to be part of God, one with God, and then although sorrow and loss continue to come, nothing can shake you any longer.

CONCLUSION

Grief is a natural response to any loss. Bereavement can feel like a crisis—the Chinese symbol for crisis means both danger and opportunity. Understanding any difficult situation can help in dealing with it. If you would like to learn more, funeral homes often have an expanding lending library of books, films, video and audio tapes on grief, personal growth, alcoholism, illness, communication etc. and you are welcome to borrow any of these.

Even though we will grieve if we lose someone we love, the love is worth the pain. In fact the grief is a reminder that we have had a relationship with someone special. In defiance of our culture's seeming paranoia about death we each need to begin living in the here and now. We can begin this by cleaning up our grief and grievances with the past. Then we can use our own mortality as a constant, friendly reminder to do and say the things which are meaningful for us, with the people who are important to us. Not from anxiety about the past or fear of loss in the future, but from the joy of sharing this very precious, present moment.

If you find that you are having trouble coping after trying any or all of the constructive concepts mentioned above, seek out some help. Asking for assistance is not a sign of weakness; it is a sign of your courage and desire to grow through your life's experiences.

HAVE A MEANINGFUL CHRISTMAS!! ONE THAT CONFRONTS THE CONFLICT OF CRITICAL TIMES AND USES CONSTRUCTIVE CONCEPTS TO CELEBRATE THE LIFE OF THE LOVED ONE WHO DIED AND UNWRAP GOD'S CHRISTMAS GIFT TO YOU.

CHAPTER 10

"It's Not Over When It's Over"— The Aftermath of Suicide

(or, Post Suicide Intervention—The Power of the Clergy and Congregation in Preventing the Next Suicide)

Rabbi Daniel A. Roberts

> Given the present state of our knowledge about suicide, proper postvention seems the most promising avenue toward reducing the large number of suicides that occur annually [1, p. 177].
>
> A father whose 16-year-old daughter took her own life says, "Suicide is not a solitary act. A beloved person thinks she is killing only herself, but she also kills a part of us" [2, p. 202].

INTRODUCTION

Although by this time many clergy (by this term are included any minister or helping person who is willing to get involved) are well acquainted with the warning signs that a potential suicide candidate displays (see Table 1), very few of us in our lifetime will deal directly with someone contemplating suicide. For the most part, it is only afterwards that we learn about the person who attempted suicide, or more dramatically, of the one who completed the act. Most of us are subsequently cast into the position of helping the members of our congregations to bring some kind of order to their lives and to make sense out of this moment of chaos. Tranquillity must not only be restored for the immediate family, but equally as well for all those who were touched in any way by this child and/or family (although the reference in this chapter is often to youths, much can be extrapolated when there is the loss of a parent or a grandparent). Suicide is a tragic event that

Table 1. Break the Silence . . . You Can Make A Difference

ALTERNATIVES TO SUICIDE—EXPLORING OPTIONS

- Think about a time in the past year when you have felt sad and hopeless
- Think about a time in the past year when you've been so excited that your joy spilled out to others . . .
- Have you ever noticed that nothing lasts forever?
- Just when you're certain you'll never get over this, along comes something or someone that you never anticipated . . .
- Just when you're certain that you're on top of the world, things take a bad turn . . .

THIS IS A PICTURE OF LIFE

MYTHS ABOUT SUICIDE

- People who talk about suicide don't attempt it
- Suicide happens without warning
- Most suicidal people are undecided about living or dying
- Improvement following a suicidal crisis indicates that the suicidal risk is over
- All suicidal individuals are mentally ill and suicide is always committed by a psychotic person
- Suicide strikes more often among the affluent

REMEMBER: YOU CAN HELP SOMEONE WHO IS DETERMINED TO COMMIT SUICIDE

WARNING SIGNS

- Suicide threats
- Statements revealing a desire to die
- Previous suicide attempts
- Sudden changes in behavior (withdrawal, apathy, moodiness)
- Final arrangements (giving away personal items, making a will)
- Tendency towards isolation

HOW TO HELP

- Take threats seriously
- Watch for clues
- Answer cries for help by listening with understanding
- Confront the problem directly
- Encourage the person to seek help
- You can give your friend HOPE

SUICIDE IS A PERMANENT SOLUTION TO A TEMPORARY PROBLEM

Information provided by the Link Counseling Center and the Union of American Hebrew Congregations National Task Force on Youth Suicide and Prevention.

leaves skeletons in the closets of everyone who knew this person. The pain that tortured the deceased is over for him or her, but for everyone else it has just begun. It is a horrendous ache which for the most part never goes away for the parents, child, siblings, grandparents, and friends. In everyone's mind the questions linger forever. Why? What could I have done to prevent this? The events leading up to the suicide will be mentally relived over and over again, and still the questions will refuse to disappear. For the most part no satisfaction will be gained from the huge number of hours spent questioning others. Eventually, most survivors will just have to learn to cope with the fact that there are no final answers, only failed hopes, unresolved emotions and for a few, a sense of troubled closure. Although some of the above reactions are not different upon sudden death occurrences; i.e., the disorientation, the unfinished business, the guilt, added to this is the feeling of being rejected, abandoned and deserted as well as an anger that this was a conscious decision by the victim to punish the survivors.

As in any death, there is nothing that we as clergy can do to undo what has already been done. We can no longer save the one who decided to end life so abruptly, but, through the role we play in this family's life, as well as through our position in the community, we have the potential to intervene, and make the remaining quality of the survivors' life a little better. In addition, since most of us are aware of a newly occurring phenomenon, *contagion* (others following the example of the deceased), and perhaps by our following through on some of the suggestions below, we might even save another human life. The words of a letter written to Rabbi Daniel Syme in reaction to his article, "Worlds to Save" remind us of how ill-equipped most of us are when it comes to handling the tremendous devastation cause by suicide [3].

> . . . As a survivor of suicide, I am continually disappointed by the void I've found in religious institutions and its leadership. My experience has been that I shouldn't look for spiritual support or answers in our tradition when it comes to the subject of suicide.
>
> . . . Robert's (not real name) suicide was a tremendous shock to the Jewish community. And one of my first responses was to counsel with the rabbis. I was looking for help in finding the Jewish responses, thought and traditions to help me gain a perspective on Robert's suicide. I wanted to find comfort and explanation through the *Jewish focus on life*. I was sure that somewhere in Jewish thought there were answers and ideas that could help me understand and be able to explain Robert's pain and despair. . . . Instead, the answer was, "It's best not to talk about it"; "It's best to forget the tragedy and go on with your life."
>
> As any survivor of suicide knows, it is never forgotten; as the daily living comes back into focus, the fact of a suicide is always there for me . . . Where and when and how is its (Reform Judaism's) leadership teaching us the Jewish traditions and resources that could bolster and secure our faith after it's so blatantly knocked off its foundation: the ultimate value of each human life?

> ... I cannot help but wonder how less painful these 3 years—and the next
> 30—might be if we had been given the spiritual basis for our daily survival as
> a Jewish family, rather than the message that it's best to forget.[1]

Much can be extrapolated from this letter for all clergy. Are we giving the message that it is best to forget the tragedy and to go on with life, thus driving people in pain away? The intent of this chapter is to examine what can be done in terms of intervention in the community to help people mourn and to prevent further escalation of death. The intent is to be **PROACTIVE** rather than **REACTIVE**. The concept is for us to realize that the power of clergy enables us to act in ways and to do things that no one else would be able and/or be *allowed* to do. We might also remember that, under the best of circumstances, most people handle death poorly and have no idea how to comfort the mourner. Thus, this is our opportunity to teach and instruct people how to get through this very chaotic moment.

HANDLING THE FIRST 48 HOURS

Consoling the Bereaved

"There are two parties to the suffering that death (from suicide) inflicts: and in the appointment of this suffering, the survivor takes the brunt," wrote historian Arnold Toynbee [4, p. 26]. Lawrence G. Calhoun and his colleagues cautiously asserted three general characterization of suicide that differentiated it from other grief [5]. These generalizations were that suicide survivors 1) feel more guilt, 2) more often search for an understanding of the death, and 3) appear to experience less social support than do survivors of deaths by other causes.

Dealing with a family which has lost one of it members through suicide (and much of what follows is probably true for homicides as well) is unlike dealing with any other family in mourning. As indicated above, the survivors will have to deal with more guilt and questions than mourners of deaths nonself-inflicted. Over and over again the bereaved will seek explanations as to why this tragedy occurred and no rational answers will seem to satisfy them. They will continually relive "final moments" and try to understand what thoughts were going through their beloved's mind, those lost dreadful secrets. The search will continue for years, even for the rest of their lives, and occasionally well into future generations. Probably the most important thing one can do during this crisis is to be personally present, thus relating to the mourners a sense that we care and do not reject them. But, let us not delude ourselves into thinking that we, as clergy, will be able to assuage their guilt, nor at this tearful time that we ought to be, God's defenders. In

---

[1] Private Communication, March 1, 1988. Permission for use granted by the writer of the letter.

fact God would probably want us, instead, to side with the sufferers and to acknowledge that an injustice has occurred. Note, it was the friends of Job, who attempted to give excuses and defend God, that were eventually chastised for their behavior. We serve God best by helping the mourners to grieve and to recover enough to cope with future crises in their lives.

Since we are often among the first to be called, we have the unique opportunity to guide and direct the survivors in ways that might be rejected had they been suggested by other well-intentioned family members or friends. We come into the situation as an "expert" on how to handle death. We also come into the situation as a trusted "family member" who is listened to because we are perceived to be interested in their best welfare. At the outset, we must encourage the family to express their feelings of guilt and hurt, their sense of responsibility, their anger, and occasionally even their relief. We must remind them that, under these circumstances, they can never share too much by talking. We should convince them that it is all right for them, even advisable, to act out their grief and their anger at the deceased by crying, shouting, screaming, or any other emotion which they wish to display. It should be pointed out that suicide is unlike other death experiences, and we need to reinforce what could be considered "normal" feelings and reactions during the months ahead: to blame themselves, to feel like they are going crazy, to feel that the pain will never subside, to be angry at the deceased for causing such great pain, to even feel a sense of relief that all the anguish during the past months is over. It is even "normal" to feel guilty for even thinking this way. We must reiterate over and over again to the mourners that they are only human and had no control over their child's (parent's) behavior and thoughts. It is essential to warn people against the use of sedatives, liquor or other drugs to deaden the pain and shock. These devices will only hinder the normal grieving process and lengthen the period of mourning.

One important area in which we can also make an immense contribution is in getting the family to decide how they are going to explain the death to others. Often, suicide brings a sense of shame, and people would love to falsify the truth, but this only leads to future deceptions and, likewise, to the denial of the truth to oneself. Thus, it could be extremely helpful to have the family rehearse how they will explain the death to their family and friends, as well as to their child's friends (or in the case of a parent, a child to his/her friends). It is vital to stress that denial of the truth will lead to a social isolation by people who most probably will have guessed the truth, but are now reluctant to openingly discussing it [6, p. 33].

This being a time of complete shock and disarray for the family, we clergy need to carefully delineate what steps should be taken. We should assist with the planning of the funeral, as well as other suggestions as to how everyone might say those "last goodbyes" (see Rituals, p. 138). In addition, we might support the extended family by helping them get organized. Since often there is an investigation surrounding the death, the family might very well be inundated by the media and by curious, but not sincere friends. A spokesperson should be appointed who will be in charge of handling this, thus relieving the immediate family of this pressure. For the most part, the family will let you know very clearly (although, at times some families will not be able to articulate it as clearly) when and if you are overextending your bounds, ultimately, it is still best for them to be in charge of their lives.

It must be emphasized over and over again that this death is unlike any other death. Under normal circumstances people know what to do and what not to do, but this situation is different. Therese Rando in her book, *Grieving: How to Go on Living When Someone You Love Dies* writes [7, p. 112]:

> A suicide is one of the most difficult deaths to cope with. Not only is it a sudden death, but it also involves a conscious choice on the part of your loved one to choose death over life. The deliberateness of this act fuels intense feeling of rejection, abandonment, and desertion in those left behind. This can contribute to a profound shattering of your self-esteem, with strong feelings of unworthiness, inadequacy, and failure.

The family and friends are at a loss as to how to allay the tremendous pain. Most people fail to understand that in this case there are no words of solace. It is important to advise the extended family as to how to protect their loved ones from the onslaught of well-wishers and callers. It is essential to emphasize the need for each of the mourners to have some private time to reflect on and evaluate the events of this highly chaotic time. The family does not have to be guarded every moment, but there must be some relief from all the hubbub. In addition, we need to make it known that there is no *one* right way to mourn for this loss; that one's choice in constructing one's own recovery is just that, a personal means of dealing with death. It is neither right nor wrong. It just is, as long as one does run away from dealing with the death.

As for the clergy, our being there physically at this time is what most families find most comforting. Yes, it is exhausting, draining, and work piles up at the office, but our personal presence brings a sort of stability in the midst of a tumultuous time, and a sense that we, as the clergy, care.

Ritual Needs

> Rituals can be particularly helpful in assisting an individual or family to successfully resolve grief, both prior to and after the death (ideally building successfully on the therapeutic foundation supplied by the funeral) [7, p. 112].

It cannot be stated enough that each death is unique, and in the case of suicide it is even more complex. So, please understand that it should not be considered morbid when it is suggested that we encourage the family, if it is their wish, to spend private time with the deceased, speaking to, touching and even holding their child (or parent). This can, strange as it sounds, truly aid healing later on, for it might be a way of releasing pent up emotions and guilt. A planned good-bye and symbolic expressions such as writing notes to put in the coffin might also be the catharsis that leads to a feeling of finality and completion. It must be remembered that rituals are not only for the immediate family but for relatives, friends, classmates and others who were involved in this person's life. As suggested above, rituals, although alien to a particular religious tradition and which under other circumstances would be discouraged should not be admonished. Most importantly, a great deal of time should be spent talking about the various traditions of mourning and their cathartic effect. Mourning ritual should not be cut short nor downplayed. It should be pointed out, too, that the most difficult time will be when mourning is completed and everyone goes home. This then will be the real time of deep loneliness, desperation and feelings of guilt. It would be greatly helpful to organize some sort of support team (see: The Community, p. 141) that will fill this void.

The Funeral

> The funeral was the first "rite of passage" that aided our grief process. It served as a ritual through which our feelings could be vented and acted out when it was too difficult to talk about them. The funeral served to affirm the basic assumptions about life that were shattered by our son's death. We had to look at meaning and purpose of life and death. The ceremony also helped us to face the truth about his death. It gave us an opportunity to say good bye [2, p. 206].

This will be one of the toughest funerals we, as clergy, will ever have to do. Unless this has been a long protracted illness wherein the decease was alienated from others, we can expect the funeral home, or sanctuary to be filled to the brim with overly emotional and shocked mourners, especially if the suicide was a young person. The family will be stricken with grief and we will be exhausted from our empathy. Our personal challenge will be to find words of comfort but *not* ones which romanticize the deceased. The eulogy must reflect honesty, and admit that we do not understand the ways of God, nor the choice of ending one's life early. Although, we might believe that the family wants to hear platitudes and wonderful words about their child (or parent/mate), we must remember that there is a great deal of animosity and anger toward the deceased for having caused all this pain. Honesty remains the best policy. We might want to suggest to the family to write parts of the tribute which could be incorporated into the eulogy. We must remember that we are eulogizing the end of a life, but not the way it ended. Writes Earl Grollman, "The person who took his/her life was still a person, with strengths as well as weaknesses. The positive aspects of the individual's life should be mentioned so that people can recall the happy times and the many ways in which life was enriched by the remembered's presence. After all, one judges a person by the total years, not by an isolated moment, cataclysmic as it may be" [8, p. 211]. We must also bear in mind that there will be many impressionable people sitting in the audience who, if the deceased is overly praised, might decide that they, too, can gain some recognition in the eyes of their parents and/or others through such an act. Don't make the deceased into a hero! Let the funeral do what it is supposed to do: to bring reality to the death and to begin the process of mourning. Let the funeral be the ritual through which feelings, which are too difficult to express verbally, can be vented and acted out. At a later date we might want to help select a cemetery marker, and then conduct some sort of ceremony for the dedication of that tombstone. A wonderful catharsis occurs upon seeing the fact of the death etched in stone.

SKELETONS IN THE CLOSET

It is said that a person who commits suicide leaves a skeleton in every survivor's closet. This is plainly seen as we now look at what needs to be done to assist in everyone's recovery from this tragic incident.

The Congregation

1. *The Clergyperson* . . . This is one of the most stressful deaths with which we, as clergy will ever have to deal. More than with any other death, we become psychologically and emotionally involved with the family. We feel their intense pain and cannot help but cry internally with them every inch of the way. We experience a frustration in that we cannot wave a magic wand and relieve them of their anguish. It is a natural tendency for us to fantasize our own reactions if this would have been our child. Suddenly, we begin to reevaluate our own lives and relationships. We become physically, emotionally and spiritually exhausted as we look ahead contemplating the things that must be done if we are to be *proactive* and help prevent another suicide from happening in the community, as well as to prevent pathological behaviour from setting in. Please keep in mind that the intensity of this time period may eventually necessitate some personal therapy for us as well. We will need to seek out a friend, a counselor, or our mate and talk—we need to talk not about the deceased and all the details, but about our feelings and how this death has affected us emotionally. When things calm down we need to plan some time away from the office even though thousands of things will have piled up on our desk to do to regain our equilibrium. Please understand, no one comes out of this event unscathed, and we are no exception.

Being in the unique position of helper, authority, and teacher on "how to mourn and how to comfort," the clergy now needs to reach out to everyone in the community to prevent further deaths. A.D. Hagin notes that "delayed, unresolved grief is a major seedbed of suicidal behaviour, particularly among adolescents following the death of a parent, classmate, grandparent, or teacher, regardless of the cause of death" [9, p. 32]. This is a special opportunity given to us—to help people resolve their grief. We must operate on the supposition that post-intervention becomes prevention. This can be accomplished in such areas as:

2. *Religious School* . . . (see also Peer Group, p. 143) Since probably everyone in the immediate community has heard about the death, this is another perfect opportunity to talk about suicide in our religious schools. [Ideally, following the suggested curriculum of the Union of American Hebrew Congregations' Task Force on Teenage Suicide Prevention,[2] discussions on teen suicide should already have been part of our religious school's curriculum. As is suggested under School Officials below, a plan should have been put into place as to what everyone in the Congregation should do if a suicide were to occur.] This conversation should be an opportunity to vent feelings and reactions concerning the deceased as well as an opportunity for cathartic relief. This discussion should not be limited to just the youngsters who were in the same grade in school as the deceased. By the fifth grade, students are capable of learning the warning signs and of being sensitive towards older brothers and sisters who may be mourning the loss of a friend. We should use this opportunity to review what leads up to a suicide, the warning signs of a potential suicide victim (see Table 1), as well as what to do if any of these signs are observed. That is, we must teach the youth to . . . *"break a confidence"* and to tell an authority when a life is in danger. This should be our central message! We must emphasize that by confiding in an adult authority figure, i.e. school principal, counselor, clergy or parent, when someone is suspected of suicidal behaviour, the "informer" may actually be saving a life. . . . In addition, this is a perfect occasion to discuss alternatives to suicide for those who are in pain and are feeling hopeless, hapless or helpless. This is also the perfect time to discuss "legitimate" coping mechanisms and how drugs and alcohol undermine and mask the distress that a person is feeling. It is also a chance to teach about self esteem and to help students understand how coping with disappointment and pain helps one's maturity. All this should end ideally with some activity that promotes life, one which is hopeful and uplifting. (As an aside, the religious school faculty and the entire congregational staff, i.e., youth advisors, administrator, secretaries, etc. should be included in a discussion of the suicide and should be educated as to how each can be involved in helping prevent this from happening to others.)

THE COMMUNITY

1. *Helping the Friends of the Suicide's Relatives* (Parents, Grandparents, Children, Grandchildren) . . . The friends of the family are the clergy's greatest allies

---

[2] Task Force on Youth Suicide Prevention, Union of American Hebrew Congregations, 838 Fifth Avenue, New York, New York 10029, 212-849-0100.

in helping the mourners. Because they care, here is a group of people who want to be involved and be helpful. However, like everyone else, they are pitifully at a loss as to how to handle the situation. Kjell Rudestam gives us some insight into the friends when he discovered in a large scale study that "the pattern was for friends to listen and be sympathetic, while at the same time avoiding the topic of death itself" [6, p. 32] In other words, he writes, "friends offered tangible support (e.g., providing meals and rides), but tended not to initiate discussion of the suicide, creating a curtain of silence around the event (author's italics) [6, p. 32]. When this happens, the survivors feel that their friends cannot or do not want to talk about the death, and thus, they feel even more isolated. We can readily see that giving solace and knowing how to console another does not come automatically. Friends and relatives need to be instructed in the art of giving comfort and must also be given permission to talk about the death. They need to be educated in what to say, such as: "It's all right to cry, I'm here with you," and not such cliches as: "I know how you feel"; "Time will heal all"; "It is time to put this behind you and get on with your life"; "Your *(child, parent, mate, sibling)* is better off now." In other words, we must teach the friends to avoid judgmental statements and confine themselves to supportive comments. They need to know that every remark that downplays the loss is offensive, and every expression that accentuates one's supportive presence is welcome and constructive. (This goes for us as clergy as well, for telling the family that this person has gone to Hell for this action is neither helpful nor supportive. If this is our theological belief, perhaps then, it is better either to keep it to ourselves or ask another clergy to take our place.)

When working with this particular group of people, one needs to keep in mind that a few might bear some guilt for not having recognized that this was going to happen. It might be necessary to talk with them about what realistically could or could not have been done to prevent this death. In addition, this might also be a time when people will worry about how they can best help their children and/or mate (or parent) cope with this tragic death, especially if the deceased was a close friend. It would be helpful to review the signs that usually appear when one is contemplating suicide in contrast to the behavior of a "normal" adolescent and/or mourner. A wonderful book that should be suggested to read is Therese Rando's *Grieving: How to Go on Living When Someone You Love Dies* [7].

A discussion of post-care and the necessity for our continued involvement in our friend's life over the weeks and months ahead should also be held. To assist us in these sessions we might want to secure one of the therapists from within or outside of the congregation to help us in confronting the issues. One might also find it advisable, as well, to select a group of mental health professionals to plan a strategy to deal with those who fall in this next category.

School Officials

Unfortunately, in this area we are most likely to meet our greatest resistance. Most school officials seem to be afraid of outside intervention, feeling that, as educators, they know best how to handle such situations. In addition, they fear that clergy will step beyond the line of separation between church and state. I cannot encourage you enough still to offer your expertise in dealing with death and mourners. School officials should be reminded that "unresolved grief is a major seedbed of suicidal behaviour," and that all students in the school system should be viewed as potential candidates for seeking negative attention. "Contagion" is and must remain our chief concern. Thus, ways must be found to help students deal with sorrow without glamorizing or dramatizing a suicide. Unfortunately, many school officials do not understand that doing nothing can be as dangerous as doing too much [10, p. 248].

Perhaps, the first thing we might do to be of assistance is to help the school staff in their own dealing with the death. There needs to be time for them to reflect on what they might or might not have done to prevent this death, and to help give a sense of closure to the subject. Next, there needs to be a discussion as to how everyone could work as a team to support the student body. (See Table 2—The Postintervention Process). It has been suggested by Karen Dunne-Maxim [10], author and Project Director of the New Jersey Youth Suicide Prevention Project, that a memorial service not be held unless this is the procedure for all school deaths. Instead, small groups should meet together with a teacher and/or counsellor and be allowed to talk about their feelings. This outward expression of grief which gives students a legitimate way of resolving grief should be accomplished without idolizing the deceased. The clergy must let school officials know that he/she is interested and willing to help, and that this assistance will be different from other professionals. It is thus hoped that through this approach the school staff will be willing to utilize our special talents. [Actually, if you are reading this chapter prior to a suicide you should be contacting your local high school principal and offering your help and expertise to develop a plan of action in the event that a suicide or sudden death should occur in the school. See questions to be resolved—Table 3 and also an example of a program of clergy intervention from a school system in Northeastern Ohio.]

Peer Groups

Regardless, whether school officials desire your involvement or not, when it comes to the close friends of the deceased, it is possible to be PROACTIVE rather than REACTIVE. These youths, particularly the most recent boyfriend/girlfriend, are in tremendous pain feeling that they were cognizant and somehow, or in some way, could have prevented the death. On the other hand, it might be possible that they feel relieved of the burden that this person has been to them and they secretly

Table 2. The Postvention Process

Student Reaction	Staff Response
1. Shock. Students may initially appear remarkably unreactive. In fact, they are in a state of shock and not yet able to accept the reality of suicide.	1. Staff needs to assume a stance of antici-patory waiting, acknowledging the shock and showing a willingness to talk about the suicide when students are ready. Hill (1984) suggests waiting 24 to 48 hours before initiating more direct action.
2. Anger and projection. Students will look for someone to blame. Initially, this may be directed at important adults in the victim's life, including school staff. "Why did they let it happen?"	2. Some expressions of anger must be allowed. Staff members may share the similar feelings they have had. However, at the same time reality must be introduced. There are limits on how much one person can be responsible for actions of another.
3. Guilt. Typically, students who knew the victim may move from blaming others to blaming themselves. "If only I had talked to him more."	3. Here, particularly, staff can be helpful by sharing their own similar reactions. And again, the reality principle is also introduced. One person cannot assume total responsibility for the act of another.
4. Anger at the victim. This is a common reaction by students, even those not closely connected to the victim. "How could he do this to us?"	4. Staff needs to be given permission for such expressions by normalizing them, perhaps tempered by questioning if the victim fully realized the impact of his act.
5. Anxiety. Students will begin worrying about themselves. "If he could kill himself because he was upset, maybe I (or my friends) could too."	5. Discussions should be guided towards helping students differentiate between themselves and the victim and towards other options for problem-solving.
6. Relief. Once the normal distortions of feelings are resolved, students can allow themselves to feel the sadness of the loss and begin the healing process.	6. Staff must guard against encouraging a pseudo-mourning process before students have worked at resolving their conflicts over the suicide.

Source: *Suicide and Its Aftermath: Understanding and Counseling the Survivors;* edited by Edward J. Dunne, John L. McIntosh, and Karen Dunne-Maxim (W. W. Norton & Company, New York, 1987), p. 267.

are glad that it is over. For many, this will be their first encounter with death and their first realization that they too are mortal. In reality, these young people will be scarred for the rest of their lives and that this moment will often invade their thoughts. The event is destined to shape and mould their entire lives. The only question is who is the one who will help them close their wounds and begin the healing process? You, as the clergy, a trusted and sensitive advisor, are the logical

Table 3. School Policies

It is particularly important to create policies to deal with certain specific questions that are likely to arise. These include:

1. How and when should students and faculty be informed of the suicide? *As soon as possible . . . use telephone chains to inform . . . meet as soon as possible.*

2. How, when and where should students be allowed to express their reactions? *In small groups with other students in school and with an appropriate adult supervisor.*

3. What should be done about the victim's close friends? *A team should decide how to best handle this.*

4. What should be done about "high risk" students? *Refer these students to counselors, psychologist, etc. . . . .*

5. Should the school hold a special assembly or memorial service? *What is done for other students who die of cancer, etc.? It is best not to have a large group together and better to work in small groups.*

6. Should there be a symbolic expression of grief, such as lowering the flag to half staff? *Do what is done for other students who die from cancer, etc. . . . Acknowledge the death but do not glamorize it.*

7. Should the school close for the funeral? *No . . . only those closely affected or those who demonstrate a desire should attend, and their parents should attend with them. If any of the youth serve as pallbearers they should be singled out to discuss their feelings and reactions to serving in such a capacity. Also, a school counselor should observe and follow up on all who seem to be overly agitated by the experience.*

8. Who should go to the funeral? *see No. 7.*

9. What kinds of commemorative activities or symbols/plaques, memorial funds, etc.—are appropriate? *None . . . but need to write notes of comfort, make food items for the house of mourning . . . work on life producing projects.*

10. Should the victim's parents be contacted and what can be offered? *Yes, contact and have come in to see how each can help the other.*

11. What should be done about the concerns of other parents? *Meet with, review signs of suicide, teach how to help their children mourn.*

12. How should the school deal with the media? *Have one person be the spokesperson and the rest of the staff refer to this person.*

13. To whom should the school turn for outside consultation of help? *Suicide prevention organizations, carefully chosen mental health workers, clergy, doctors, etc.*

Note: Italics are the author's suggestions.
Source: *Suicide and Its Aftermath: Understanding and Counseling the Survivors;* edited by Edward J. Dunne, John L. McIntosh, and Karen Dunne-Maxim (W. W. Norton & Company, New York, 1987), p. 247.

person to gather these friends together and provide an atmosphere in which they can mourn. Simply getting everyone together and giving them the opportunity to openly talk and express their grief with one another can be the catalyst for healing to begin. Allowing everyone to reflect on the situation and to articulate their guilt more becomes a catharsis. It is also important as well to put a halt to the cycle of accusations that generally happens when a sudden death occurs, for each person has the tendency for self-blame or to blame others for the death. This easily becomes a vicious circle. Everyone needs to realize that no one is really to be blamed, and that there will always be "why's" that will remain unanswered.

One way to relieve everyone's sense of responsibility is to invite these friends to contribute information for the eulogy by writing down their thoughts and/or to write a letter to their companion to be placed in the coffin. [Should this meeting take place after the funeral this writing exercise is still very cathartic. These can be buried in the cemetery at a later time by the group.] Another idea is to have everyone bring a picture of the deceased and to talk about the event in the photograph and all the memories it invokes. This too will prove to be a cleansing process.

In addition it would be important to help these schoolmates and family members to think of ways they might be able to channel feelings into constructive action without making a martyr of the deceased. Suggestions such as: donating to charities, learning more about suicide prevention, teaching others about the signs of suicide, reaching out and helping others who might be in danger by manning a telephone hotline, or constructing plans to prevent "contagion" might be good ideas. This occasion should also be used to educate these young people in the art of comforting their deceased friend's parents, i.e., what to say and not say, when to visit and when to leave. Along with this it is critical to instruct these young people how to console one another, for if their grief is not resolved they are the ones greatest at risk to follow suit.

One wonderful suggestion I heard was for us to call friends of the deceased who are away at college and to discuss with them what happened and the mourning activities in which they might engage.

The Peers' Parents

Since these friends are among those greatest at risk to be the next suicide victims, someone needs as well to instruct their parents in the skills of comforting their child. Imagine the frustration these parents must be experiencing as they watch their child mourn and they don't know how to help them or to relieve their pain, let alone to recognize what might be pathological behavior. A meeting should be held to discuss normal grieving versus behaviour evident of deeper problems. Parents should be encouraged to attend the funeral with their child and not to take this occurrence lightly by letting their child go through this event alone.

The parents should be given some suggestions as to how they can talk with their child about feelings and to not allow the conversation to remain on the level of just details. They should be reminded not to lecture their child on how awful the deceased was to have caused such suffering, but rather, to assist their child in seeing both the good and the bad qualities of the deceased. I believe this conference will help reduce anxieties, and will instruct parents as to how to open new lines of communication between themselves and their child(ren), which thus could prove to be a redeeming factor to this death.

THE SURVIVORS

In assisting family survival in the aftermath of suicide, Nancy Hogan speaks to the importance of "commitment of the survival of the family," as well as "commitment to the memory of the deceased." These two aspects are essential for positive resolution [2, p. 209].

1. *Parents-Grandparents-Children* . . . (Reread the beginning of "First 48 Hours") It is said that there is no worse death than the death of a child. This is only superseded by the loss of a child through suicide, or homicide. The agony of the parents (the following applies to grandparents and children who have lost a parent as well) is insurmountable and will haunt them for the rest of their lives. They will continually search for answers as to "why" this occurred and will question over and over again what they could have, should have, might have done to prevent this death. They will go through a madness unknown to other mourners of sudden death (see chart on reaction to Suicide-Table 4). Unlike other deaths where with time the pain subsides, the best that most surviving parents of suicide can expect to do is learn to cope with the daily pain much like the arthritis patient learns to cope with the agony of movement. For years afterwards, the parents will probably continue to go through a plethora of feelings and emotions, i.e., they will attend graduations and/or weddings of friend's children, and old wounds will be opened anew. Thoughts that it could have been their child standing up there will run rampant through their minds, and the ache returns once more. For the most part they will probably never quit blaming themselves and questioning "why."

Often others will wonder why these survivors do not get out and attend community events or even come to church just to get their minds off their troubles? Perhaps the words of an Atlanta counselor and one who lost her son, gives us some insight. "I used to drive down the street thinking I had a sign on my car that said, 'MY SON KILLED HIMSELF'. Another car would pass me and I would think, 'Now they know' " [11, p. 17]. A woman who lost her sixteen-year-old son stated, "Losing my son was painful enough, but the whispers, feeling like a leper, being avoided, having people act like nothing happened, never mentioning the death, changing the subject, people being afraid it's contagious, as if they touch me or reach out to me, it may happen to them—is almost worse" [11, p. 17]. Wherever these survivors go it is not unusual to feel as if a part of them were

Table 4. Survivor Reactions

Manifestations	Consequences
I. Physical	
Increased organic and psychosomatic complaints and symptoms	Visits to physicians
II. Psychological	
A. Affective	Feels guilt, self blame, anger
Relief	Scapegoating, triangling with family or therapist
Anger/Hostility	Lawsuits
Sadness/Depression	Increased suicide risk
B. Cognitive	
Shock/Disbelief	Fuels denial, fear of "going crazy"
Guilt/Self-reproach	Obsessive reviewing for acts of omission/commission
	Myth-making about murder/accidents
Denial	Search for meaning, explanation
One-way communication:	Anger toward deceased
"I choose not to live with you"	Closed-off communications
Shame/Secrecy associated with stigma	Emotional cut-offs
	Geographic moves
Fear of "going crazy"	Avoidance of therapy as further stigma associated with sickness
Identification with deceased	Suicidal construct as means of coping, personal solution
	Accident proneness, suicide attempts
C. Behavioral	
Loss of patterns of conduct	
III. Psychosocial	
Absence of social role for survivors, secondary to stigma	Truncated, pathological mourning

Prepared by Frank A. Jones, Jr., M.D. from material presented in Calhoun, Selby, and Selby (1982)

Source: *Suicide and Its Aftermath: Understanding and Counseling the Survivors;* edited by Edward J. Dunne, John L. McIntosh, and Karen Dunne-Maxim (W. W. Norton & Company, New York, 1987), p. 68.

missing or to recognize that their status has changed. As in the case of a parent's or sibling's suicide, a young person might sit in the classroom and speculate on how they are now different from the other students, i.e., they no longer have a father/mother or brother/sister. Suddenly, life takes on a new dimension. These people are much more serious about living and the possibility of its ending with a single act. To add to the complexity of the situation, most youths have a difficult time putting words to their feelings and thus making it difficult for them in the beginning to fully deal with this death. A wonderful book to read on young people's reactions to death is, *Teenagers Face to Face with Bereavement* [12].

If we truly want to help all these survivors, we need to reach out and provide them with those things which because of their exhaustion from struggling with the death they would never obtain for themselves. On their behalf, we might gather books on surviving suicide, find existing support groups, put the family in contact with social services and arrange for those in the congregation who would like to befriend them to get started.

In addition, we might also share with them the article by Iris Bolton, in the appendix, which gives everyone permission to feel and express feelings and emotions (see Table 5). Families need to know, that if they so choose, they can survive this nightmare. Nancy Hogan writing in the Compassionate Friends News letter adds that family members "need to be assured that the disorganization that occurs with tragedy is normal and that in time (the) family will have under-standable rhythms again" [2]. They must be reminded that there has to be not only a commitment to the memory of the deceased, but to the continuation of the family and to each individual in that family as well. Interestingly enough, the best way to commemorate the deceased's memory is by commitment to life. The family must be told that they will probably never understand the suicide and that it is not a necessity to do so in order to go on with life. They need to be reminded that the deceased should not have the power from the grave to destroy the "lives" of those who survive.

More intensively than other "sudden death" mourners, the survivors of suicide will undergo an elongated period of exhaustion and physical weakness. Often in an attempt to find some momentary relief, they will try as soon as possible, to return to "normal activities," yet, they will find that thoughts of the deceased will continually hound them. The small events of daily living suddenly become major traumas and take much more energy to complete. Activities involving the surviving siblings, as well as work, will no longer have the enjoyment they once had and will require every ounce of energy to perform. It is our function to indicate that all of these feelings, emotions and exhaustion are normal, and that these survivors must learn to say, "no" to most new requests at this time in order to preserve their strength. We must remind them that their self-esteem is at its lowest point and, subsequently, they will be vulnerable to any traumas that arise. Yet, we need to encourage them ultimately to find ways that they can do and give to others for this is one of the best paths to "recovery."

Table 5. Beyond Surviving: Suggestions for Surviving by Iris M. Bolton

Hundreds of books have been written about loss and grief. Few have addressed the aftermath of suicide for survivors. Here again, there are no answers; only suggestions from those who have lived through and beyond the event. I've compiled their thoughts.

1. Know you can survive. You may not think so, but you can.

2. Struggle with "why" it happened until you no longer need to know "why" or until you are satisfied with partial answers.

3. Know you may feel overwhelmed by the intensity of your feelings but all your feelings are normal.

4. Anger, guilt, confusion, forgetfulness are common responses. You are not crazy; you are in mourning.

5. Be aware you may feel appropriate anger at the person, at the world, at God, at yourself. It's okay to express it.

6. You may feel guilty for what you think you did or did not do. Guilt can turn into regret, through forgiveness.

7. Having suicidal thoughts is common. It does not mean that you will act on those thoughts.

8. Remember to take one moment or one day at a time.

9. Find a good listener with whom to share. Call someone if you need to talk.

10. Don't be afraid to cry. Tears are healing.

11. Give yourself time to heal.

12. Remember, the choice was not yours. No one is the sole influence in another's life.

13. Expect setbacks. If emotions return like a tidal wave, you may be experiencing a remnant of grief, an unfinished piece.

14. Try to put off major decisions.

15. Give yourself permission to get professional help.

16. Be aware of the pain of your family and friends.

17. Be patient with yourself and with others who may not understand.

18. Set your own limits and learn to say no.

19. Steer clear of people who want to tell you what or how to feel.

20. Know that there are support groups that can be helpful, such as Compassionate Friends or Survivors of Suicide groups. If not, ask a professional to help start one.

21. Call on your personal faith to help you through.

22. It is common to experience physical reactions to your grief, e.g., headaches, loss of appetite, inability to sleep.

23. The willingness to laugh with others and at yourself is healing.

24. Wear out your questions, anger, guilt, or other feelings until you can let them go. Letting go doesn't mean forgetting.

25. Know that you will never be the same again, but you can survive and even go beyond just surviving.

Source: *Suicide and Its Aftermath: Understanding and Counseling the Survivors;* edited by Edward J. Dunne, John L. McIntosh, and Karen Dunne-Maxim (W. W. Norton & Company, New York, 1987), p. 280-290.

As clergy we need to remind the mourners that each will experience this recovery differently. Unlike other death experiences in which people have the support of their mate, and/or their parents, with suicide everyone in the family is going through this torture simultaneously—yet, each is different, eg., men, who are traditionally poor at expressing their feeling generally state that "they do not need to talk and can handle this by themselves." On the other hand, women, who are more in touch with their feelings and are better able to express their emotions, find it easier to talk and share. Females often feel let down by their mate who is silent and distant, and thus they often question their mate's love for his child since he does not talk nor express the same emotion as she does. For the male it is usually on the weekend that the loss is most acute. This was the time when he generally spent rough-housing, playing sports or was most involved with his child. Subsequently the male's grief declines more rapidly and he is often able to escape his emotions by burying himself in work. On the other hand, the woman's most intimate contact with her child was much more regular, i.e., after school and in the evenings. Thus woman's depth of emotion is much greater and more acute and grieving can be intense for up to two years. As clergy we can help these parents and grandparents to look at some of the issues that must be resolved in order to make it through this period of their lives, such as: appropriate times to talk about the deceased and when it is better to remain silent; when one needs a respite from the emotions and when one needs to share the memories; when one really needs to talk and share feelings with the other and when one needs to just sit and listen without commenting; how to return to a loving sexual relationship and when one is not feeling amorous how to let the other know that they are not being rejected for any thoughts of anger; how to regain some sort of social life and with whom that will be, and how to experience joy in living life again without feeling guilty; and lastly, how to get over placing blame on the other and how to forgive others. We must point out as well that each will need to search again for the meaning to life and that each one's coping mechanism will be different. Lastly, it is important for each to come to terms with the fact that the lessening of grief does not indicate that their love for the deceased is any less.

Most of the events described above can be handled by friends once they understand how they can be of assistance. However, our role should be of the architect who diagrams the restructuring of this family. The psychological components should indeed be handled by a competent counselor, but we might have to suggest who that trained person might be. Please remember that a suggestion of psychological help might have to be repeated many times, for the family may resist thinking they need help and believe that they can get through this alone especially if there is some of the perceived stigma in receiving psychological help.

Let us not overlook the tremendous pain that the grandparents are experiencing too, for with this death they loose not only their future, but they loose their own child as well to uncontrolled grief. They must sit and watch all the pain and hurt that their child is going through and there is nothing they can do to relieve it. They feel impotent and are caught wondering why they did not die rather than their sweet innocent grandchild.

As clergy we ironically often overlook one area of our expertise which can be of enormous help and that is in the area of faith and prayer. Think how many people endured the Holocaust because of the strength of their belief and hope! (See: *Man's Search for Meaning* by Victor Frankl.) I believe we can assist a family to build upon the faith which has gotten them through life to this point. Our role, as stated before, is not to argue on God's behalf. These devastated people may be angry with God, and what we must do is give them permission to express that anger out loud. My teacher, Rabbi Zvi Yehuda, reminded me, "people of faith can relate to God by either loving God or hating God, by resignation or protestation, thus, they are not indifferent to God." We have to assure this family that even though they feel this anger and, perhaps, feel guilty for such emotions, they can still be within the boundaries of their religious beliefs.

By bringing these survivors to the sanctuary and helping them to articulate their emotions to God, we might ultimately assist them in finding a source of comfort which they might otherwise ignore. Their utilization of prayer should not be depreciated just because the first question they asked was, "How can there be a God who lets my wonderful (*child/mate/parent*) die?" Even though at first the family appears to reject God, I remind you that there has been a history of belief and faith which has carried this family through other life events.

Although, it is impossible to undo that which has already been done, it is possible to help these survivors walk away from this event with more meaningful, purposeful, compassionate, forgiving and loving lives. The challenge is ours.

2. *Siblings* . . . With all that goes on during this time siblings are often the *forgotten mourners.* Linda Rosenfeld and Marilynne Prupas comment in their study of survivors, "It seems siblings often assume the responsibility for taking care of things, postponing their own needs" [13, p. 77]. The authors also warn of the identification siblings may feel with the deceased and the fear that they too may commit suicide. A 1967 study of a St. Louis Suicide Prevention Center showed that 33 percent of the callers had had a previous suicide in their family [11, p. 15]. Thus, we can fathom that it is very important to pay attention to this population. On the other hand, it is also possible, as S.R. Morse noted, that suicide survivorship can be a "force of growth" for siblings [14, p. 82]. Even if this were the case, there is a long painful road to travel before it becomes a "face of growth" for the siblings often carry for years the fantasy that they could have prevented this death. In truth, there might be some basis to this belief, for the deceased probably did confide feelings and thoughts about suicide and most likely did exhibit some of the symptoms. These signs probably can be much better understood now that the siblings can view everything retrospectively. Nonetheless, these survivors must be convinced that constantly harbouring guilt is unwarranted and unproductive, and that this guilt must now be channelled toward something productive. On

the other hand we must also bear in mind that these siblings may be relieved that all the turmoil and attention showered upon their brother/sister is finally over. Getting these children to emote is of the utmost importance. Giving permission for them to verbalize their guilt and then to speculate on what power they actually had to change or prevent the situation, especially when others more qualified, i.e., parents, counselors, etc. could not change what happened, is crucial. This concept of retrospective reconstruction is one way to make the situation more manageable [7, p. 92]. We might also let these siblings know that many times during the course of the next year they will feel anger towards the deceased for causing all this pain, both to themselves and to their parents. They should also not be surprised to discover that they are infuriated that long after the death their sibling still seems to be getting all the attention. They also need to know that they will probably chastise themselves for feeling jealousy towards their beloved brother/sister, who is dead and of whom everyone else now speaks about in glowing terms. However, they should be told that all of this is perfectly normal. (Much of what has been said above also holds true for a child who loses a parent.)

In addition, we need to teach these children how they might comfort their parents. They must be helped to think realistically what they can expect from their parents in the months ahead. They must understand the torment and anguish their parents are experiencing, as well as, how difficult it will be for their father or mother to derive joy from their accomplishments or to muster any energy to participate in their activities. Yes, they will probably feel resentful and angry, but this is normal. We must encourage this group of survivors to find people outside of the family with whom they can talk and share their feelings. (A suggestion of perhaps two or three psychologists, psychiatrists, or social workers should be prepared and given to the child and the parents—the parents should be informed of their surviving child(ren)'s need for psychological help.) We can also be of assistance to these siblings in rehearsing how and what they will tell their friends, as well as how they will publicly deal with the issue that their sibling (or as the case may be, a parent, etc.) committed suicide. We might also explore with them constructive ways to channel their energies. There is no better way to recovery than to get this *at risk population* to turn this adversity into something positive, especially if we can get them to go out and help others. Dr. Sol Gordon, author of *When Living Hurts*, (see address for U.A.H.C.) calls this "Mitzva Therapy."

CONCLUSION

Being the comforter to the family and friends of a suicide victim is one of the hardest tasks we, as clergy, will ever be called upon to perform. Yet, by the very nature of our position as clergy, and the almost unique respect that our position commands, we have the unique opportunity to influence many people's lives, and, in reality, maybe even to save one. With our help people might discover how to bury the skeleton remaining in their psychological closets which, without us, might continue there indefinitely. Through our perception and understanding, we often can aid others in their quest to make sense out of a chaotic period of time, to find meaning out of disarray and to gain direction to a less painful life. With our care and concern it is possible that some might even be able to achieve a more satisfying life and to build tomorrow's dreams upon the grave of yesterday's bitterness.

APPENDIX
Suicide Prevention
Clergy Crisis Team Procedure

STEP 1:

Director of Pupil Personnel Services from the school system contact Interfaith Council representative(s) when a crisis occurs that requires additional personnel. They are informed of the nature of the crisis, all facts known at the time are shared, and directions regarding building needs are given.

STEP 2:

Clergy crisis team reports to the building principal. The most current factual information is provided to them. (Example: for a death of a student—who and how died, what is known, and what will be done, etc.)

STEP 3:

Clergy Crisis Team will be provided with designated areas for counseling students who voluntarily come, individually or in small groups, seeking support and assistance.

NOTE: Decisions for clergy to work in individual classroom will be made by the building principal.

Suggested Counseling Methods Consist of the Following:

A. Actively listening to the students in a non-judgmental climate.

B. Validate what the student is saying as significant and important. Avoid telling a student "You shouldn't feel that way," or "You should have done it differently," etc. By validating the student, it reduces the need and risk of that student going to his/her peer group and receiving inaccurate information or engaging in unhealthy alternatives.

C. Clergy does not need to have all the answers. Sharing with the students allows for the development of a support network (i.e., "I wish I had more answers for you; I hurt as well and maybe we can work on this together").

D. It would be helpful for the clergy to inform the students that it is okay to have feelings and to utilize the support available if needed. It is important that clergy relay their acceptance of the students' vulnerability by being aware of their own voice tone and body language.

NOTE: Help prepare students for the attendance at funeral services (for those students who wish to go and for whom attendance is appropriate).

STEP 4:
Clergy crisis team will be available to meet with building personnel to review the events of the day. They will need to share information and assess initial reactions of students to crisis. This includes a review of individual students who, because of their 1) proximity to the crisis, 2) emotional involvement with the crisis, 3) lack of support systems, or 4) emotional immaturity, might be at special risk.

ACKNOWLEDGMENT

Quotes on p. 138 [7, p. 112] are reprinted with the permission of Lexington Books, an imprint of Macmillan, Inc., from *Grieving: How to Go On Living When Someone You Love Dies* by Therese A. Rando, Ph.D. Copyright © 1988 by Lexington Books.

REFERENCES

1. H. Resnik, Psychological Resynthesis: A Clinical Approach to the Survivors of a Death by Suicide, in *Survivors of Suicide*, A. C. Cain (ed.), Charles C. Thomas, Springfield, Illinois, 1972.
2. I. Bolton, Death of a Child by Suicide, in *Parental Loss of a Child,* Research Press, Champaign, Illinois, 1986.
3. D. Syme, Words to Save, in *Hadassah Magazine,* 1987.
4. R. Toynbee, *Man's Concern with Death,* McGraw-Hill, New York, 1969.
5. M. J. Hauser, Special Aspects of Grief After a Suicide, in *Suicide and Its Aftermath,* E. Dunne, J. McIntosh, and K. Dunne-Maxim (eds.), W. W. Norton, New York, 1987.
6. K. E. Rudestam, Public Perceptions of Suicide Survivors, in *Suicide and Its Aftermath,* E. Dunne, J. McIntosh and K. Dunne-Maxim (eds.), W. W. Norton, New York, 1987.
7. T. Rando, *Grieving: How to Go on Living When Someone You Love Dies,* Lexington Books, Lexington, Massachusetts, 1988.

8. E. Grollman, First-Line Help Following a Funeral, in *Suicide, The Will to Live vs. The Will to Die,* N. Lizner (ed.), Human Sciences, New York, 1984.

9. A. D. Hagin, Understanding Suicide, in *Suicide Prevention and Caring,* National Funeral Directors Association, Milwaukee, Wisconsin, 19??.

10. F. Lamb and K. Dunne-Maxim, Postvention in Schools: Policy and Process, in *Suicide and Its Aftermath,* E. Dunne, J. McIntosh and K. Dunne-Maxim (eds.), W. W. Norton, New York, 1987.

11. G. H. Colt, The History of the Suicide Survivor: The Mark of Cain, in *Suicide and Its Aftermath,* E. Dunne, J. McIntosh, and K. Dunne-Maxim (eds.), W. W. Norton, New York, 1987.

12. K. Gravelle and C. Haskins, *Teenagers Face to Face with Bereavement,* Julian Messner, New York, 1989.

13. L. Rosenfeld and M. Prupas, *Left Alive: After a Suicide in the Family,* Charles C. Thomas, Springfield, 1984.

14. J. L. McIntosh, Survivor Family Relationships: Literature Review, in *Suicide and Its Aftermath,* E. Dunne, J. McIntosh, and K. Dunne-Maxim (eds.), W. W. Norton, New York, 1987.

CHAPTER 11

Role of Organ Donation in Helping Family Members Cope with Grief*

Maryse Pelletier

This chapter will examine the donor family members' appraisal of the most stressful situations experienced from losing a loved one and from consenting to organ/tissue donation. It also will explain the type of coping strategies used to manage these sources of stress and the impact of organ donation on their grief.

Spouses, parents, and siblings from the provinces of New Brunswick and Prince Edward Island who had lost a loved one unexpectedly and had consented to organ and/or tissue donation in 1988 were interviewed in their homes [1]. The time lapse between the loss of the loved one and the interview with family members ranged from ten to fifteen months. The critical care areas in which the loved one was identified as a organ/tissue donor included: the Intensive Care Unit (ICU), Neuro-Intensive Care Unit (NICU), Emergency department and the Coronary Care Unit (CCU). Organ donation had been a subject of previous family discussion in six of seven families and recollection of such discussion facilitated the family members' decision to donate. Four families consented to donate a combination of organs and corneas and three families donated corneas only [1]. Lazarus and Folkman stress and coping theory guided the development and interpretation of the study [2]. The instrument used for data collection consisted of a semistructured interview. A series of open-ended questions were designed by the investigator to capture the richness and completeness of the individual family member's perceptions. The interviews were audiotaped and subsequently transcribed for content analysis.

*Parts of this chapter have been reprinted with permission from Blackwell Scientific Publications, Oxford, *Journal of Advanced Nursing 17*, pp. 90-97, 1992.

Family members recounted in vivid detail the story of their journey through the grieving process and experience with organ donation. They shared fond memories of who their loved one was, and disclosed what their hopes and dreams had been. Family members' stories will be illustrated by the use of excerpts from the interviews.

The findings of this study showed that although the situations family members appraised as having been most stressful, the emotions they reported experiencing, and the coping strategies they remember using were similar to other bereaved families, there were also significant differences.

MOST STRESSFUL SITUATIONS

The most stressful situations that family members identified in response to the unexpected event centred around two main issues: the processes of organ donation and the loss of a loved one.

Processes of Organ Donation

Family members were confronted with many stressful issues related to the processes of organ donation. Specifically, the stressfulness resulted from being informed of the diagnosis of brain death, consenting to organ donation, and waiting for the organ/tissue retrieval to be completed [1].

Diagnosis of Brain Death

All family members reported being unprepared when told of the diagnosis of brain death. They concurred that health professionals' failure to explain brain death sufficiently—or indeed tell them "anything about the meaning of brain death" made the diagnosis difficult to comprehend. Additional factors that made it difficult for them to understand the diagnosis included signs of viability, such as breathing or a beating heart; normal body function, such as warmth, growing beard, or perspiration; as well as the absence of cuts and bruises [1]. One spouse remembered that "his [her husband's] heart was pumping away when he was pronounced dead. He appeared alive, yet, the physician had just told me that he was dead. How could I believe that he was dead?" Health professionals' discomfort when discussing this subject has been suggested as one cause of family member's misunderstanding of brain death [3]. However, informing family members about the irreversible nature of the illness can be a major step in helping them prepare for the reality of the impending loss which is, in essence the first task of grieving [4]. Consequently, several family members experienced cognitive dissonance as a result of having to accept brain death as being synonymous with their personal knowledge of, beliefs about, and experience with death. Although all families gave consent to organ donation, most obviously did so without a clear understanding of brain death. This finding suggests that health professionals need to assess individual family members' understanding of the meaning of brain death and provide the type of information needed to enhance their understanding of such concept.

Consenting to Organ Donation

In relation to giving consent to organ donation, family members identified four particular stressful situations which have not been previously reported by donor families in earlier studies. For most, these included the failure of health professionals to approach families about organ/tissue donation, to identify their loved one as a potential donor, to discuss the type of organ/tissue they could donate, and to respond to their wishes to donate [1]. Most family members reported that if they had not asserted their wishes to donate organs, the opportunity to donate might never have been offered by health professionals. One mother described her experience emotionally by stating, "I had to go and make the effort and like almost begging. Please, use what you can use" [1]. Evidence shows that the health professionals' reluctance to approach and discuss organ donation with grieving families is often related to their fear of adding to their grief [5-7]. However, according to Health and Welfare Canada this reluctance has been identified "as the most significant barrier to an increased organ and tissue supply" [8, p. 3]. By not offering family members the opportunity to donate organ/tissue, health professionals may inadvertently be denying them the opportunity to decide to donate and depriving them the opportunity both to fulfil their loved one's wishes and to find some comfort at their time of loss [9]. It was clear from the findings that "not being approached" to consider organ donation was more stressful for families than "being approached." This suggests that health professionals need to be less fearful about presenting the option of organ donation and that they should continue to initiate with sensitivity the subject with families [1].

Waiting for Retrieval or Organ/Tissue

The family members reported that once consent was given for organ donation, the situation once again became very stressful. This was due to delays in tissue-typing and organ/tissue retrieval, parting with the loved one before the organ/tissue retrieval was completed, and/or not being called following completion of the procedure. These "unknowns" generated unanswered questions and unresolved doubts about death. Some researchers have suggested that such situations may prevent family members from facing the reality of their loss and reaching a sense of closure [10, 11]. As health professionals, we have a vital role in offering family members the opportunity to be contacted if there are any delays in the scheduled surgical time, to spend private time with the loved one before and/or after retrieval, and to be called after retrieval is completed. Such strategies may help family members "achieve emotional closure" [4, p. 68].

Loss of Loved One

It was evident that the impact and meaning of losing a loved one varied among individual family members [1]. Lazarus and Folkman suggest that these variations may be due to differences in sensitivity, interpretations, vulnerability, and reactions to similar events [2]. Furthermore, the family members reported that the sudden and untimely loss of the loved one was a significant factor influencing the extent to which they appraised their loss as stressful [1]. As explained by Lazarus and Folkman, an "off time event" can be more threatening as it can deprive one of a chance to prepare for new roles, to solicit peer support, and to engage in anticipatory coping.

For the family members like those in earlier studies, the most stressful consequences of their loss, were having to deal with discontinuity in patterns of living, poignant reminders, the loss of a significant relationship, and inappropriate support received from family and friends.

Discontinuity in Patterns of Living

All family members reported stressfulness associated with adjusting to new roles and responsibilities, disruptions in daily routines, and/or unexpected alterations in future plans. Most spouses found that it was very stressful to take over daily living tasks, learn new skills previously performed by their partner, assume "new roles and make decisions" on their own. Other family members described how their loss had irreparably changed their daily routines and shattered their hopes and dreams for the future. Clearly, for parents, their children represented the beginning of life, the future, and, in a sense, immortality. One mother's sorrowful revelation seemed to illustrate the meaning of losing a child: "It's like part of yourself, your heart and your soul is just wiped out. Like someone came and scooped [out] everything that makes you tick" [1]. In contrast, spouses described the untimely loss of their partner as a sense of deprivation for what could have been. One spouse explained, "I expected us to die of old age, I never thought of him dying before me. So there's a lot of things we didn't get a chance to do."

Poignant Reminders

Family members described poignant reminders which triggered memories of their loved one. They found that special events and circumstances such as holidays, special dates, times of special meaning, everyday encounters, or the loss of an another family member evoked painful emotions with renewed intensity [1].

Loss of a Significant Relationship

The impact of losing a significant relationship was especially stressful for the spouses. For them, this meant losing the person with whom they confided, shared their feelings or thoughts, problem-solved, and/or from whom they drew strength, support, or reassurance from during difficult times [1]. One husband described how "not being able to share things with her the way we did before has been difficult. Like if anything bad or irritating happened . . . it would be eased by sharing it with her."

Inappropriate Social Support

Family members revealed that the type of support received from family and friends changed as the process of grief unfolded. Shortly after their loss, support from a variety of sources was readily available and mostly helpful. However, as time evolved the type of support received was characterized as insufficient or inappropriate. For example, some family members reported a lack of intrafamily support that was manifested by a reluctance to talk about the loved one. One spouse described how differently her husband coped with the loss of their son, as "there were times when I felt like talking about him but he wouldn't be interested in talking. Instead he'd just quietly walk away." Such avoidance may have impeded communication which could have been mutually beneficial and this may have interfered with keeping the memories alive in families. Other family members commented on the lack of support received from friends they had previously counted on, while others were annoyed by how inept people were at providing consolation. Most people suggested "give yourself time, you'll be OK." This lack of support may reflect society's discomfort with discussing issues of death and dying [11-13]. As a result, family members reported not only feeling inhibited in talking about their loss but also recognized grief as something to be shared only with selected confidants. Given the overwhelming grief emotions experienced, perhaps the manner in which these were expressed deterred and/or made it difficult for others to extend support [14]. As well, the type of coping strategy that family members used may have influenced the type of support others provided. For example, some family members exercised control over their emotions by acting strong to keep others from knowing about their feelings or upsetting them. They wanted to prove that they did not "wallow in their sorrow." As well, several used positive reappraisal, which involved seeing their loss in a favorable way. Consequently, these coping strategies may have provided cues to relatives and friends that they were not distressed and appeared to be coping well, and therefore, support was not needed [15].

According to Pittman, nurses working with bereaved families have a responsibility to "provide support to the family members beyond the hospital setting" [16, p. 570]. Such support could be provided by means of home visits and/or phone calls three to four weeks after the loss and thereafter, as requested [17]. Providing an opportunity for family members to accept or decline follow-up support may allow them to ask questions and express concerns. As well, follow-up visits may enable nurses to assess the family members' feelings about the loss, coping abilities, and availability of emotional support. In turn, this may guide the development of early and specific nursing interventions to meet family members' unique needs and to provide them with information about self-help or bereavement groups.

Emotional Response

All family members experienced a combination of intense grief emotions such as loneliness, hurt, fear, guilt, and/or numbness as they attempted to deal with the loss of the loved one. For most family members, the feeling of loneliness persisted and was difficult to endure. For one father, this feeling was accompanied by a deep, aching desire to "put my arm around him [his son], give him a hug, or squeeze him."

Other family members revealed that their loss left them with a constant sense of unrelenting hurt, which seemed to lose some of its intensity but never completely subsided. One spouse described the pain "like being injured . . . it's like a raw wound inside and I'm waiting [for it] to heal. . . . It festers . . . [and] it's always there to remind me that he is never coming back." For another spouse, the truth that her husband was gone forever was not denied but was conveyed by a feeling of numbness that she described as lasting "for a whole year."

A mother whose son had committed suicide searched for things she might have done to have prevented the tragedy from occurring and to have helped him in times of need. She reported feeling guilty and hurt for not having intervened.

Coping Strategies

Family members reported using a combination of eight different types of coping strategies to manage the new demands, threats, challenges and grief emotions resulting from the loss of their loved one. The variety of strategies supports Folkman and Lazarus's premise that individual cope in complex ways when confronted with stressful situations [14]. Making the suggestion to donate, positively reappraising their loss, keeping the connection, and using escape avoidance were the most frequently reported helpful strategies. A summary of categories and subcategories of coping strategies is found in Table 1.

Making the Suggestion to Donate

One of the most striking and significantly different way family members coped was by making the suggestion for organ donation. In fact, five of seven families took the initiative and requested organ donation, while two families who were approached by the physician readily consented. It is interesting that organ donation had been a subject of previous family discussions in six of these families and recollection of such wishes facilitated their decision to donate [1]. They approached the physicians within hours or days of their loved one's admission to

Table 1. Coping Strategies

Major Categories:	
1. Escape-Avoidance Subcategories: A. Wishing/hoping B. Denying C. Avoiding	6. Seeking Emotional Support Subcategories: A. Accepting Support B. Sharing Feelings/Story C. Asking for Support
2. Planful Problem-Solving A. Considering Issues Logically B. Drawing on Past Experiences C. Taking Time to Consider Probabilities	7. Keeping the Connection Subcategories: A. Remaining Near B. Keeping the Memories Alive
3. Searching for Information	
4. Making the Suggestion to Donate	8. Exercising Control Subcategories: A. Acting Strong B. Distancing
5. Positive Reappraisal Subcategories: A. Experiencing Positive Growth B. Drawing on God's Strength C. Finding Positive Meaning D. Adapting	

a critical care area and before the confirmation of the diagnosis of brain death. For one spouse, the thought of donating his wife's organs/tissues was comforting in that it gave him something positive to focus [on]. One mother recounted how her decision was made easier. Once approached by the physician, she remembered "what her son wanted. . . . It was the doctor who made me think of what he wanted. If he [the physician] hadn't come in and said, 'Consider giving up his organs,' I wouldn't have thought of it [myself]. . . . I don't think I could have lived with knowing I was going against his wishes" [1]. Clearly, a strong respect for the loved one's wishes to donate, an unquestionable commitment to fulfil that wish, and a strong belief that organ donation presented an opportunity to gain some control over the sudden loss of a loved one motivated family members to initiate the approach and to give consent.

Positive Reappraisal

In spite of the many stressful implications associated with the sudden loss of their loved one and organ/tissue donation, all family members were able to positively reappraise their loss. They focused on the positive aspects by comparing their situation to that of less fortunate people or situations, drawing on God's strength, rediscovering important aspects of life, and finding positive meaning in organ/tissue donation. Such strategies contributed to their morale, gave them courage, and provided comfort. The fact that all family members had positive feelings about organ donation is consistent with the findings of earlier studies on donor families. All reported finding comfort and solace in knowing that other persons' lives had been saved or enriched as a result of organ/tissue donation. One mother seemed to speak for all family members when she described "feeling good inside that I did something good for somebody." Most importantly, all believed that organ/tissue donation had provided them with an opportunity to change the horrendous outcome into something more positive.

Although, consenting to organ donation was undoubtedly perceived as a positive experience, the extent to which organ donation helped family members with their grief varied. Sometimes it provided comfort and thus, reduced distress, while sometimes it prolonged a period where death could not be confirmed. One mother explained how organ donation had created unresolved doubts about the reality of her son's death and had prevented her from attaining a sense of closure: "I can't accept that he is completely dead. I'll always wonder whether he is really resting in peace because. . . .there are parts [organs/tissues] of him still alive somewhere in this world. So to me it's like he's not completely dead" [1]. Nevertheless, all family members agreed that organ donation has been a consistent source of support in their acceptance, healing, and growth. In fact, for two parents "organ donation has been the only thing that has given us a bit of peace and comfort."

Keeping the Connection and Escape-Avoidance

The finding that both keeping the connection and escape avoidance were frequently reported by all family members suggests that individuals used seemingly contradictory coping strategies. In one sense, keeping the connection allowed family members to keep the memories of the loved one alive. They reported remembering their loved one on an on-going basis by either "visiting the grave site," "looking at photos," "recalling stories and memories of the past," or "keeping a diary" of the events. On the other hand, using escape-avoidance patterns of coping, such as keeping busy by doing hobbies, working, visiting, and/or participating in social and leisure activities with family, groups, and friends distracted them from thinking about their loss. Such activities have been found to be significantly helpful in providing a brief respite from the pain and loneliness associated with a loss. According to Folkman and Lazarus, employing contradictory coping strategies is significantly useful when one strategy does not effectively help to master, reduce, or tolerate stressful situations [14]. Alternately, if using escape-avoidance along with keeping the connection helped to mitigate the latter's emotional impact, then their functions could be considered complimentary.

In conclusion it is clear that for most family members the loss of a loved one impacted to varying degrees on facets of their emotional, physical, social, and/or spiritual well-being. Although all reported experiencing incredible anguish as a result of losing a loved one, most revealed that their loss had helped them to grow into stronger and wiser individuals whose values and life priorities now have a more meaningful focus.

As the family members shared their stories, it was moving to hear how their generosity had provided a gift of hope and life to a stranger in need. It was evident that for most family members, the opportunity to donate organs/tissues has been a valuable experience in the grieving and healing process. Although progress has been made in field of organ/tissue transplantation, much remains to be done in relation to the donation process. In order to enhance this valuable experience for families of donors, "nurses and physicians need to work collaboratively to support each other through the phases of donation . . . with open communication and understanding of each other's perspectives" [18, p. 1].

REFERENCES

1. M. Pelletier, The Organ Donor Family Members' Perception of Stressful Situations During the Organ Donation Experience, *Journal of Advanced Nursing, 17,* pp. 90-97, 1992.
2. R. S. Lazarus and S. Folkman, *Stress, Appraisal and Coping,* Springer Publishing Company, New York, 1984.
3. D. T. Savaria, M. A. Rovellie, and R. T. Schweizer, Donor Family Surveys Provide Useful Information for Organ Procurement, *Transplantation Proceedings, 22*:2, pp. 316-317, 1990.
4. M. Antonacci, Sudden Death: Helping Bereaved Parents in the PICU, *Critical Care Nurse, 10*:4, pp. 65-70, 1990.
5. E. Etheredge, M. Maeser, G. Sicard, and C. Anderson, A Natural Resource: Prevalence of Cadaver Organs for Transplantation and Research, *Journal of American Medical Association, 241,* pp. 2287-2289, 1979.
6. L. R. Sophie, J. C. Salloway, G. Sorock, P. Volek, and F. K. Merkel, Intensive Care Nurses' Perceptions of Cadaver Organ Procurement, *Heart & Lung, 12,* pp. 261-267, 1983.
7. F. P. Stark, A. L. Reiley, and L. Cook, Attitude Affecting Organ Donation in the Intensive Care Unit, *Heart & Lung, 13,* pp. 400-404, 1984.
8. J. A. Banning, A Time of Reflection, *Canadian Nurse, 4,* p. 3, 1987.
9. M. Bartucci and P. Bishop, The Meaning of Organ Donation to Donor Families, *ANNA Journal, 6,* pp. 369-410, 1987.
10. M. S. Caplin and D. L. Sexton, Stresses Experienced by Spouses of Patients in Coronary Care Unit with Myocardial Infarction, *Focus on Critical Care, 15,* pp. 31-40, 1988.

11. A. Miles, Caring for Families When a Child Dies, *Paediatric Nursing, 16,* pp. 346-347, 1990.
12. B. Heffner, Shattered Dreams, *Issues of Comprehensive Paediatric Nursing, 12,* pp. 303-308, 1989.
13. J. Wiler, Grieving Alone: A Single Mother's Loss, *Issues in Comprehensive Nursing, 12,* pp. 299-302, 1989.
14. S. Folkman and R. S. Lazarus, The Relationship between Coping and Emotions: Implications for Theory and Research, *Social Science Medical Journal, 26,* pp. 309-317, 1988.
15. C. Dunkel-Schetter, S. Folkman, and R. S. Lazarus, Correlates of Social Support, *Journal of Personality and Psychology, 53*:1, pp. 71-80, 1987.
16. S. Pittman, Alpha and Omega: The Grief of the Heart Donor Family, *The Medical Journal of Australia, 143,* p. 570, 1985.
17. P. Miam, Sudden Bereavement: Nursing Interventions in the ED, *Critical Care Nursing, 10,* pp. 30-40, 1990.
18. Canadian Nurses Association, CNA Statement on the Role of Nurses in Organ and Tissue Donation, Retrieval, and Transplantation, *Canadian Nurse, 83*:3, p. 14, 1988.

CHAPTER 12

SIDS: Parents' Responses

Linda Ernst and John DeFrain

> Thirty-seven years have passed, and until four years ago I was not allowed to talk about it. Not to my husband and family or friends. I wasn't allowed to talk or cry myself out. No one wanted to know. I was blamed for letting the baby sleep on his stomach. I am seventy-two years old, and not until recently when a friend of my daughter's had a neighbor who went through the same thing was I finally able to talk and receive some comfort.

INTRODUCTION

Many parents have for years felt isolated in their feelings of guilt and failure as a parent because their child died suddenly with no explanation for the death. Although research about Sudden Infant Death Syndrome (SIDS) and recognition of the syndrome has increased since the middle of the 1970s, many parents still wrestle with the self-doubt, blame, and guilt that goes with a child dying without any identifiable cause.

By definition SIDS is:

> The sudden death of an infant or young child which is unexpected by history and for which a thorough autopsy examination fails to demonstrate an adequate cause of death [1].

The goal of research in the past years has been to find out what causes SIDS and, ultimately, to prevent SIDS from occurring.

The effects of SIDS on surviving family members warrants focused research because blame is often placed on family members since there is no medical explanation for the death. Family members also internalize this blame and feel they should have been able to do something to protect the child. Parents may think that "if only they had taken the child to the doctor," or "if only they had checked on the child earlier," or "if only they had tried harder to revive the child." These parents are often isolated because of feelings of blame on the part of extended family members and others in society. They cannot reach out for comfort in the same way as survivors from other kinds of deaths. The strain placed upon individual family members as well as the family as a whole becomes severe.

THE STUDY

The information in this chapter was taken from a much larger study which was conducted with 127 parents, eighty grandparents, and seventy-three siblings of babies who died of SIDS. This larger study is reported in a book, *Sudden Infant Death: Enduring the Loss* [2]. The parents responded to a twenty-three-page questionnaire with open-ended questions. For example, one question follows:

> Could you describe at length (and we know this is terribly difficult) what happened at the time of your baby's death? Who was caring for the child? Who found the child? What did they see? What happened after the child was found? Please tell the story of the first day or so after the death.

This one question was followed by a half page of blank space for parents to write their answer. Parents would usually fill up that space and added other pages to tell their story. Many parents told us they had to put the questionnaire away several times because they could not finish at one sitting.

This chapter focuses on the responses of the 127 parents to questions about what happened the day the baby died, their initial thoughts about the death, and feelings about an autopsy being performed. The chapter begins with an account of one mother's experience with SIDS and ends with a discussion of implications of the findings for those in helping professions.

AN OVERVIEW: ONE MOTHER'S STORY

> In the beginning I lost all sense of being. The second day after the funeral, I went out and tried to dig up her grave. I thought I could see her in her walker or hear her cry. I stayed up all day and night checking the other kids. I'd leave them several times a week and go to the cemetery and sit by her grave all afternoon. At the time I was four months pregnant. After my little boy was born, my husband and I took turns with four-hour shifts, watching the baby for several weeks. Then I would dress him in her clothes, until one day I put her shoes on him and I had to get my oldest child to take them off.
>
> I wouldn't allow her to be put in a casket until the day of the funeral. We had taken pictures of her at the funeral home, but my husband wouldn't allow me to look at them. But they seemed to be some sort of help. I can't really explain

in words how they helped me. I had never had but one other picture of her, and it was when she was a newborn. The best I can explain this is that just being able to look at her, it seemed she wasn't so far away. The pictures from the funeral home were not taken of her in a casket and she looked as though she were asleep.

I still have periods of fear of losing the other children. Right after my baby died, my niece, four years old, drowned. Then my father was shot and killed. I lost all sense of reality. My husband started drinking, and I hated him. I couldn't sleep. If I did, I had dreams about bugs eating her, or I'd dream of the funeral. Somewhere in the back of my mind I decided if I could just stop loving the kids, my husband, and parents, I could never by hurt by anyone or anything.

I knew I needed counseling, but my mom and husband were totally against anything like that. It was only for crazy people. But I finally went to one doctor for almost a year, and I lived in my grief and could talk to him, and am thankful to God he told me what a selfish mother I was being. Oh, I hated him at the time, but he is the only one who really helped me out of the loneliness, because I'd shut myself off from any feeling relationships.

My stepfather made some harsh statements; some people thought we were really to blame. When it happened we were visiting my mother and the baby was in bed with us; my husband had been drinking and thought he had suffocated her. My husband wanted to send the pictures we had taken of her to his mother. I hated him and blamed him. She had awoke for a two o'clock feeding, and we played and she laughed and cooed, and at six o'clock she was dead. My husband never said so in so many words, nor did I, but we just became distrustful of each other.

THE DAY THE BABY DIED

The above account provides a description of one mother's experience with SIDS. The following section provides a broader scope of what happened to other parents in the study. These accounts become important for family members and those providing support for families because parents keep reliving this day in their minds for years to come.

Babies in the Care of Baby-Sitters

Approximately one-third of the babies in this study died in the care of baby-sitters. This is to be expected when high numbers of women are in the work force. Although most communities have support and educational services available for parents of babies who died of SIDS, most communities do not have programs for other care givers. One parent provided some clues as to the possible agony baby-sitters experience when a child died in their care:

> She called 911 and could not get herself to apply CPR because she had gone through the same thing three years earlier with another infant boy. She told me she knew there was no hope, but apologized that she hadn't tried CPR anyway. I had to console her when I arrived at her home. She was literally a madwoman, tearing her hair out, walking from room to room amidst all the police and rescue people. I finally got her attention, and all she could do was apologize. . . . My sitter was taken to the hospital by her family and had to be under sedation for a couple of days. The next day we tried to see her, but she was still at the hospital, so we didn't try again for several days.

It is apparent that support and educational services need to be provided for other care givers as well as family members. This care giver is likely to be unrecognized as a grieving individual who is greatly affected by SIDS.

Premonitions About the Baby Dying

As some parents described what happened the day their baby died, they began the story by saying they either knew their baby would die very young or had dreams about the baby dying. One woman who knew her child would die very young was afraid to tell anyone but her husband, because people would think she was crazy. Another parent described her experience with a dream about the baby dying:

> When I awoke again, I noticed the clock read 9 a.m. Since I had a dream that someone was telling me, "The baby is dead," I was scared to go and look in on him. I noticed that my older son was up and watching cartoons in the living room, and he had to look at the baby before leaving the room, since he had slept in the same room with him that night. Then my husband got up and rushed to the bathroom to shower. He ordinarily looked in on the baby also, so I figured the dream was absurd.

Although many parents may have such feelings about their children's futures, for this parent her worst fears have come true.

Parents' Immediate Responses to the Death

Parents who experience the sudden death of child often feel they are going crazy or that their responses are somehow abnormal. The parents in this study, however, had a wide range of feelings and responses. The experiences of these parents may be of comfort to others. After leaving the hospital, one parent drank beer for the next several days. Another parent bent a metal chair with his hands in the hospital waiting room as he told his parents on the telephone what had happened. Another ran out of the hospital and gave a piercing scream after he was told his child was dead. Another put his fist through the wall after calling 911 from his home. Another went home and quickly packed up all the baby's things and had them put into storage. Although these reactions may seem extreme, the stress of losing a child so suddenly creates all kinds of feelings and responses unique to that day and time.

Some Less-Typical Examples

Most parents found their child dead after being asleep. In some cases the body was cold and the child had been dead for awhile. In other cases the body was warm and efforts at resuscitation were unsuccessful. Some deaths occurred in ways which are less typical and provides a further understanding of SIDS. One child died in the back seat of a car while the mother was driving:

> My father and I were returning to my home on the central California coast after visiting my college friend and her new baby in Portland, Oregon. I put him down for a nap right behind me while I drove. We stopped at a gas station and parked for dinner. He had been asleep for almost three hours. I turned him over and he was dead, newly dead, because he was still quite warm, except for his hands.

Another couple was watching their baby sleep and were talking about their feelings of being parents. As they were looking at the baby, he started turning blue and they were unable to revive him.

These two examples should be of comfort to parents who feel their baby suffered or died under great stress. These parents did not have indications of suffering on the part of their babies.

Some of the babies were found not breathing and neither parents nor medical professionals were able to start the heart beating again. For some parents there was hope, for a little while, that the child might live. This anxiety, however, of not knowing whether their child might live and possibly have extensive brain damage, or might die at some later date, created additional stress for these parents.

One couple rushed the baby to the hospital while administering CPR. After about half an hour, the doctor announced there was a heartbeat:

> The pediatrician said my child was a sick boy with internal bleeding. . . . We waited through three hours of anxiety, with his blood pressure rising and falling. Around daylight the medical team from Boston arrived. Their prognosis was also grim. "If he lives he'll be a very sick child." Later, a doctor pulled us into a room and we heard the words "I'm sorry to say your baby could not be saved."

Another couple found their baby not breathing and also administered CPR until the paramedics came to their home.

At the hospital his heart was started after a shot of adrenalin, and he was flown by life-flight helicopter to Toledo. . . . We couldn't know how much damage the baby had suffered from lack of air. Total recuperation, a coma for weeks, brain damage to some degree, death? I really wondered which would be harder to face, a brain-damaged child after having had a lively, happy, normally developing, bright child, or death. Both alternatives seemed so devastating. He was stabilized, still unconscious and unable to breathe by himself. . . . The doctor called to say that part of his intestines had been eliminated, indicating organ death from lack of oxygen, and that he would die within hours. We returned immediately to the hospital and sat by his bed just watching the heart monitor lose ground beat by beat. I was able to hold him once there was no hope, and, therefore, no concern over causing further brain damage by moving his head. He had so many tubes hooked up to him. I just rocked him and stroked his soft head until his heart stopped beating. It was so hard to lay him on the bed and leave the hospital. One child lived for four days after what medical personnel referred to as "interrupted SIDS." The baby was taken to the hospital with no pulse or heartbeat. The child was on a respirator and was unconscious.

We were told he was dying and they couldn't help him. He had been too long without oxygen. Even if he did live he would be a vegetable. His brain and all other organs were devastated. He would never be our beautiful baby we knew and loved. When we were allowed to see him, my heart just shattered. He was connected to machines from everywhere on his body, and he was having terrible seizures. How could this have been true? He was fine at 6:30. Why would God let this happen? My whole life was dying in front of my eyes, and no one could stop it. The things my precious baby went through took a little piece of me away every minute. . . . Those days were full of hope, despair, tears, and asking why and how one hundred times a day.

These parents had a little more time to prepare for the baby's death. That time, however, was very stressful and sometimes filled with difficult decisions.

The Way the Babies Looked When They were Found

This may appear to be an unnecessary part of studying families who have had a baby die of SIDS. It is important to remember, however, that this image is part of what parents carry with them as they relive the death many times a day.

Some of the parents found their baby limp and very white or blue. Usually they went to check on the child in the morning or after a nap.

He was face down in the pillow! I turned on the light and quickly lifted him. He was like a pale rag doll.

He was limp like a rag doll. He still had his color but was not breathing.

> The baby did not look dead when I found him. He just looked as though he was sleeping.

> He was dead, newly dead, because he was still quite warm except for his hands, but all blue.

Other parents found the baby stiff and cold. Some babies looked bruised because blood had settled to the lower extremities after death. Others looked black. Some babies had vomit on the bed, and some had blood on their noses.

> I picked him up and he was kind of stiff and cold. I shook him and called his name. Then, as best I can remember, I started to scream. I covered him up with a blanket. I remember thinking he might be cold.

> She was cold and stiff, and her face was black.

> I knew he was dead because there was a spot of blood on the sheets.

> As I walked into her room, I noticed the underside of her hand was purple. Her head was face down into the covers.

> I picked up her hand, and her stiff body turned right over. She looked like she had been beaten.

The vomit or blood-tinged mucus from the nose or mouth results from the pressure changes in the chest cavity after death. It is mucus discharge from the lungs.

Many of these descriptions are very negative images for parents to carry with them. Some of the images may elicit thoughts of abuse or a struggle on the part of the baby. Some parents think their child choked or suffocated because of the vomit. These thoughts and concerns might need to be discussed and explained by those in helping professions.

Parents' Responses to the Death

What follows are descriptions of a range of responses that parents had to the death. Other parents may read these accounts and realize their actions or feelings were not unique and did not mean they were crazy.

> I remember going to a restaurant and not being able to stop eating. I couldn't fill up.

> I remember sitting on our bed holding myself and rocking. I hit my head on our cast iron-bed (hard) and thought, I'm going crazy and can't let myself do it.

[The next day] I went into the hills and burned the bassinet pad, sheets, and blankets he had slept in last.

The first night after she died was awful. I wandered around all night crying and looking for her. I didn't know where her body was: at the hospital, morgue, or funeral home. . . .The next night I slept better knowing where her body was.

I couldn't keep warm enough. I constantly had a blanket wrapped around me. That night when everyone left, we were so tired, but we just couldn't get to sleep. My husband got up and wrote a poem to the baby.

[The day after the baby died] we went out that day and bought a brown teddy bear for our baby—something I had been wanting to do but kept putting off. Now it seemed the most important thing that I had to do.

Clearly, anything parents do after their baby dies suddenly is "normal."

Holding the Baby After the Death

Most parents appreciated the opportunity to hold their baby and spend some quiet time with the child after it died. A few choose not to do so and, in fact, did not want to look at the child.

Some babies died at home and parents held the baby while waiting for the medical examiner. One mother described how her child was pronounced dead and the family waited three hours for the mortician to come. During that time "we held and cried over him until they took him. That was very comforting."

Another parent described the experience:

We went into the intensive care room, and I held him for a long time. I was so glad that they let me do that because I felt that I at least got to hold him for one last time. It was so hard to put him down, because I knew that I would never get to hold him again. He just looked like he was sleeping and would wake up at any minute.

Generally the hospital personnel were caring and compassionate and were sensitive to the needs of grieving parents. They also made efforts to make the visual image of the child positive. For example, they would wash the baby or disconnect medical equipment. Some parents, however, saw their baby with needle pricks or with "cuts and marks all over the baby's skin from the tremendous effort to save him."

INITIAL THOUGHTS ABOUT WHY THE BABY DIED

An important part of this story is the parents' immediate thoughts about why the baby died. For many parents these immediate thoughts, even though they may be incorrect, stayed with them for a long time. Some parents, for example, who thought the child died because of their neglect still have these thoughts in the back of their minds even though they have been told many times it is not their fault.

Death Resulted from Lack of Oxygen

More than one-third of the parents thought their baby had in some way suffocated and died from lack of oxygen. One parent said the baby died because the mattress was too soft. Another thought the baby died because she was lying on a pillow. One parent said, "I knew I killed my baby because I laid him on my bed." One parent thought the baby had strangled itself in clothing. One parent said, "I thought I had not burped him well enough after his last feeding, and he had spit up and gagged to death." One father thought his wife suffocated the baby.

Death Resulted from SIDS

Approximately one-fourth of the parents from the very beginning felt their child died of SIDS. These parents had some previous experience with SIDS with a family member or a friend, or they had read about it. One parent had recently read that breast-fed babies do not die of SIDS, and because she had just stopped breast-feeding, thought the baby died of SIDS.

Other Thoughts About the Cause

The remaining parents had a wide range of thoughts about the cause of death. Following are some examples:

I was sure I had killed him!

I thought someone had broken in and beaten her up.

I thought our cat could have done it. I've always heard that cats will suck the baby's breath out of them. I also remember putting the cat out before the ambulance arrived.

I thought it was punishment for what I had done and said to my husband.

I thought it was because of the medicine I had given him for his cold.

I thought it was because I let bottles sit on the counter after taking them out of the refrigerator.

I thought it was caused by an accident or child abuse from the sitter.

Many of these initial thoughts lingered for a long time. Many have implications for feelings of guilt or self-blame. Because there is no medical explanation, parents and others have a need to create their own explanation.

WHEN AUTOPSIES ARE PERFORMED

Approximately 10 percent of the parents did not have an autopsy performed to provide them with an explanation for the death. One parent said, "I wish there had been one done. Maybe I wouldn't have these feelings of guilt." Another parent said, "We just assumed an autopsy would be performed and didn't realize until it was too late that one was not performed." The results of most of the autopsies indicated that nothing was abnormal enough to have caused the death of these children.

A vast majority of parents who had an autopsy performed were satisfied with the results. A few parents indicated, however, that even though an autopsy was performed and the result was SIDS, this was still not enough. When asked whether they were satisfied with the results of the autopsy, these parents responded:

> I have to say yes and no, because I knew I could have other children without worrying about birth defects or disease. But not to know *exactly* why he is dead is a hard thing ever to accept.

> I didn't get any answers to why he died.

> Healthy, normal babies should not just die for no reason.

> As satisfied as humanly possible when told there was no reason for the death.

There is no doubt that autopsies should be performed when SIDS is suspected. It needs to be understood, however, that the autopsy findings does not always provide enough of an answer for many parents.

IMPLICATIONS FOR THOSE IN HELPING PROFESSIONS

Even though SIDS has been recognized since the mid-1970s and parents are told that their child died of SIDS, many parents still feel that they were somehow responsible. The guilt and blame remains and those in helping professions need to recognize those feelings are embedded in parents' grief.

Day care providers are sometimes caring for children when they die of SIDS. Their grief may not be recognized and there may not be support or counseling focused on their needs. This group must be recognized as being left out of the grieving process, but who also experience the feeling that they did something wrong.

The education and intervention which results when there is a SIDS death must continue. Initially one-fourth of the parents in this study thought their baby died of SIDS because they were familiar with the syndrome. The remaining parents had other thoughts about causes, many of which resulted in self-blame. The continued education will make more people aware of SIDS and intervention can provide accurate information when parents blame themselves or others. In addition, those in helping professions must recognize that those initial thoughts when parents learned of the death are never forgotten and may need to be talked about over and over again. Parents in this study had many flashbacks to the time when they found their child dead or learned of the death. The feelings that go with that time are not easily resolved.

Although the results of autopsies are an important aspect in helping the grieving process, those in helping professions must also recognize that the fact that even with an autopsy there is still *no cause* for the death. Some parents feel even an autopsy does not provide closure to an understanding of why this happened.

The parents in this study made it clear that SIDS is the kind of death which adds unique qualities to the grieving process. There is self-blame and guilt from not having protected their child from the death. This blame can also be directed at their spouse or other family members and can cause strain within the family. There can also be feelings of isolation which results from blame placed on the parents on the part of extended family and others in the community. Until a cause or causes of SIDS is found we must continue to provide added support and understanding to families experiencing SIDS.

REFERENCES

1. A. B. Bergman, J. B. Beckwith, and C. G. Ray, Sudden Infant Death Syndrome, in *Proceedings of the Second International Conference on Causes of Sudden Infant Death,* A. B. Bergman, J. B. Beckwith, and C. G. Ray (eds.), University of Washington Press, Seattle, 1970.
2. J. DeFrain, L. Ernst, D. Jakob, and J. Taylor, *Sudden Infant Death: Enduring the Loss,* Lexington Books, Lexington, Massachusetts, 1991.

CHAPTER 13

Growing Beyond Survival: Grief Experiences of Children from Dysfunctional Families

Judy Oaks

It is important to me to introduce this chapter by sharing background information about myself. Although this chapter will address intellectual information, woven into it for explanatory purposes, will be personal anecdotal stories. My perspective on dysfunctional families has been gained from learning experiences that compliment my own recovery from losses.

I grew up in a large family of eight children. My mother also birthed a stillborn daughter and miscarried once. I would describe my mother as struggling with depression much of her life. My father was a coal miner for thirty-five years. He was the hero child of an alcoholic father. Both parents were children of poverty. Because of our large family I am also a child of poverty. My entire family worked very hard to survive. Each child was expected to contribute to child care, household chores, care of farm animals, and gardening. We raised and preserved the majority of our food supply. Because of the large family, the limited resources, and the necessity of work, emotional nurturance as well as many of the developmental needs and tasks were inadequately met. Since both of my parents were reared in similar circumstances, their parenting skills were limited as well.

Understanding a dysfunctional family involves study of multi-generational issues, including not only those people who wounded us but also those people who nurtured us. Uncle Wayne was the only male in my life who was unconditionally loving. In college I married a man quite like Uncle Wayne. Eight years later an accident left me widowed at the age of thirty. My sons were two and seven. I returned to graduate school following my husband's death and completed a doctoral dissertation on "Adjustment to Bereavement." I was learning how to survive the loss I had experienced. Five years later I married again to a man like my father. Gary was the hero child of an alcoholic. Two years after we married, his alcoholic father strangled to death while on a binge drunk. Gary experienced a delayed grief reaction.

When I met Gary he was a counselor in a detoxication center. When we married, he was the director of two half-way houses for recovering alcoholics. He has a degree in psychology which describes his intelligence and education, but he was still wounded because he had not completed any recovery work as an adult child. He was a Vietnam veteran who experienced post-traumatic stress disorder. As he conducted his life review, his anger and his inability to express his feelings festered into rage. Although I was able to convince him to enter therapy, he was unwilling to stay in treatment when his own alcohol addiction began to surface. He was handicapped by the typical defense mechanisms developed by an addict, but also experienced confusion created by flooding of feelings regarding all his life experiences of trauma. He threatened suicide twice, but chose instead to escape in his own "art therapy" and alcohol. We separated after he withdrew from family therapy. Our divorce was final six weeks after my oldest son died as the result of an automobile accident.

With every loss personal growth can occur. My own healing and recovery began with the death of my first husband. That healing continued at a phenomenal pace after the separation and divorce from my second husband. It was my own codependent trying to "fix" Gary which led me to understand that my choice in the second husband was to fulfil a "hunger attachment" create by my emotionally unavailable father. The "observer's" position I held in analyzing Gary's behaviour was so revealing and served as a catalyst to begin my own recovery from childhood traumas. While Gary's family was more dysfunctional than my own, I knew that I had unresolved issues. The key indicator of that was understanding what needs in my own programming had led me to marry him in the first place. For example, in recalling my husband's death and funeral, I held no memory of my father's presence. I remember Uncle Wayne being there in a loving and supportive manner. My father was physically present but emotionally unavailable. Seeking answers to "why" and "if only" questions led me to discover many unresolved losses of my own.

Life is filled with "mini" losses as well as "many" losses. Too often professionals in the grief area do not give enough attention to the accumulation of "mini" losses. The addiction literature is mushrooming now with information on healing from earlier childhood traumas and losses. A short bibliography follows this chapter to facilitate your exploration of this area in greater detail.

The recovery movement for children from dysfunctional families requires that survivors get in touch with those early traumatic experiences and the feelings which accompanied these traumas. Defense mechanisms such as repression, denial, psychic numbing, and disassociation protect the child at the time, but they represent survival techniques. Loss of memory of childhood experiences is a good indicator of abuse or of depression. These defense mechanisms, if employed, will impede the healthy resolution of loss. This phenomenon of unresolved grief is connected to what grief experts would label as delayed, inhibited, or chronic grief reactions. To clarify the connection between dysfunctional families and dysfunctional grief, a description of dysfunctional families follows.

DYSFUNCTIONAL FAMILIES

My usage of two descriptors need clarification. I am often asked "what do your mean by an adult child?" Professional colleagues in education have suggested that it sounds almost derogatory to refer to an adult as a child. Dysfunctional families have become the norm. Yet, many educators are uninformed. Part of the reason for this ignorance is that many adult children are educators or counselors. These adult children have evolved at a very high level intellectually but emotionally still carry unhealed wounds from their own childhood traumas.

Another area where some people are not well versed is "What represents abuse?" Just recently I was talking about a woman who was abused. The male colleague listening to my description first response was "Did he hit her? Is that what you mean by abuse?" Abuse in a dysfunctional family covers a wide range of behaviors and is experienced by family members in different ways. Physical abuse is an invasion of our personal privacy and physical boundaries. We have a clearer understanding of physical boundary invasion. We also readily understand that sexual abuse is another invasion of the physical boundary. However, sexual abuse is also an invasion of one's emotional and spiritual boundaries; it is a total disregard for the self.

Emotional and verbal abuse are extremely destructive to one's sense of self. The wounds for both are difficult to "make real." Emotional abuse is less recognized, less understood, and more difficult to overcome. Emotional invasion can be really devastating and virtually leave the child without a sense of protective boundaries. Emotional incest occurs when an adult shares intimate, painful information about the other parent with a child. This emotional intimacy invasion is also referred to as enmeshment. Because the child does not possess the developmental skills nor the power to address the problem, the experience is emotionally traumatizing. Depending upon the level of dysfunction in the family, multiple boundary invasion may occur.

A model has been proposed which allows us to understand that dysfunctional families occur for many reasons and not merely because of drug addiction. A family can become dysfunctional if any compulsive behavior is present, mental illness, rigid rules, religiosity and any situation where the outer circumstances seek control rather than facilitate the emergence of a strong inner sense of self, personal power, and life skill competency development. We know that dysfunctional families continue to re-emerge in different forms in the second and third generation unless recovery is accomplished. The family does not suddenly become healthy when the drinking or compulsive behavior stops.

Dysfunctional families are universal. Addiction treatment professionals suggest 80-95 percent of families are dysfunctional to some degree. If the norm is dysfunctional, then what attributes describe a functional family? A functional family provides children with a safe and nurturing environment, supports learning during the different developmental stages, affirms the child's worth and nurtures a sense of self confidence and autonomy. If the addiction treatment community is correct, the majority of people reading this chapter have experienced some wounding that may need healing. The life experiences that caused those wounds will most likely be included in the life review when a family member who caused, or failed to protect child from harm, dies. My response to my second husband's grief and research into dysfunctional families led me to begin my own recovery. My father and mother are both elderly and ill. I began an "anticipatory grief" reaction with the deliberate intent to finish my unfinished business with them before they died.

Those of us who grew up in a dysfunctional family or who were neglected or abused in different ways are disenfranchised in our grief. Our losses in childhood have not been honored; they have been disregarded. As children from dysfunctional families, we have disowned our true self; we did so to survive. Let me add that I love both my parents and recognize that they were better parents than their mothers and fathers. Part of the recovery process of this disenfranchised grief also includes forgiveness and making peace with one's parents. When I began my recovery work, I did not feel comfortable being with my parents. It was too easy to slip back into use of the defense mechanisms and to become caught up in the roles and messages. Later as I became stronger, being with my family was helpful. I could remain detached and therefore observed their behavior and my responses more realistically. As in the numbing and denial phases of grief, children of trauma also have difficulty making their losses real. Support groups where persons can validate your experiences are necessary or the loss may never be resolved.

ROLES IN THE DYSFUNCTIONAL FAMILY

Imagine a child's mobile. Each represent a family role. Roles are played out subconsciously in an effort to keep the family on an even keel. Roles may be exchanged and different family members may play more than one role. The first role is played by the person with the principal dysfunction. That person's behavior is out-of-control. The role of the enabler balances the addict. The enabler gradually assumes greater responsibility for the family and attempts to control the behavior of the addict. As the addict loses control over his or her behavior, the enabler attempts to regain control and balance. Both are preoccupied with this interactive dance. If these two persons represent parents in a family system, one can easily understand the lack of appropriate nurturance and role modelling for children.

Another role played in the family system which is intended to maintain balance is the hero child. The hero child looks really good, tries to be perfect, makes straight A's, may be captain of the football team, attends school regularly, participates in many school functions, and then comes home to help take care of the other children. The hero assumes a great deal of family responsibility when the sick person starts acting out. The enabler tries to control the craziness, and both parents abandon the children. Abandonment is a common issue in dysfunctional families. The hero child abandons his/her childhood, the children are abandoned by the parents; the spouse is abandoned by the addict. Therefore, loss is a frequent occurrence in dysfunctional families. Death represents the ultimate abandonment.

The hero tries to pick up the slack of both parents. The hero is the family member who tries to excel in life. He/she may become a doctor, therapist, teacher, etc. Heroes are extremely responsible and productive. However, they are failures in the area where they contribute the most energy. They fail to protect the family from pain. The addiction literature suggest that hero children are likely to commit suicide as a way of escaping this realization.

To balance this family mobile, however, someone has to be responsible for all the family pain. The scapegoat role is represented by the child who wrecks the car, gets pregnant, gets someone pregnant, gets into fights, steals, abuses drugs, etc. His/her behavior is negative. The scapegoat is frequently told that if he/she were more like the hero, the family would be o.k. When a death occurs, the scapegoat is often not an invited guest to the funeral. Much anger and resentment is projected upon this individual prior to the death and during the mourning period.

The next role is the mascot. The mascot is the child who tries to bring humor and joy to the family. The mascot plans parties, buys presents, and is generally a good stand-up comic. When the pain becomes too intense, the mascot tries to find a way to make the family laugh.

The final role played in the dysfunctional family is the lost child. If you tried to visualize all the people in your high school class, lost children are the people whose names you can not remember. He/she makes average grades, is quiet, and basically tries to fade into the wall. The lost child is trying to avoid pain. The lost child obviously wants to escape. Running away or taking "long-distance" cures by moving hundreds of mile from family are two strategies often employed. The lost child is most likely to commit suicide. The lost child is also the least likely to attend the funeral.

Each family member becomes disassociated from his/her real self. Everyone becomes a reactor. Thus codependency emerges. Control is the major issue for anyone who grows up in a dysfunctional family. Each person needs to be in control and wants desperately to keep the peace.

By comparing the traits of the authentic self to the codependent self and considering negative messages/negative rules in these families, we can begin to understand the belief system that creates so much conflict for bereaved persons.

These lists of descriptors are taken from Dr. Charles Whitfield's book *Healing the Child Within* [1, p. 10].

Real Self	Codependent Self
• authentic	• alienated from self
	• unauthentic
• true self	• false
• genuine	• ingenuine
	• acts "as if" personality
• spontaneous	• plans and plots
• expansive	• contracting
• loving	• fearful
• giving	• withholding
	• envious
• communicating	• critical
• accepting of self and others	• idealized
	• perfectionistic
	• other oriented
• compassionate	• overly conforming
• love unconditionally	• loves conditionally
• feels feelings including appropriate and spontaneous current anger	• denies or hides feelings including long held anger and resentment
• assertive	• aggressive or passive/aggressive
• intuitive	• is rational and logical rather than intuitive
• honors inner child	• overdeveloped adult scripts
• natural child plays and has fun	• super responsible people who avoid playing and having fun
• vulnerable	• pretend always to be strong
• powerful	• limited personal power
• trusting	• distrusting
• enjoys being nurtured	• avoids being nurtured
• surrenders	• lacks self control
	• withdraws
• self indulgent	• self righteous
• open to the unconscious	• blocks some conscious material
• remembers our oneness	• forgets our oneness
	• feels separate
• free to grow	• tend to act out unconsciously
	• repeats painful patterns especially marriages and relationships like those modelled by parents
• private self	• public self

Negative rules and negative messages complete the belief system in a dysfunctional family. If you want a more indepth analysis of your own belief system, consult C. Steiner's *Scripts People Live* [2]. You can probably get some idea of your family scripts by paying attention to those statements that "trigger" you as you read the following list.

Universal rules in a family system are don't talk, don't trust, don't feel. The need for rules is pretty obvious. You don't talk about the real problem; your parents are unreliable so you can not trust them; there is a lot of pain in the family which no one will recognize so feelings are unimportant; don't express your feelings; don't get angry; don't get upset; don't cry; do as I say not as I do; be good; be nice; be perfect; avoid conflict or avoid dealing with conflict.

Negative Messages

Shame on you
You're not good enough
I wish I had never had you
Your needs are not all right with me
Hurry up and grow up
Be dependent
Be a man
Always look good
I'm always right; you're always
   wrong
Always be in control
Maintain the status quo
Everyone in the family must be an
   enabler
I'm sacrificing myself for you
You're driving me crazy
You'll never amount to anything
It really didn't hurt
You're so selfish
You'll be the death of me yet

That's not true
I promise, then promises are broken
Don't think or talk, just follow rules
Do well in school
Don't ask questions
Don't betray the family
Don't discuss the family with
   outsiders
Keep the family secret
Be seen and not heard
No backtalk
Don't contradict me
Big boys don't cry
Don't be like that
Act like a girl or lady
You don't feel that way
You're so stupid or bad
You caused it
You owe it to me
Of course we love you

The "looking good" dysfunctional family for all outward appearances seems to be functional. They wear the right clothes, say the right things, belong to the right groups; they look perfect on the outside, but no true intimacy exists. Family members' emotional needs are not met. Again the question of suicide emerges. We all know "good" families were a member has committed suicide and the entire community is shocked. The family has difficulty understanding also, because their view is that the family was meeting all the individual's needs.

UNIFYING MODEL

We now have a unifying model of codependency and compulsive behaviors described by John and Linda Friel in their book *Secrets of Dysfunctional Families* [3]. The model is referred to as an iceberg model because frozen core feelings and issues depicted below the water line are common to all children from dysfunctional families. At the very bottom, the inner core issue is a fear of abandonment. Shame and guilt are next but there is a difference in shame and guilt. Guilt is described as a conflict in your behaviors and values. The message is "you're behaviour is inappropriate." The message reflected in shame is "You're no good. You're bad to the core." Shame issues are identified by listening to feelings which is difficult for children of trauma. Above that is a layer identified as codependency and intimacy problems. Codependents either have difficulty attaching or they act like leaches. They have no separate self; they become so obsessed and involved with another person that they don't know what they think or what they believe. They go along with whatever the other persons wants, thinks, and needs. Codependent's whose spouse die, for example, have more difficulty making decisions because they no longer can assess what the spouse would do. Those codependents quickly transfer their dependency to children or another adult.

Please note that Figure 1 depicts a projection of resulting problems in many different forms; compulsive behaviors that include chemical addiction, eating disorders, relationship addictions; stress disorders; depression; compulsions.

I propose that another layer be added in the frozen feelings area, directly above guilt. That layer would be entitled "unresolved grief from losses." The recovery process for adult children parallels Dr. William Worden's [4] four tasks of mourning; accepting the reality; being with the feelings; adjusting roles and responsibilities; renewing life. In the addiction literature the first stage is emerging awareness which includes an understanding that what happened in the family was not o.k. The person begins to "make real" the pain that was felt. Bibliotherapy is helpful in removing the layers of denial. I encourage journaling along with bibliotherapy to assist the person in staying touch with feelings and events associated with them. Dreams are also important at this time. I also find it helpful to "highlight" a book that is particulary meaningful because subsequent readings will reveal even more important data. Because of repression, denial, and psychic numbing, the person's psychic is protected from revealing too much information quickly. If this does occur, "flooding" and "flashbacks" will result. The person may shut down altogether as a survival strategy. The individual is encouraged to conduct the life review slowly during this time. The second stage in identifying core issues such as need to control, fear of intimacy, neglecting needs, etc. The third stage is transformation. Integration occurs when the individual begins to change the way he/she responds. Giant steps in personal growth are taken during the transformation and integration stages.

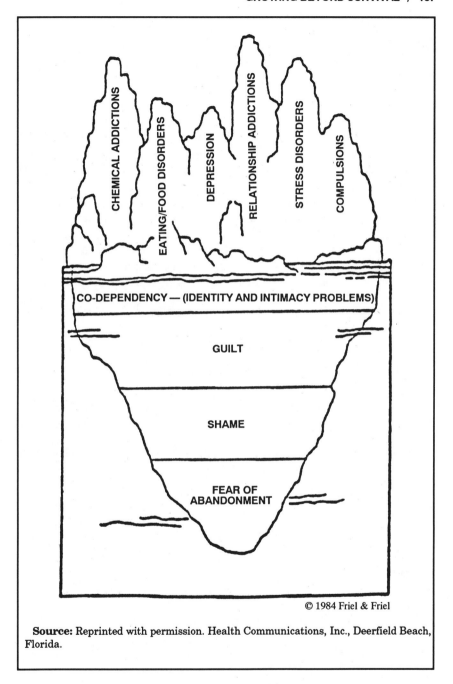

Figure 1. Unifying model of co-dependency and addictions.

Again, the addiction literature is helpful in summarizing how healing occurs. According to Charles Whitfield, the first step for an adult child is to discover and practise being our real self [1]. Many people recovering from a death find that they become more centred, more whole, more aligned with the self.

The second step is to identify our ongoing physical, mental, emotional, and spiritual needs and practice getting these needs met with safe and supportive people. A safe person is someone who will listen, accept your feelings, honor your feelings, does not discount or invalidate feelings, honours your confidence, and will not attempt to tell you what to do. These are few and far between in the grieving person's world. These safe people empower you to believe in yourself. They do not betray you.

Thirdly, Dr. Whitfield suggests we must identify, re-experience, and grieve the pain of our losses and traumas in the presence of safe and supportive people. The fourth step is to identify and work through our core issues and be responsible for our own recovery. It is amazing how closely these steps parallel grief recovery. There is much that grief counselors and death educators can learn from the adult children's recovery movement. More research is needed regarding suicide and correlates to dysfunctional family rules, messages, and roles. It is quite possible that studies in the dysfunctional family area will provide the key to facilitating the resolution of dysfunctional or pathological grief.

REFERENCES

1. C. Whitfield, *Healing the Child Within: Discovery and Recovery for Adult Children of Dysfunctional Families,* Health Communications, Deerfield Beach, Florida, 1987.
2. C. Steiner, *Scripts People Live: Transactional Analysis of Life,* Grove Press, New York, 1974.
3. J. Friel and L. Friel, Adult Children: The Secrets of Dysfunctional Families, Health Communications, Deerfield Beach, Florida, 1988.
4. J. W. Worden, Grief Counseling and Grief Therapy: A Handbook for the Mental Health Practitioner, Springer, New York, 1982.

BIBLIOGRAPHY

Bradshaw, J., *Bradshaw on: Healing the Shame that Binds You,* Health Communications,Deerfield Beach, Florida, 1988.
Middleton-Moz, J., *Children of Trauma: Rediscovering Your Discarded Self,* Health Communications, Deerfield Beach, Florida, 1989.
Weiss, L. and Weiss, J.B., *Recovery From Co-Dependency: It's Never Too Late to Reclaim Your Childhood,* Health Communications, Deerfield Beach, Florida, 1989.

PART III

Lessons from Traditions

CHAPTER 14

Native American Burial Practices

Gerry R. Cox and Ronald J. Fundis

Burial practices offer a way to know about the values of a culture. Historically, anthropologists have analyzed burial practices and what people included in burial sites to try to understand the cultures of the past. The burial record can give little beyond a cultural chronology and something of the demographic patterns of a people [1]. But for those with an interest in dying and death, an analysis of burial practices can yield an understanding of a people's attitudes toward dying and death and the dead.

The rich traditions of the three hundred or so Native American tribes in North America can be expressed through an analysis of their burial practices. Such cultures have been present for thirty thousand or more years and have left behind a burial record complete with rituals, artifacts, and customs. Burial practices are the one remnant that is left of all cultures.

By studying the burial and mortuary customs, one can learn much of the philosophy and the religion of a people. When possible, an attempt should be made to uncover cultural universals or at least the basis for diverse practices. Sociologist Emile Durkheim stressed that rituals were related to institutions and that while there was variety in form and structure, there were elements common to all practices [2].

The common elements of burial and mortuary practices reflect the values of a culture. Depending upon who died, the amount of public display will vary. The more display, the more highly valued the deceased. Public display suggests high social value. A tribal chief, a great hunter, or even a child could have high social value for one tribe while in another tribe a holy person, a grandfather, or a story-teller might have high social value. The length and intensity of grieving also tends to reflect one's social value.

Disposal methods may reflect attitudes toward the dead. Cremation as a method of disposal may reflect attitudes toward the dead. Cremation may be used to send the soul of the deceased skyward to an afterlife. It may be used to try to help the deceased on the journey out of love and respect for the deceased. Cremation may also be used to destroy the corpse so that the deceased cannot come back to inflict injury or harm upon the living. By destroying the corpse, one is done with it, and it can no longer harm you [3].

Mummification can be used to preserve the corpse for various reasons as well. Mummification could be used simply to preserve the body from decay out of love for the deceased to aid the grieving process. On the other hand, mummification could be used to secure personal survival for the deceased to allow them to live in an afterworld [3].

Tree burial may reflect a culture living in trees historically and attempting to return to their "roots." It may simply be a product of their attempt to return the deceased to nature as quickly as possible by allowing birds, animals, and insects to consume the body. This reflects a naturalist philosophy. It is also possible that tree burial may be the result of a person dying in the winter when the ground was simply too hard to dig.

Mound builders are also quite common in North America. The mounds may have been built to provide the deceased with the necessary provisions to make their journey to the afterworld in a fashion similar to the Egyptians. It may have been a method to prevent the deceased from coming back to disturb the living. Those who used stones to cover the grave, whether from piling them over the grave or from causing a rock slide to cover the corpse, may have done so to keep the ghost of the deceased from returning to haunt the living [4]. Rocks may have been used to protect the deceased from the ravages of animals and other scavengers. It is also possible that rocks were used to mark graves.

The practice of leaving items of property and food for the deceased in the grave may have originated from a fear of the corpse and the belief that if such items were left for the deceased, he or she would not return to disturb the living [4]. These practices may be the desire of the living to further honor the deceased by giving treasured items to be buried with those who were loved by the living. What is left also reflects who is in the grave. In a child's grave, one might find toys; in a warrior's grave, one might find weapons, beads, or paint; in a woman's grave, one might find food or tools for pottery or tanning; and in a farmer's grave, one might find food, implements, and tools [5].

An analysis of mortuary and burial practices would not yield a complete picture of the attitudes and values of a people toward dying and death. One would need to observe hundreds of funerals to uncover the subtle practices that distinguish one funeral from another even in the same culture. Variation may be caused by the age, sex, social position of either the deceased or the survivors. The cause of death, time of year, or even the personality of the deceased or of survivors might impact what occurs after the death.

SOUTHWESTERN TRIBAL BURIAL PRACTICES

Navajo Burial Practices

The Navajo are generally thought to be of the Athapaskan family as are the Apaches. Some questions exist as to when the Navajo arrived in the Southwest and whether or not they did cross the Bering Straits to reach North America. Perhaps they did come from below from the underworld where no light from the sun or stars existed [6]. The Navajo refer to themselves as the people or the Dineh. The Navajo borrowed from the tribes around them. Unlike the other Southwestern tribes, the Navajo were not farmers, but rather made their living from hunting and banditry. The largest of the United States tribes today, the Navajo are also thought to be the last to settle in the Southwest. From the Pueblos they borrowed the loom, grew cotton, and learned to grow corn. From the Spanish, they borrowed horses, sheep, wool, and silversmithing. The Navajo would steal and capture not only material goods, but people. They would marry them and borrow their culture as well [7]. Whether the Navajo moved to the Anasazi land or were descendants of the Anasazi, they choose not to inhabit their deserted big towns. Instead, they built their traditional hogans of mud, logs, bushes, and sticks [7].

The Navajo believe that as life begins when the wind enters the body through the orifices and particularly the ears, death occurs when the wind leaves the body through the fingers [8]. Death is the end of all good things to the people. No Navajo looks forward to life in the next world as a reward for good deeds on earth. At best, life in the afterworld is uninviting. To the living, the dead are objects of horror who must be buried with elaborate precautions to protect the living from having the ghosts of the dead returning to cause problems for the living [8]. One must even avoid whistling after dark to avoid attracting ghosts [9]. To bury the dead, one must prepare by going through rituals. This may include removing clothes and using a yucca leaf to cover oneself, bathing, using sign language to communicate, and to eat only certain foods [10]. When possible, the Navajo gets a white man who serves as a teacher or missionary to the tribe to do the burial, and if that is not possible, the Navajo hires another Navajo who is not a relative to conduct the burial and associated tasks [8]. Depending upon whether the deceased was an infant, elderly, or another age group, the Navajo choose two or four people to become mourners for the deceased. One of these is a near relative or clansman of the deceased; another is commonly from the clan of the father, wife, or husband of the deceased. One of these is chosen to direct the rite. They will bathe the corpse; dress it in fine clothes; put the right moccasin on the left foot and the left moccasin on the right foot. If the dying person was not removed from the hogan before death, they will remove the body from the hogan through a hole made in the forth side of the hogan. The mourners will carry the body to the burial site in a prescribed fashion using only sign language to communicate along the way. They will bury the body in a deep hole a long way from the hogan with the saddle, blankets, and other treasures placed in the grave. Then they will kill the deceased's horse at the grave site followed by breaking the digging tools and leaving them on the grave site [10]. One of the mourners will lead the horse carrying the possessions of the deceased to the grave site, two others will carry the corpse to the grave site, and the fourth will warn people not to cross the death line or the route taken with the corpse until the four days of mourning are complete [11]. Mourners are also warned not to spit, to maintain silence, not to turn even a stone on its side, to skip and hop on their return, to avoid stepping on brush or cactus, and to return via a different route than they used to go to the burial site [11].

Because the Navajo often bury valuable items including cash with the deceased, grave robbers are a problem [12]. Since the ghost of the deceased is at the very bottom of the grave, those who rob graves must, therefore, purify themselves after robbing a grave before they can touch another person [10].

During the mourning period, horses or sheep may be killed, dishes broken, the hogan may be destroyed if the death occurred there, eating and other behaviors restricted. Family members may weep silently in another hogan, people may remain apart for four days, and mourners will purify themselves with the smoke of a sage fire [8]. Should the ground be too hard due to winter weather, the body will be placed in the hogan, and the hogan will be torn down to cover the body [8].

The Navajo death beliefs are filled with dreams, omens, and portents relating to death and the dead. They do not have a belief in a glorious afterlife for the soul, but rather have a vague conception of an afterlife as an ephemeral and shadowy existence with the end of all that is good [13]. Not only is death to be avoided as long as possible, but those who are dead are a threat to the living. Homes of the dead are haunted as are the ruins of the Anasazi and other ancient peoples. The Ghostway and Ghost Dance ritual are used to stave off offended ghosts [10]. All ghosts are feared. The dead are thought to be the source of all sickness and disease whether physical or mental. Holy Way Chants, Life Way Chants, Ghost Dance rituals, astrological rituals, and so forth are used to deal with malevolent ghosts. Even the hogan is constructed and blessed with an awareness of astronomical directions and concern for the traditions of the past [14].

In recent years, the Navajo have dropped many of their traditional ways of dealing with the dead. Today, the burial of the dead is surrendered to the white men whenever possible. Navajo allow missionaries to bury their dead whenever possible [15]. Schools have been provided with coffins or at least lumber for them, and staff members take responsibility for burial [8]. Since World War II, even more changes have occurred. Since white soldiers were publicly buried with honor, the Navajo gave their own dead soldiers public burial [16]. The Navajo still have a strong fear of contact with the dead [12].

THE APACHE

The Apache were the last of the hostile tribes to submit to the whites and were, like the Navajo, thought to be descendants of the Athapaskan-speaking peoples. While there is debate as to where and when the Apache arrived as with the Navajo, they quickly left their mark as a fierce and warlike tribe. Like the Navajo, the Apache in banditry, but unlike the Navajo, they also engaged in war as a way of life. The Jicarilla and Mescalero Apaches seem to have borrowed from the plains Indians and have lived in tipis, used braids, and wore buckskin as did plains Indians. The Chiricahua and other Apache groups live in wickiups which is basically a grass and bush covering over young trees. Unlike the Navajo, the Apache did not develop arts and crafts to any extent. The burial and mortuary practices of the Apache groups are similar.

The Apache seemed to have a great fear of death and communicated this fear to children at an early age. The Apache also practiced methods with children that are largely not recommended today such as not allowing children to be around the dying or even viewing the dead and preventing children from associating with other children who are grieving until they have been cleansed [17]. The Apache also believed that when a person dies, his or her spirit does not go immediately to the underworld at the instant of death, but rather, it stays for a while which means that those relatives who touch the body are likely to get ghost sickness [18]. One of the reasons given for burying the deceased goods with the corpse is to prevent ghost sickness [19].

When an Apache dies, the dead person is dressed in the best clothes that are available, wrapped in a blanket, carried to the hills, thrown into a crevice in the rocks, or buried in a shallow grave [19]. For the Western Apache, ashes and pollen would be sprinkled in a circle around the grave beginning at the southwest corner to offer the soul a safe journey to heaven after which the crevice or shallow grave would be covered to prevent coyotes from getting to the corpse [20]. The Apache would use as small of a place as possible to put the corpse such as a place where a rock had shifted or a stump had fallen, and then they would put back the rock or stump to cover the body [20]. The Apache, who pride themselves on caring for those in need such as the ill, elderly, orphans, and others in need, often leave a jug of water for the deceased to drink that can be traced back to an earlier legend that the Gahan or Mountain Spirit will come to rescue the thirsty and take them to the mountains to dwell with the mountain spirits [6].

The Apache did have a wake and did cry and wail for the deceased. The Apache would also set aside a part of their fields for the dead and would not cultivate the field for a period of time to honor the deceased [21]. Like the Navajo with the hogan, the Apache would sometimes leave the body in the wickiup and push it down on top of the body [21]. The Chiricahua Apache wives and children would often cut their hair short, cover their faces with mud and ashes, and dance to keep the ghosts from capturing them after the death of a warrior [21]. The

Mescalero Apache saw death as the final foe and did not perform rites upon the death of a loved one [21]. For all Apache groups, the death of a warrior aroused much grief while the death of a squaw seemed almost unnoticed except for intimate friends and relatives [20].

Like the Navajo, the Apache saw death as the enemy and expressed no great desire to be among the dead or their ghosts. Both tribes also saw ghosts as responsible for sickness and death and feared the threat of deceased relatives, and yet because of their fear of the dead, both tribes felt a tremendous need to properly dispose of the dead to protect themselves [22].

Hopi Burial Practices

As a southwestern tribe in the midst of the Navajo the Hopi are called the peaceful ones. Though some of the Navajo may call them old women. They have also been called Moqui or the dead. The Hopi left behind many ruins for the archaeologist to study. As a pueblo people, they built and abandoned many sites and left behind their exquisite basketry and pottery. For the Hopi, the perfect individual is one who obeys the laws and conforms to the pure and perfect pattern laid down by the Creator and then becomes a Kachina when he dies and goes immediately to the next universe without having to pass through all of the intermediate worlds or stages of existence [23]. The Hopi culture is very much like that of the Anasazi culture [17]. The Hopi suggest that life is a process of childhood, youth, adulthood, and old age along a path that leads to the sun [24]. They also hold the belief that long ago people lived in the underworld where there was much rain and crops grew very well. But people began to quarrel as they do today so they had to journey to the upper world and wander until the Bear Clan group arrived at Shungopovi and took possession of the land [24].

Unlike the Navajo and Apache, the Hopi do not seem to have such great fear of the ghost. The Hopi suggest that the dead return as Kachinas, intermediaries or messengers rather than gods, to help mankind continue its evolutionary journey [23]. The famous and valuable Kachina dolls represent Kachinas but are not invested with power. They help children to know the masks and names of real Kachinas [23]. The Hopi liken the individual's history to that of their people; one follows the path of life and at death the individual is allowed to return to the lowerworld through the place of emergence to the ultimate home where the souls of the dead live like those living on earth [24]. The souls of the dead often revisit the upperworld in the form of clouds represented by the masked dancers called Kachinas to bring rain and other necessities to the living [24].

Like the Navajo and Apache, the Hopi seem to feel that excessive handling of the dead body could cause illness [25]. While all three tribes exhibit great fear of death and the dead, the Hopi remain in the house where the death took place and do not destroy it as the Navajo or Apache often do [22]. When one is dying, the young leave the house of death so that they do not become frightened or even die because of their fear and only the brave remain with the dying [22]. Whichever adult chooses to stay, will attend the dying and prepare the corpse. A man will be wrapped in buckskin and a woman in her wedding blanket with both being buried in the clothes that he or she was wearing at the time of death [22]. The Hopi do not wash or prepare the body in any way other than to wash the hair with yucca suds and to tie the hair with yucca fibre They place the corpse in a sitting position with the knees and arms flexed and tied with yucca if necessary [22]. After the death, the father of the dead person or a man in the clan of the deceased will immediately make prayer feathers and tie one to the corpse's hair, one to each boot to take the deceased to the next world, under each hand, and still another over the navel where the breath of a man lives [22]. The face will be covered with raw cotton to signify the future existence of the deceased as a cloud, and piki bread and a small gourd of water will be placed in the pockets of the deceased to provide lunch for the journey to the next world [25]. One of the men will carry the corpse to the cemetery, dig a hole, place the body in it, fill the grave, and place a stick on the grave to provide a ladder to climb to the next world [22].

The Hopi believe that Masau'u is the God of Death and is in charge of the underworld where dead spirits go and that a touch of his club brings death. Masau'u is in the dark which leads the Hopi to fear the dark [25]. Traditionally, the Hopi made a great show of not mourning for their dead; but now that they, like the Navajo, let the missionaries bury their dead, the Hopi do mourn [25]. Like the Anasazi, the Hopi use Kivas for rituals and bury their deceased beneath Kivas [26]. The hole in the floor of the Kiva represents the place of emergence in the path of life [24].

Anasazi Burial Practices

The Anasazi culture is perhaps the most famous of the prehistoric tribes because of Mesa Verde National Park. It is also one of the newest of the prehistoric tribes with a rich cultural heritage. For over a thousand years, the Anasazi culture flourished. They developed weaving of baskets, foot coverings, utensils, clothing, and storage containers of many and purposes [7]. The pit house which ultimately evolved into the Kiva was developed along with basketry was also developed to include the making of burial shrouds [27]. The Anasazi culture covered a great territory and numerous communities that supported hundreds of people. Many of the artifacts left behind still have the bright colours and exhibit craftsmanship that belie their age of hundreds of years [27]. While no explanation exists as to what happened to these people, there is no evidence of any warfare or destruction by another culture [7].

While not much is known of their burial practices, they did leave behind artifacts that provide clues of some of their basic practices. When a death occurred, the Anasazi placed the deceased in a tight flexed position with the knees to the chest and buried them with many possessions such as beads, sandals, digging sticks, blankets, smoking pipes, and mats. The body was placed in a basket and mats laid over the body before the grave was covered [27]. At times, the Anasazi apparently buried their dead beneath garbage piles and rock slides. In other eras, there is no evidence of burials of any sort. At other times, the Anasazi sealed their dead in rooms of their houses where they still remain [28]. It is possible that many of these rooms still exist and could explain why no burials were found during some periods of Anasazi culture.

Like the later Hopi and Zuni tribes, the Anasazi made Kivas of two distinct types. Some were circular, others rectangular, some had roofs and others had none [26]. Since the Anasazi buried their dead where they lived and provided them with possessions for an afterlife, it would appear that they had no great fear of the dead.

PLAINS TRIBAL BURIAL PRACTICES

Sioux Burial Practices

There is probably more generalized knowledge of Plains tribes since they are most often portrayed in movies and television. Unlike the more sedentary tribes of the Southwest, the Plains tribes were mobile on a large scale. With the great temperature variations of the great plains, the inhabitants needed to adapt to all kinds of climatic changes. They were primarily dependent upon the bison as a source of food, clothing, and shelter. Other animals and plant life were also major sources of food, but the bison offered the most dramatic picture of the life of the plains tribes. There were sedentary tribes, but the various groups that spoke the Siouan language were the hunters and nomads of film and television. The coming of the horse following the arrival of the Europeans added greatly to their prowess as warriors and as hunters. A war-like tribe, they have made their name in history by fighting against the European-Americans in such famous battles as "Little Big Horn" and "Wounded Knee."

The eight (seven main tribes and one, the Assiniboin, were outside of the loose confederation) Sioux tribes were relatively similar in their burial and mortuary practices. Like many other Western tribes, the Plains tribes believed that everything in the world around them was filled with spirits and powers that affected their lives whether from the sun, the mountains, the buffalo, or the eagle [29].

Like the tribes previously discussed, the Sioux feared the dead and would burn the dwelling of the deceased, forbid using his name, and bury personal goods with the corpse to keep the ghost of the deceased from coming along to live with friends and relatives [30]. Yet, death in old age was not feared nor were their ghosts who were often thought to remain for a time after their death [27].

The Sioux took the position that death will occur to all regardless of one's achievements, fame, wisdom, bravery, or whatever and that the mortuary practices allowed the living a way of showing their reverent respect for the dead [31]. The Dakota (Lakota or Sioux) tribes would prepare a tipi to honour the deceased. In front of the tipi, they would place a rack upon which robes and articles of clothing would be displayed while inside the tipi mourners would prepare themselves for their bereavement [31]. If the deceased was a young person, and particularly if a child, the mourners would gash their arms and legs and engage in ritual crying [27]. When death occurred in the home, the burial would be delayed for a day and a half in hopes that the deceased might revive [31]. The body would be dressed in the finest available clothes provided by a relative if the deceased had none. It would be wrapped tightly in robes with the weapons, tools, medicines, and pipe included with the corpse; and then, the bundle would be placed on a scaffold for air burial with food and drink placed beneath the scaffold [27].

Some Dakota or Sioux groups used earth burial. There is evidence that in earlier times they used mound burial [27]. During winter when scaffolds could not be built, trees were often used for burial [31]. After the body was prepared and properly wrapped, the adult members of the family began wacekiyapi or worship rite for the deceased in which men might run pegs through their arms and legs, women might slash their limbs and cut off their little fingers at the first joint, and both men and women might cut their hair and express their grief by singing, wailing, or weeping [31]. The favorite horse of the deceased would be killed beneath the scaffold of its owner and its tail tied to the scaffold, and the mourning would continue for as long as a year [32]. By placing the corpse in a tree or scaffold, the Dakotas and other similar tribes believed the soul would then be free to rise into the sky if the person died of natural causes. If the person died in battle, the Dakotas would often leave the person on the plains were he was slain to rise into the sky [29]. For the Dakota or Sioux, the spirits of the dead are not gone and lost to humankind, but rather continue to exist here and can be reached by the living for support and aid [33].

Burial Practices of the Cheyenne

The Cheyenne lived among the Blackfoot, Crow, Dakota (Sioux), and Comanche among others. The Cheyenne joined the Sioux and Arapahos to defeat George Armstrong Custer in 1876 [34]. Like the other Plains tribes, the Cheyenne believed that a supernatural power permeates every phase of being including peace, war, hunting, courtship, art, and music [35]. Like the other Plains tribes, the Cheyenne came to depend upon the bison. The burial practices of the Cheyenne were like those of the Arapaho, Comanche, Kiowa, Kiowa Apache, and Sioux or Dakota tribes [32]. When the Cheyenne buried their dead in the ground, they would cover the grave with rocks, and those who passed by would place a rock on the grave to give honor to the deceased [36]. Another slight difference from other tribes was that the Cheyenne would give the property not buried with a warrior to his widow or to the daughters and give the sons almost nothing with the idea that the sons could steal their own goods from enemies [37].

Burial Practices of the Mounds Builders

The early history of the United States tribes is not known. Perhaps, between 25,000 and 40,000 years ago, tribes began to occupy what is now the United States. The early Folsom discovery indicates that the early tribes were skilled hunters who destroyed mammoths, muskox, and bison, but they did not keep any records or leave any remains to allow knowledge of what kind of culture and people that they were. What is available for study is the enormous number of mounds that are scattered from southern Mexico to the Great Lakes to Florida. A great deal of controversy does, however, surrounds the mounds builders.

One argument is that the mounds builders were a superior group when compared to ordinary Native Americans and are descendants of a vanished people who were of the Israelite tribe of Joseph built the mounds [38]. Powell suggests that there was not a single group or tribe who built the mounds and that any search for the original tribe was simply fruitless [39]. Henry C. Schoolcraft, in a masterful six volume text, suggests that there is nothing to suggest that the mounds builders had Asiatic or European origins from the artifacts left behind nor that the tribes had any connection with one another [40].

The Angel site, the Clovis site, the Cahokia site, the Hopewell site, Moundville (Alabama) and numerous others are similar to one another, but there is no real evidence of what rituals or attitudes the people who buried their deceased had nor is there any evidence of the social differentiation of who was buried in what fashion. Mounds range from rooms constructed for burial as in the Angel site to burial in a trash heap in Arizona. While there are thousands of mounds all across the United States, much that was buried has rotted and disappeared leaving only things made of stone, copper, shell, and bone behind [28]. What little information that does exist suggests that the peoples who built mounds must have had a farming culture and been able to support a large population. It is possible that North American tribes began farming as early as 9000 to 7000 B.C. [34]. The mounds cover areas from hundreds of acres to just a small hill and range in design from a pyramid shape to a small mound of dirt [7].

Mounds were constructed with flat stones, dirt, poles, twigs, grass, mud coatings, mud plaster, slab lids, and whatever else could be found including garbage [41]. The mounds have included gifts and supplies for the dead to use on spirit journeys [28]. Rather than being a culture of mound builders, it seems probable that what occurred was simply various tribes disposed of their dead in similar ways. Some built pyramids while others built humps. Typically, all tribes have offered goods and gifts to the deceased. The mound builders may have offered such gifts and simply placed the body on the ground and covered it over creating a mound. A lack of digging tools or whatever could explain their practices.

Burial Practices of United States Tribes

There is evidence that United States tribes used all known methods of disposal of the dead ranging from burial (both ground and air), cremation, and mummification. It is also probable that the cause of death, where the death occurred, the age of the deceased, the sex of the deceased, and the social status of the deceased impacted the mortuary and burial practices of the tribe, but sufficient information about how such factors influence burial practices conclusive. Evidence tends to show a general pattern that the tribes exhibit a fear of the dead. It is also likely that climate, weather, availability of materials to dispose of the body, and religious beliefs were major determinants in how bodies of the dead were disposed. Burial practices also seemed to remain stable for a remarkably long period of time among the tribes [42]. Almost universally, tribes provide provisions for a spirit journey whether for a single or for a group burial [5]. If nothing else is known, it is that tribal groups did not abandon their dead. They provided them with ceremony and disposal.

REFERENCES

1. J. Brown, Introduction, in *Approaches to the Social Dimensions of Mortuary Practices*, American Antiquity, 30:3, Part 2, July, 1971.
2. E. Durkheim, *Elementary Forms of the Religious Life*, Free Press, New York, 1915.
3. B. Malinowski, *Magic, Science, and Religion and Other Essays*, Doubleday, Garden City, New York, 1955.
4. J. G. Frazer, On Certain Burial Customs as Illustrative of Primitive Theory of the Soul, *Royal Anthropological Institute of Great Britain and Ireland Journal, 15*, pp. 64-104, 1886.
5. M. Atkinson, *Indians of the Southwest*, Naylor, San Antonio, Texas, 1935.
6. B. Dutton and C. Olin, *Myths and Legends of the Indians of the Southwest: Navajo, Plma, Apache, Bellerophon Books, Santa Barbara, California, 1979.*
7. J. U. Terrell, *American Indian Almanac*, World, New York, 1971.
8. D. Leighton and C. Kluckhorn, *Children of the People: The Navaho Individual and His Development*, Harvard University, Cambridge, 1948.
9. Franciscan Fathers, *An Ethnol Logic Dictionary of the Navajo Language*, The Franciscan Fathers, Saint Michaels, Arizona, 1910.
10. C. Frisbie and D. P. McAllester (eds.), *Navajo Blessingway Singer: The Autobiography of Frank Mitchell, 1881-1967*, University of Arizona, Tucson, Arizona, 1978.
11. G. A. Reichard, *Social Life of the Navajo Indians: With Some Attention to Minor Ceremonies*, Columbia University, New York, 1928.
12. R. W. Young, *The Navajo Yearbook*, Arizona Navajo Agency, Window Rock, Arizona, 1961.
13. R. W. Haberstein and W. M. Lamers, *Funeral Customs the World Over*, Bulfin, Milwaukee, 1963.
14. J. G. Monroe and R. A. Williamson, *They Dance in the Sky: Native American Star Myths*, Houghton Mifflin, Boston, 1987.

15. E. C. Vogt, Navajo, in *Perspectives in American Indian Culture Change,* Edward H. Spicer, University of Chicago, Chicago, 1961.
16. R. Underhill, *The Navajos,* University of Oklahoma, Norman, Oklahoma, 1976.
17. V. E. Tiller, *The Jicarilla Apache Tribe: A History, 1846-1970,* University of Nebraska, Lincoln, Nebraska, 1983.
18. J. L. Haley, *Apaches: A History and Culture Portrait,* Doubleday, New York, 1981.
19. J. C. Cremony, *Life Among the Apaches: 1849-1864,* A. Roman, San Francisco, 1951.
20. J. C. Cremony, *Life Among the Apaches,* Glorieta, Rio Grande, Glorieta, New Mexico, 1969.
21. T. E. Mails, *The People Called Apache,* Prentice-Hall, Englewood Cliffs, New Jersey, 1974.
22. E. Beaglehole and P. Beaglehole, *Hopi of the Second Mesa,* Reprint, Millwood, New York, 1976.
23. F. Waters, *Book of the Hopi,* Viking, New York, 1963.
24. L. Thompson, *Culture in Crisis: A Study of The Hopi Indians,* Harper and Brothers, New York, 1950.
25. M. Titiev, *The Hopi Indians of Old Oraibi: Change and Continuity,* University of Michigan, Ann Arbor, Michigan, 1972.
26. J. W. Fewkes, *Preliminary Report on a Visit to the Navaho National Monument Arizona,* United States Government Printing Office, Washington, 1911.
27. R. F. Spencer and J. D. Jennings, et al., *The Native Americans,* Harper and Row, New York, 1965.
28. S. E. Fletcher, *The American Indian,* Grossett and Dunlap, New York, 1954.
29. B. Capps, *The Indians,* Time-Life Books, New York, 1973.
30. O. LaFarge, *A Pictorial History of the American Indian,* Crown, New York, 1956.
31. R. B. Hassrick, *The Sioux: Life and Customs of a Warrior Society,* University of Oklahoma, Norman, Oklahoma, 1964.
32. W. K. Powers, *Indians of the Southern Plains,* Capricorn, New York, 1971.
33. R. J. DeMallie and D. R. Parks (eds.), *Sioux Indian Religion: Tradition and Innovation,* University of Oklahoma, Norman, Oklahoma, 1987.
34. H. E. Driver, *Indians of North America,* University of Chicago, Chicago, 1969.
35. G. A. Dorsey, *The Cheyenne,* Rio Grande, Glorieta, New Mexico, 1971.
36. M. Sandoz, *Cheyenne Autumn,* Hastings House, New York, 1953.
37. K. N. Llewellyn and E. A. Hoebel, *The Cheyenne Way: Conflict and Case Law in Primitive Jurisprudence,* University of Oklahoma, Norman, Oklahoma, 1941.
38. R. Silverberg, *Mound Builders of Ancient America: The Archaeology of a Myth,* New York Graphic Society, Greenwich, Connecticut, 1968.
39. J. W. Powell, On Limitations to Use of Some Anthropological Data, in *Smithsonian Institution, Bureau of Ethnology,* First Annual Report, 1879-1880, 1881.
40. H. C. Schoolcraft, *Historical and Statistical Information Respecting the History, Condition, and Prospects of the Indian Tribes of the United States (1851-1853),* Vols. 1-6, 1855.
41. F. H. H. Roberts, Jr., Archaeological Remains in the Whitewater District of East Arizona: Part I House Types, *Smithsonian Institution, Bureau of American Ethnology,* United States Government Printing Office, Washington, 1939.
42. E. W. Voegelin, *Mortuary Customs of the Shawnee and Other Eastern Tribes,* Indiana Historical Society, Indianapolis, 1944.

BIBLIOGRAPHY

Ceram, C. W., *The First American: A Story of North American Archaeology,* Harcout Brace Joanovich, New York, 1971.

Hoebel, E. A., *The Cheyennes: Indians of the Great Plains,* Holt, Rinehart, and Winston, New York, 1960.

Hurtz, R., *Death and the Right Hand,* R. Needham and C. Needham (trans.), Free Press, Glencoe, Illinois, 1960.

Lockwood, F. C., *The Apache Indians,* Macmillan, New York, 1938.

Opler, M. E. and W. E. Bittle, The Death Practices of the Kiowa Apache, in *The North American Indians: A Sourcebook,* R. C. Owen, J. J. F. Deetz, and A. D. Fisher, Macmillan, New York, 1967.

Roberts, F. H. H., Jr., Archaeological Remains in the Whitewater District of East Arizona: Part I House Types. *Smithsonian Institution, Bureau of American Ethnology,* United States Government Printing Office, Washington, 1940.

CHAPTER 15

Suicide Prevention Consultation In Canada's Northwest Territories: A Personal Account

Ross E. Gray

This chapter is about a process aimed at preventing suicide in Canada's north. The government of the Northwest Territories, recognizing that suicide has become a major problem, recently invested money and time in a series of community consultations focused on prevention. My intent in this chapter is to provide an entirely personal perspective on this process of consultation, drawing from my experiences as an outside consultant freshly initiated into the mysteries of the north.

RANKIN INLET

I travel to Rankin Inlet on a plane with maybe ten seats and no room for my legs. The engine throbs right through me. Looking out the window all I see is ice, with no way of determining where the land ends and the Hudson Bay begins. Not a single tree or bush. Desolate!

I'm supposed to be met at the airport, but no one is there. I wait. People milling around in the small building. Mothers with infants strapped on their backs. No one in a hurry. Not a rolodex in the place.

I take a taxi to the hotel. All the roads end at the edge of town, beyond which there are only snowmobile trails. Lots of large dogs tied up. Houses are small and box-like. Even in the brilliant April sun I can feel the shadow of oppressive darkness and unrelenting cold. What must it be like here in January? The taxi driver is a tall Inuit man, who it turns out is a delegate at the Conference.

I'm scared! What do they expect from me? I have no reference points in my experience to help me anticipate what my audience will be like. I know they are "grassroots" people from across the Northwest Territories, and that the majority are of aboriginal ancestry. Among the participants are an Inuit woman who is a local mayor; a Dene chief from the Western Arctic; a Metis woman representing a political organization; a pentecostal minister; a Royal Canadian Mounted Police officer; and a government person there to listen.

What a grand adventure for a psychologist from Toronto. An incredible juxtaposition of worlds. The challenge of being flexible enough to be useful in this radically different context. I hope I can be relevant.

Why am I here? To consult about the personal aspects of suicide—loss and grief. Somewhere in the planning process it occurred to the conference organizers that many of the people who would be attending had experienced the suicide of a family member or close friend. And what would happen when the fierce grief of all these people combined in one time and place? Faced with their own frightening fantasies about what could go wrong, the organizers decided they should call in an "expert" (ironically, there is no word for expert in the Inuit language, Inuktitut). Someone who could help them think about these issues and be present to help "manage" difficulties should they arise. That's me!

Initially, I'm faced with a dozen or so people who will be the facilitators for small group work once the main conference gets underway. Most are mental health workers or drug and alcohol counselors. They have a grab-bag of training—doing the best they can with what they have. I'm impressed with them. They're not impressed, sizing me up. There is a natural leeriness of "southern" professionals come to enlighten northerners about the nature of reality. Theory detached from practice is a luxury not even to be considered. There is too much to be done.

So I start the only place it seems possible to start, with my own experience. How my dad became so discouraged that he would choose to take his own life. How could that be? Telling this story shakes my bones. Am I a bereavement expert or a ten year old boy lost in confusion? After me, others tell their stories of loss; it goes slowly. Everyone has a lot to say. I begin to worry we are taking too long and try to hurry things up. My first mistake!

When we've all had a chance to speak there's a tangible lessening of tension. I talk about the range of experiences people commonly report after a loss, and describe a couple of conceptual maps of bereavement. People are hungry for this information. They have things they want to talk about—not waiting for me to lead. At the end of the day, I sense that the group is more confident about dealing with loss, ready now for the conference to begin.

The main consultation process involves a lot of small group work. Brainstorming about essential questions. What are the causes of suicide in the north? How can suicidal intent be recognized? What ways do communities currently have for dealing with suicides that occur? What can be done to prevent suicide? Struggling with these questions is hard work!

This is one of those events that surprises people. They find themselves being less petty and mean-spirited; opening up to common suffering, common longing. Somehow as a group we move closer to a mutuality that should be, that our hearts hope for. I'm talking with a Metis man who held two brothers in his arms while they died of self-inflicted gunshot wounds. What fault should I find in this person? What should I withhold? My heart is breaking with him. All of our hearts are breaking together.

I sit listening to people talk about why suicide has become such a problem. Such an overwhelming number of possible contributing factors, from economic realities to cultural disintegration to family breakdown to self-inflicted abuse. There's nothing for me to say. Soaking in it, trying to understand. Solutions are discussed, but there seems no easy way out of the "environment of suicide." Is there a politician, scientist, or religious leader who could point a clear way to the alleviation of this suffering?

I know that much suffering goes on in Toronto. The difference is that it is so often hidden behind layers of appearances. Not so here. It's as plain as the proverbial nose on your face. People suffer! But they also laugh. Belly laughs at silly things. I am enjoying myself.

I feel close to these people, yet I am clearly an outsider. There is *so* much I don't know about what it means to live in Rankin Inlet and be one or two generations separated from nomadic hunting as a way of life. I want to understand what I can, but I know this will be limited. I must resist the temptation to try to interpret the lives of northerners to people in Toronto. It is O.K. to be an outsider. It's part of the value of my being here.

As an outsider, I bring validation through my acceptance and excitement about the suicide prevention consultation. Ironically, my status as expert allows people here to feel better about their own work. My valuing them is like a mirroring of their capabilities. Perhaps this validation should be unnecessary. Perhaps it has only become helpful because of the power trips played out historically by southerners, such that northerners have come to feel habitually insecure. Whatever the case, at least at this point in time it seems helpful. I'm told it's helpful.

Also as an outsider, I am a safe person to talk to. You would think that in an area as huge as the Northwest Territories, confidentiality would not be a problem. But with not even two hundred thousand people, all the "players" know each other. If I'm having personal problems in Toronto, I can seek out a therapist I don't know. This isn't Toronto.

BAKER LAKE

In the wake of the Rankin Inlet success, the government decides to hold smaller consultations using a similar approach in each of the regions of the Northwest Territories. I am invited to be part of a core group that will organize and lead these consultations. Again, I am along to talk about and manage the personal fallout of losses through suicide. The core organizing group changes slightly from one consultation to the next, but most of its members come from Yellowknife, capital of the Territories. It is a fine group of people, characterized most of all by a discipline of respect for the people in local communities.

Baker Lake, like Rankin Inlet, is in the Keewatin region, on the shore of a large inland lake. Two days before my arrival in October a large herd of caribou crossed the sloping hills near town. Carcasses and bones give evidence. Small boats are frozen into the ice. I check in to the Iglu Hotel.

There's a sculpting workshop happening this week, where local carvers are learning to use a new stone medium. I buy a print by a local artist from a neglected corner of the Co-op store.

The group attending this consultation is much more homogenous than in Rankin Inlet. They are mostly Inuit, from a variety of local communities. Several participants never make it to the meeting, having missed their plane connection because of bad weather. With no other flights for two or three days they are out of luck. Some other participants are late arriving. The chartered plane that was to bring them in was used instead for a medical emergency, flying an ill person south to hospital. The simultaneous interpretation equipment doesn't arrive and this is a problem given that about half the people are unilingual in Inuktitut. Although the organizers are upset about these developments, I sense an underlying acceptance that such things tend to happen in the north. Everything is tenuous. Projects like this hang together by a thread and can be scuttled at any moment by a change in weather, not to mention a change in political winds.

So I'm faced with trying to talk about difficult personal matters and facilitating discussion working with an interpreter. This is a new and very revealing exercise in flexibility. What really *needs* to be said?

Suicide makes people angry. When we talk about feelings that people have had following suicides, we don't get past talking about anger. Anger fills the room, crackling with intensity.

There has not been enough time scheduled for participants to discuss the personal aspects of loss through suicide. I try to compensate by inviting only selected comments regarding peoples' experiences. This is unsuccessful, as the Inuit men and women want to tell the whole story, starting at the beginning and covering all the major points. As a result, only a portion of participants are able to share within the allotted time.

The issue of how much time to devote to personal aspects of loss preoccupies me even after my return to Toronto. It seems that participants' need to recount personal experiences is to some degree at odds with the government's agenda of coming up with specific plans for suicide prevention. I struggle with this, wanting the consultation to be successful from a policy perspective, but believing that it cannot be successful unless there is adequate clearing away of emotional debris. I begin to doubt my perceptions. Am I "psychologizing" things too much, forcing the consultation in a personal, emotional direction because that's what I know how to do and because I look for personal pain out of the bad habits of a psycho-therapist? In the end, I trust my perceptions and suggest to the organizers that more time is needed for discussion of personal experiences. I've come to believe that this is an essential step in the development of community generated policy. Fortunately, they agree, and the schedule is to be changed for future workshops.

One of the themes raised repeatedly during consultations, and especially in Baker Lake, is that of the need for strong ties to traditional cultural ways. Indeed, from what I'm told, it seems that those communities that have traditional values have suffered the least from social disintegration. The breakdown of traditional ways is seen as contributing to an environment which makes suicide attractive. For example, the breakdown of family functioning as it was previously known is seen as leading to despair. There is a commonly expressed notion that children in the North have too many choices these days. Perhaps young people should be subject to the authority of their parents as they were in the past—even into adulthood.

It seems to me that, compared to young people in Toronto, youth here have very few choices. Many of the so-called choices are illusory, existing in theory but impossible in practice. Suppose a young person from Baker Lake wanted to become a physician and help care for his/her people. In practice, this would involve a minimum of six to eight years living as a stranger in a foreign city. How real is this choice? I realize my own values are challenged by the thought of increasing control over children. Perhaps even more so by the thought of women sentenced to traditional female roles. Nevertheless, life in the north makes it much more difficult to hold to one-sided views. I'm talking to a woman who grieves for the collapse of her traditional Inuit values, and who sees the construction of safe houses for battered women as yet another lever to pry people loose from a cohesive way of life. Yet this same woman has used the safe house after being beaten by her husband, and has then found herself being blamed and ostracized by the extended family. She has mixed feelings about what it means to hold to traditional ways. It's easy to see why.

COPPERMINE

The first two attempts at holding the Coppermine consultation were can-celled—once because all the interpreters had gone to a conference, and then because the only restaurant in town burnt down. So now it's January! Bitter cold and strong winds. The sun peeks over the horizon in the late morning and disappears again by mid-afternoon. Coppermine is on the coast of the Coronation Gulf, which is connected to the Arctic Ocean. My imagination is fired by bits and pieces from my schoolboy memory—European adventurers looking for the Northwest passage. Strange that I don't remember studying anything about the people who were already living here.

It's a lively group in Coppermine. Early on a woman talks about the recent death of a family member. This opens the gates to everyone's sorrow. And there is a lot of it! As in the other consultations, there is a private room where people can retreat to should they feel overwhelmed, and identified people to talk to on an individual basis.

I'm in a small group where four of us have had a suicide in our immediate family and the other two people in the group have made attempts. Of those who had a suicide in the family, it has been talked of rarely, if at all. Words come slowly. Pain flashes out. And then relief and comradery. Laughter.

Several people here talk to us about the style of this consultation. They say it reminds them of the way things were in the past, when there would be much community discussion of issues, with decisions arising out of the discussions. More recently, consultations from government and others have tended to be top-down. Hierarchical notions of wisdom, with travelling experts dispatching information to needy recipients. People have become disconnected from their own wisdom, overwhelmed by what they don't know. They are grateful to be part of this process. In the language of the day, this is "empowering."

Most of the participants in the consultation are helpers in their local community. I'm struck by how difficult this role is in the north. The boundaries of the regular work day is no protection when everyone in town knows where you live, and where there is little cultural permission to say no to someone in need. One of the outcomes of the suicide prevention consultation here is an agreement for helpers to meet regularly to support each other. Another outcome is to seek further training in interventions with suicidal persons.

It's during the Coppermine consultation that the world learns of the Allied attack on Iraqi forces. People break into tears. I'm somewhat surprised by the sensitivity to international conflict, given that we are so far away from the centers of political power. But here there is a strong feeling for the suffering of others, and a recognition that we all share responsibility for what happens on this planet. I am reminded of the small Inuit community that decided to donate its entire municipal budget to Ethiopia during a time of famine.

On the last night of the consultation we are able to attend a community event in the large recreational complex. Animal skins hang on the walls. Traditional drum dancing starts things off, with one person at a time drumming and dancing in the centre. Then the square dancing begins. What a joy to dance. And to be welcomed as a participant despite stunning inadequacy.

FORT SIMPSON

Fort Simpson is brilliant sun in an evergreen paradise, situated at the juncture of two great rivers. Here the majority of people are Slavey Indians, members of one of a number of tribes referring to themselves collectively as Dene.

From the beginning, this consultation has a different flavor. It is difficult for people to speak about their suffering. The opening welcome from a local dignitary can't be completed as the speaker becomes overwhelmed by feeling and lapses into painful silence. I give a talk about bereavement and despite my best efforts there are few comments and questions. I'm told later that people were listening attentively, but that for whatever reason were unable to engage further. In a small group, I hear a local counselor say she has never heard a discussion about any of the suicides that have occurred in the community over the last ten or fifteen years. This seems an exceptionally strong taboo. As the workshop progresses, it feels like walking into a strong head wind. People are making efforts and are moving forward, but against resistance.

A group of respected elders have been invited from another community to attend the suicide prevention consultation. I'm told that many people seek out the elders in the evenings—looking to their wisdom for guidance. Surely this too relates to suicide prevention. There must be many paths to prevention and not all of them will fit into a "how-to" manual. The notion of a single program for suicide prevention seems impossible, and probably not a good idea.

I'm invited to speak to two classes of students at the local school. First, the grade seven class. They eye me like a target at a shooting booth. And then they start to fire the questions. Why would a person want to commit suicide? What should you do if a friend wanted you to promise to keep secret his plans for suicide? How did you deal with your father's death? Lively interest. Any remnants of a taboo quickly abandoned in free-wheeling discussion. The older group of students is more alert to social posturing and the dangers of appearing too interested in anything. Nevertheless, there is a marked contrast between the youths' eagerness to talk and the reticence of adults participating in the consultation. The interaction in the school leaves me feeling hopeful.

SUMMING UP

The problems related to suicide in the Northwest Territories are many and deep. Some of the most fundamental difficulties are tied to national and global trends in economics, politics, and social values, and thus are not easily addressed through individual and community action. In some ways, efforts at this level are like a person with a bucket trying to stop a tidal wave. In light of this hard reality, it is easy to feel cynical about government-sponsored consultations on suicide prevention. Even if the government remains committed to addressing the issue over time, and provides necessary funds to follow up on the initial regional consultations, the road will be long and hard. It is probably unrealistic to expect an observable lessening of suicide rates, especially in the short term.

Does this mean that the suicide consultations have been useless or unwarranted? Not at all! I'm convinced something essential has been happening through this process of trying to address the problem of suicide. A giving voice to suffering. A sparking of hope. A reckoning of what can be done to make things better. An identification of what cannot currently be changed. Surely this consultation process is not the answer to suicide prevention. But just as surely it is making a difference, pointing us in the direction of a healed society.

Through my involvement in the suicide prevention consultations I met many people dedicated to driving away the darkness of despair in Canada's north. What courage! Your effort gives us all hope!

CHAPTER 16

Psychocultural Influences on African-American Attitudes towards Death, Dying and Funeral Rites

Ronald K. Barrett

The works of notable forerunners [1, 2] in the area of death and dying (thana-tology) suggest a general bereavement response pattern that is universal. Much of the theory, research, and clinical observations of practitioners in the area of thanatology support the notion of a seemingly universal set of complex behaviors characterizing the bereavement process for those experiencing loss. However, Kalish and Reynolds propose a psycho-cultural approach to death rooted in ethnicity, suggesting variations and subtle patterns unique to specific ethnic and cultural groups [3]. Few references provide a cross-cultural perspective on death and dying. Too few provide insight into the attitudes of African-Americans towards death, dying, and the current funeral rites.

The author provides cross-cultural evidence and insights from his clinical experiences with African-American terminally ill AIDS patients, their families, and significant others. Results from a national survey of funeral directors and cemetery operators as well as the author's experiences as a facilitator of grief-recovery groups, and as a behavioral consultant with the Los Angeles County Coroner's Office will be highlighted in this presentation.

The nature of any culture's influence and impact on human behavior is evident in the varied mosaic of human behaviors—including responses to death. This philosophical insight, by Jacques Choron [4], has anthropological implications: "the issue of death throws into relief the most important cultural values by which people live their lives and evaluate their experiences" [5, p. 2]. Rosenblatt conducted an extensive cross-cultural study of seventy-eight world societies from an historical prospective utilizing ethnographic literature and diaries [6]. The Rosenblatt study reported both qualitative and quantitative differences in the evidence and descriptions of bereavement for all societies. Rosenblatt's cross-cultural and historical perspective provides some sense that grief is a basic human phenomenon. The cross-cultural and historical information also suggests that grief in response to death is subject to variations in individual and cultural expressions [7]. Thus, the cross-cultural literature supports the view that people vary significantly in their responses to a death.

Significantly, no ethnographic accounts of any cultures describe people who are indifferent to the death of someone close. Habenstein and Lamers note that there is no group, however primitive at the one extreme or civilized at the other, which left freely to itself and within its means, does not dispose of its dead without ceremony [8]. So true is this universal fact of ceremonial funeralization that it seems reasonable to conclude that it flows out of human nature. The manner by which the members of any given family handles death seems to depend upon many factors: their cultural background; religious beliefs; constraints of their cultural, social, economic, and political context; their individual psychology, and their family history [7]. At the moment of death, survivors in some societies remain rather calm, others cry, while others slash their bodies. Some societies prefer to dispose of the corpse by earth burial, others place the corpse in a tree, some leave it alone for the animals to remove, and others burn the body. Within hours after burial, some cultures dictate that close relatives of the deceased remove the body, scrape the meat off the bones, and distribute the bones to the next of kin as keepsakes. While some societies officially mourn for months, others complete the ritual within hours. In addition, family involvement in preparation of the corpse for the funeral ritual exists in many societies, while others call professional morticians to handle the job. While they surely vary, nonetheless, all societies seem to have some social mechanism for managing death-related emotions and re-constructing family interactive patterns modified by death. Many of the customs (familial and cultural) are passed down from generation to generation and are an integral part of a society's way of coping with a major event like death [9].

Given the reality that death is an inevitable part of the human life cycle, all societies have established patterns of behavior to assist individuals in coping with a death. Loss of a significant other produces a state or experience of grief. The process of grieving or mourning occurs in a social context and is subject to influence of expression and interpretation. These ritualized mourning behavior norms provide the mourners (and survivors) with "blue prints" or "scripts" to follow providing symbolic mourning behavior, fulfilling the need to mourn while enabling those who mourn to do so in "appropriate" ways [9, 10].

The varieties of behavior which society may demand of the individual during bereavement are considerable [11]. This has led Durkheim to proclaim that [12, p. 397]:

Mourning is not a natural movement of private feelings wounded by a cruel loss; it is duty imposed by the group. One weeps, not simply because he is sad, but because he is forced to weep. It is a ritual attitude which he is forced to adapt out of respect for custom, but which is in a large measure, independent of his affective state.

Averill argues that "bereavement behaviours" refers to the complex series of responses following the loss of a significant other [11]. Mourning and grief are both integral components of Averill's conception of bereavement behavior. Both serve to reinforce the social structure, although mourning is mainly of cultural origin while grief is the product of biological evolution [11, p. 721].

Each culture must address the eternal search for the meaning of life and death [13]. Anthropologist Clifford Geerty uses the term "cultural ethos" to refer to the veil of order and meaning that societies construct against disturbing chaos [14, p. 127]. Death poses the most fundamental threat to the order and meaning that social systems erect to shield their members from the anomic terrors of chaos [13]. A culture's world view and subjective reality determines the cultural vision of death. The death ethos, similarly, affects the behaviors of the living. Kearl reports that many societies organize much of their social life around the ever present reality of death, with all cultures having varying recipes for dealing with the challenge [13].

In summary, death is a universal human experience, yet the response it elicits is shaped by the attitude towards it and beliefs about it that are prevalent in a particular culture or society. This shared consciousness among its members makes a culture distinct and it gives a particular cast to experience and the meanings ascribed to it, and death is such an experience. The broader global perspective in our consideration of the human response to death gives us a sense of contrast to attitudes and behavior that are often different from our own. In many respects, culture greatly influences attitudes and behavioral responses to death. While many customs, behaviors, and traditions at first seem unfamiliar or even exotic, all cultures and societies share a common struggle—coming to terms with the meaning of life and the significance of death [12, 15-17].

AMERICAN SOCIO-CULTURAL ATTITUDES TOWARD DEATH AND DYING

Death is universal, but each culture has its own beliefs, mores, norms, standards, and dictates regarding the standards to be followed in response to death. These support or prohibit certain behaviors and determine the repertoire of responses from which mourners can choose [18]. In order to appreciate and understand fully the Western cultural response to death, likewise, one must consider the cultural context in which grief, mourning, and bereavement behavior occur. The individual's attitudes towards death are also meaningfully influenced by family and early childhood experiences [18].

While there are significant differences among individuals, depending upon one's ethnic, social, religious, and regional backgrounds, there is a fairly significant set of socio-cultural attitudes towards death that characterizes a typically American response to death (the term "American" is used to specifically refer to those of North-American origin and residents of the continental U.S.A.). Theresa Rando refers to the United States as a "death-denying" culture [18]. There is a widespread refusal to confront death. There are fewer rituals for recognizing death, and in their place we have contrivances for coping with it. Death is viewed as antithetical to living and not a natural part of the human existence. Many Americans go to great lengths to shield themselves from the realities of death. Rando supports this view by pointing out that the majority of Americans no longer die in their own homes, but are sent to nursing homes, hospitals, or hospices to die, away from family and friends. While this growing practice is rationalized as practical and in the best interest of the patient, family members also benefit and are spared the discomfort of watching their loved ones die. Elisabeth Kübler-Ross describes dying in the United States today as occurring "offstage," away from the arena of familiar surroundings of kin and friends with over 70 percent of deaths occurring in institutional settings—hospitals, hospices, and nursing homes [9].

Elisabeth Kübler-Ross describes a more natural and less distanced attitude towards care of the dying in her classic work [2] where she describes a more natural setting for dying—the home where traditional family members assisted in the care for the dying patient, and consequently, came to a more "natural" acceptance for loss and death as part of life. Kübler-Ross suggests that when a patient is allowed to complete his life in the familiar and beloved home environment, it requires less adjustment. In context of the home, children are allowed to actively participate in the dying process and receive more support for their grief. It is in this more "natural" context that children come to view death as part of life.

Numerous studies [6] suggest that there are many benefits to caring for the patient at home, which enrich the lives of the grieving family care-givers as well as the patient. Kübler-Ross' work has contributed to the "thanatology movement" and has assisted in the progress in recent years towards discussing death more openly. However, the American culture in general still takes great pains to deny and avoid death.

Robert Kavanaugh conducted an extensive poll among college students and found that 92 percent had yet to witness a death [19]. According to Kavanaugh, American society has done little formally to socialize its members to deal with dying and death on personal and emotional levels.

American attitudes toward the disposition of the dead reflect even deeper levels of denial and avoidance of death as a natural part of the human life cycle. The dead are carried away by professionals (e.g., funeral directors, morticians, etc.) to funeral homes and beautifully displayed in "slumber rooms." The mortuary (funeral home) is judged most critically in terms of its ability to make the dead look life-like. Phrases like "passed on" and "at rest" are used preferentially [18]. Similarly, the final resting place of the human remains is in modern cemeteries, which are aesthetically attractive, garden-like environments called "memorial parks." Most are private institutions which are professionally managed and operated.

Herman Feifel's essay, "The Meaning of Death in American Society: Implications for Education," attempts to explain the American difficulty in accepting death [20]. He contrasts today with the Middle Ages, when death was viewed as the emergence into a new life. The Christian idea of death as a continuation of life, albeit changed from before, was prevalent. Death was the reunification with the Creator; death would result in a final reward. Today, with the disintegration of family ties and other supportive group interactions, plus the upsurge in technology and its resulting depersonalization and alienation [20, p. 4], there is a

> . . . waning of providential faith, death no longer signals atonement and redemption as much as man's loneliness and a threat to his pursuit of happiness. Fear of death reveals less concern with judgement, and more with total annihilation and loss of identity.

Americans no longer have the sense of continuity with others that might help them transcend death in a meaningful way, leaving them with existential anxiety [18].

The thanatology movement in the 1970s was a concerted effort to bring an open discussion and awareness of behaviors and emotions related to dying, death, and bereavement. This movement has been significantly impacted by Geoffrey Gorer's work, "The Pornography of Death," in which he showed that death was the taboo topic of modern civilization [21]. In 1959, Herman Feifel edited *The Meaning of Death*, an interdisciplinary attempt to restore death to cultural consciousness [22]. In 1963, Jessica Mitford blasted "the American way of Death" in her book of the same title [23]. In 1969, Elisabeth Kübler-Ross's *On Death and Dying* advised Americans that they can play a significant role in the lives of the dying [2]. According to Leming and Dickinson [9], most writers have promoted the Puritan position, "Life is not comprehended truly or lived fully unless the idea of death is grappled with honesty."

American attitudes and funeral traditions were significantly impacted by the Puritan position of fear of death. Consistent with this view (following death), they prayed not for the soul of the deceased but for the comfort and instruction of the living. The funeral was the main social institution channelling the grief of Puritan survivors. The "Enlightenment position" of Unitarianism and Evangelicalism accepted the view of death as a natural occurrence rather than a time of judgement. With the emergence of the American middle class between 1830 and 1945 the "dying of death" occurred as funeral institutions were designed to keep death out of sight and mind. Additional influences on "the dying of death" included the important intellectual influences of romanticism, sentimentalism, scientific naturalism, and liberal religion [9].

THE AMERICAN FUNERAL RITES

An historical and retrospective look at the American funeralization process over a four-hundred-year period reveals a number of changes and evolving traditions, demonstrating causality and coincidence in the evolution of the contemporary American funeral industry [24]. In the early years of our country the abundance of lumber and land allowed people to build large homes to shelter often large, extended families. Many of their ceremonial occasions were held in the home. The 1880s characterized the undertaker as a tradesman and merchant who supplied materials and funeral paraphernalia (i.e., caskets, carriages, door badges and scarfs, special clothing, memorial cards, chairs, candles, and other ornaments). By the end of the 19th century the undertakers began to assume a much larger role—assisting more with the deposition of the dead. After the Civil War, embalming became increasingly a conventional American custom, and most states required funeral directors and embalmers to be certified by state licensing. In the 1880s the National Funeral Directors Association began to regulate the profession and established minimum standards of service. With the advent of smaller houses and increasing urbanization, the funeral "parlour" became the place for the preparation of the dead, replacing the family parlor. Although the one-room funeral parlor became the substitute ceremonial room as people no longer used their homes, the custom of survivors sitting up in a vigil with the dead until burial, called the "wake," was often held in the family parlor [15].

The contemporary funeralization process is initialized by the authorization of the funeral home, which removes the body from the place of death. Frequently, upon removing the body, the funeral home begins to prepare the body via bathing, embalming, and dressing. Afterwards it is placed in a casket selected by the family. The traditional wake is an opportunity for members of the community to "pay their respects" and visit with the family prior to the formal funeral service. The preference for viewing or having the body present is optional. Similarly, arrangements for the ceremony and the details of the funeral ritual (i.e., time, place, type of service, etc.) vary and often depend upon family preferences, religion, and ethnicity. In most contemporary American funerals a public rite or ceremony with a religious content is typical in 75 percent of funerals [24]. Following the funeral ceremony, the final disposition of the body is made. The survivors must choose between either burial (85%), cremation (10%), or entombment (5%) [9].[1]

THE AFRICAN PERSPECTIVE ON DEATH
AND FUNERAL RITES

The African cultural heritage provides enormous resources for understanding of life and death. According to Opuku [25], these resources are the product of many centuries of experienced and mature reflection and represent Africa's own insights into the meaning and significance of life and death.

According to Chief Musamasli Nangol, the traditional African belief is that in the beginning God intended man to live forever [26]. African scholar and writer John B. Mbiti supports this view [27]. According to Mbiti, there are hundreds of myths in Africa concerning ideas about the origin of death—some documented and researched, others are unrecorded and undocumented. According to traditional African beliefs, God gave the first men one or more of the three gifts of immortality, resurrection, and the ability to become young again. But all three gifts were somehow lost and death came into the world. There are many different explanations as to how the loss took place and how death came about [28].

The variation in myths reflects a general belief that death came about by mistake, but has since remained due to some blame laid upon people themselves (especially women), animals, and, in some cases, evil spirits or monsters. Death therefore spoiled the original paradise of men, separating God from men and bringing many associated sorrows and agonies to men. While there are many variations in beliefs about the origin of death there are no myths in Africa about how death might one day be overcome or removed from the world [27].

Death was accepted as one of the rhythms of life, firmly integrated into the totality of life as an unalterable sequence. Life without death was viewed as clearly contrary to our nature as human beings [25]. A traditional Asante myth illustrates this traditional African view. The Asante believe that when the early human beings started experiencing death, they pleaded with God to put a stop to death. Their request was granted and for three years no one died; however, strangely enough, no one gave birth to a child during this time. The people found this situation unbearable and again pleaded with God, this time to grant them the ability to have children even if it meant accepting death also. Consequently, among the Asante, death and birth are complementary—death taking away members from the society, while birth compensates for the losses death inflicts on the community [25].

---

[1] The percentages are based on national averages and may vary by geographic region.

Therefore, the traditional African attitude towards death is positive and accepting and comprehensively integrated into the totality of life. Life in the African cultural tradition is so whole that death does not destroy its wholeness. Death becomes, therefore, a prolongation of life. And, instead of a break between life and death, there is continuity between the two [29, p. 138]. According to Mbiti, death is regarded as a journey to man's original place as home, and not as an end or an annihilation [30, p. 157]. The deceased goes to join the ancestors, to live in the land of the spirits ("Living dead").

This means that the relationship between the living and the "Living dead," as Mbiti describes them, remains unbroken and that the community of the living and the community of the "living dead" experience a reciprocal permeability characterized by a constant interaction between the two communities. This wholeness of life expresses itself in the fact that the African family as community is made up of the living as well as the dead. Therefore, the belief in a supernatural or extra-human dimension of the family and community is an extension of the traditional African belief system and world view of life and death [25].

The traditional African funeral rites and ritual reflect a view of death as sorrowful and important. Even though death is accepted as part of life, it is regarded as impolite to state bluntly that someone is dead. It reflects good breeding and courteous comportment to refer to the death of someone in euphemistic terms (i.e., "has gone home," "has joined the ancestors," etc.). Throughout the mourning period, which may last up to three moons, the close relatives of the deceased may not do any work. These tasks are eagerly performed by distant relatives and community friends. Women tend to wail, while men sing and dance, often in praise of the departed one. According to African customs, men are not to cry in front of women because they would appear weak before the very group they are to protect. It is therefore reasonable to assume the traditional funeral masks worn by men may have served as a cover of facial affect as well as a funeral ritual ornament. The body of the deceased is displayed either inside the house or outside on a veranda for public view. The body is displayed until all the relatives have gathered and paid their respects. Any relative who fails to show up for the funeral is often accused or suspected of having bewitched the deceased. A failure to acknowledge the dead is a social offense which is punishable in some communities. Traditional African customs require that gifts of money be given to the family of the deceased to help defray funeral expenses [25].

The African funeral rites vary according to the social status and importance of the deceased. The funeral for children and unmarried people is usually simple and often attended by only close relatives, whereas the funeral for a chief or a king could take on the significance of a national affair requiring much preparation, pomp, and expense [27]. African customs vary considerably in terms of the extent and methods used to prepare the body—sometimes ritually and others times without formality. Generally, the disposal of the body takes place the same day or the next day due to the effects of the tropical heat that accelerate decomposition.

In most parts of Africa the traditional ground burial is most commonly favored, although there are vast variations in terms of place of burial, position of the grave, the position of the body in the grave, and grave markings [25-27].

Often after the initial shock of a death and the customary funeral rites, the atmosphere of sadness is soon replaced by laughter and the sharing of funny stories about the dead. When the deceased is a person of note, such as a chief or king, the burial often assumes a carnival atmosphere accompanied with music from drums, dancing, and food for the assembled mourners. Often, the funeral festivities may go on for some time until the community agrees that the important person has been properly acknowledged and properly escorted to the next world. According to custom and tradition, a child of the same sex as the deceased will be born into the family and, according to African custom and tradition, given the name of the deceased—honoring the deceased and symbolizing the wholeness of life [25, 26, 31].

THE AFRICAN-AMERICAN PERSPECTIVE ON DEATH AND FUNERAL RITES

The African-American contemporary response to death is intimately connected and deeply rooted in the traditional African tradition, yet tempered by the American socio-cultural experience [32]. Much has been written about the traditional African response to death, yet very few people have acknowledged the African-American response. The African-American funeralization practices and customs have evolved over centuries, reflecting a characteristic disposition and tradition rich in cultural symbolism and customs deeply rooted in and resembling the African experience (see Figure 1).

The earliest, most authoritative work on African-American attitudes towards death and dying is contained in a classic cross-cultural study by Kalish and Reynolds [3]. In this largest study of its type, the researchers examine 100 or more persons in four ethnic groups (African-American, Japanese-American, Mexican-American, and Anglo). Inevitably, a number of ethnic differences were found.

To be an African-American in America is to be part of a history told in terms of contact with death and coping with death. For the Black race in the era of slavery, death or other forms of personal loss could come at any time, at any age, randomly, and often at the whim of someone else [3]. According to Chapman, African-American artists reflect this history in artistic expression in music, spirituals, poetry, novels, drama, and visual arts [34]. Kalish and Reynolds' survey data indicate that contemporary Black Americans also have significantly more contact with homicide, accidents, and war-time deaths than any other group.

The American sociocultural attitudes and behavior in response to death have been termed "death-avoiding" [1] and "death denying" [18, 20]. However, African-Americans tend to be more accepting and less fearful of death than the three other ethnic groups studied [3]. In a study by Myers, Wass, and Murphey,

Cultural Groups	Orientation		Life View		Ritual Priority		Funeral Social Sig.		Investment		Funeral Disposition
	Avoid	Accept	Life-Death	Death-Birth	Primary	Secondary	Low	High	Low	High	
AFRICAN		✓		✓	✓			✓		✓	GROUND BURIAL
AFRICAN-AMERICAN		✓		✓	✓			✓		✓	GROUND BURIAL

Figure 1. Comparative and descriptive model of traditional African and African-American Funeral Rites.

222

| CULTURAL GROUPS | ORIENTATION | |
	AVOIDANCE	ACCEPTANCE
AFRICAN		Opuku (1989) Nangol (1986) Mbiti (1975) Parinder (1976)
AFRICAN-AMERICAN	Myers, Wass & Murphy (1980)	Kalish and Reynolds (1981) Martin & Wrightsman (1965) Lewis (1971) Nichols (1989) Fenn (1989) Connor (1989)
AMERICAN	Rando (1984) Kübler-Ross (1969) Leming and Dickinson (1985) Kavanaugh (1972) Feifel (1959) Feifel (1971) Mitford (1963) Kastenbaum and Aisenberg (1972)	

Figure 2. Cultural influences on attitudes towards death.

elderly African-Americans showed a higher level of fear towards death than elderly whites [34]. However, researchers [2, 3] argue that devout and true believers can cope with death more effectively than those with vague or ambivalent views. Kalish and Reynolds report findings that African-Americans perceive themselves as more religious than Anglos and tend to rely on their belief systems more in times of crisis and need [3]. This observation lends more support to the perception of Blacks as less fearful of death than Anglos [35].

The various art forms (i.e., music, literature, theatre, and visual arts, etc.) mirror the attitudes of African-Americans towards death [36]. A consistent theme of death is reflected and often connected to a sense of solace in a theology and belief in the afterlife and promise of a better life [33]. Similarly, another study conducted in Detroit showed that African-Americans, substantially more than Anglos, believed that people should live as long as they can, and that helplessness, but not pain and suffering, would justify dying [37]. Kalish and Reynolds report findings that African-Americans are more likely than Anglos to disapprove of allowing people who want to die to do so [3]. The basic premise appears to hold true: whether it is their religiousness or their survival ordeal, African-Americans express a high acceptance of life and death [3].

CULTURAL GROUPS	LIFE VIEW	
	LIFE-DEATH	DEATH-BIRTH
AFRICAN		Opuku (1989) Mbiti (1969) Methuh (1982) Mulago (1969)
AFRICAN-AMERICAN		Lomax (1970) Chapman (1968) Nichols (1989) Fenn (1989) Conner (1989)
AMERICAN	Rando (1984) Leming and Dickinson (1985) Kastenbaum and Aisenberg (1972) Kearl (1989) Ranum (1974)	

Figure 3. Cultural influences on attitudes towards death.

CULTURAL GROUPS	RITUAL PRIORITY		FUNERAL SOCIAL SIG.	
	PRIMARY	SECONDARY	LOW	HIGH
AMERICAN	Opuku (1969) Mbiti (1969) Nangol (1969)			Opuku (1989) Mbiti (1969) Nangol (1969)

AFRICAN-AMERICAN	Kalish and
	  Reynolds (1981)
	Chapman (1968)
	Nelson (1971)
	Carter (1971)
	Nichols (1989)
	Fielding (1989)
	Fenn (1989)
	Conner (1989)
				Kalish and
				  Reynolds (1981)
				Chapman (1968)
				Nelson (1971)
				Carter (1971)
				Nichols (1989)
				Fielding (1989)
				Fenn (1989)
				Conner (1989)

AMERICAN	Mitford (1963)	Reather (1971) Kübler-Ross Gorer (1955)	Reather (1971) Gorer (1955) Harmer (1971)	Mitford (1963) Fulton (1965)

Figure 4. Cultural influences on attitudes towards death.

CULTURAL GROUPS	INVESTMENT		FUNERAL DISPOSITION
	LOW	HIGH	
AFRICAN		Opuku (1989) Nangol (1986) Mbiti (1975)	Ground Burial Opuku (1989) Nangol (1986) Mbiti (1975) Fenn (1989) Nichols (1989)
AFRICAN-AMERICAN		Kalish and Reynolds (1981) Nichols (1989) Fenn (1989) Conner (1989) Fielding (1989)	Ground Burial Kalish and Reynolds (1981) Nichols (1989) Fenn (1989) Conner (1989) Fielding (1989)
AMERICAN		Mitford (1963) Raether (1971) De Spelder and Strickland (1987) Tegg (1876)	Ground Burial Cremation (10%) Emtombment (5%) Leming and Dickinson (1985)

Figure 5. Cultural influences on attitudes towards death.

Elaine Nichols' *The Last Miles of the Way* is the most comprehensive and authoritative documented anthropological study of African-American cultural traditions and funeral rituals in the southeastern United States (i.e. the South Carolina low-lands) [32]. Nichols' work supports and carefully documents the African cultured origin of many African-American beliefs, traditions, and practices in funeral rites. Nichols' efforts also illustrate and detail the intricate symbolism of burials and grave markings. Fenn also supports Nichols' thesis of African cultural roots in grave markings as Fenn documents methods and symbolism rooted in African Kogo traditions [38]. An anthropological analysis of African-American mortuary practices by Conner [39], also supports Elaine Nichols' classic and insightful scholarly work.[2] While a number of aspects of Nichols' findings may be unique to the southeastern region of the United States (i.e., South Carolina), striking similarities in the African-American experience in

[2] Elaine Nichols' unprecedented anthropological work involved the procurement and analysis of physical evidence and cultural artifacts obtained from both library research and private individual collectors that are a part of a special exhibit in the South Carolina State Museum scheduled for a national tour.

other regions lend support to the generalizability of similar cultured influences and behaviors in the subculture of the African-American experience.

The available research [3, 39, 40] provides documented support of the thesis that many of the attitudes, beliefs, and traditions regarding funeral rites, death and dying are deeply rooted in African cultural traditions. The African-American attitudes, beliefs, and funeral rites are also significantly influenced by American attitudes, beliefs, and cultural traditions regarding death, dying, and funeral rites. These studies make a significant contribution to our knowledge and understanding of the African-American experience, however, more research and study is needed to understand better death related behaviors and also provide needed documentation of a very important and regarded sacred psychocultural complex tradition.

African-American attitudes toward funeral rites have remained for too long largely undocumented and lacking in systematic study and observation. Halloween Lewis' [41] analysis of the role of the church and religion in the life of southern Blacks suggests that the religious connection took on special meaning in funeral customs. Lewis notes variations occurring according to the community reputation of the deceased, family wishes, and local church practices. As is common among Protestants, most African-American Protestant churches have no formally prescribed funeral ritual dictated by church hierarchy. Local church custom is followed [42]. According to the denominational procedure outlined in Habenstein and Lamers [8], the only generalizations that can really be made are: 1) that family members can select the equipment, music, participants, and place of service without dogmatic restriction, and 2) that the minister leads the procession from church to the funeral coach and from the coach to grave site, positioning himself at the head of the grave. This leaves room for considerable variation [3].

While regional and denominational backgrounds influencing the African-American funeral rites vary, there are some striking similarities linked to traditional African-American beliefs and traditions. In a social context where people are treated like objects and with minimal respect, and the channels by which respect can be achieved are blocked, it is understandable for victims to desperately seek a way to affirm themselves and confirm some sense of self-worth and positive self-identity [3]. African-American funerals in the African-American subculture represent a posthumous attempt for dignity and esteem denied and limited by the dominant culture [32, 40]. Funerals in the African-American experience historically are "primary rituals" of symbolic importance. Kalish and Reynolds'[3] survey reveals that African-Americans were more likely to have taken out life and burial insurance than any other group surveyed [3]. It appears that

---

[3] The term "primary ritual" is used in this context to refer to an event of primary, major importance in that social context. (Contrastingly, a "secondary ritual" is an event of lesser social priority or significance—informal gatherings, family meetings, local holidays, etc.)

funeral pre-arrangements, wills, and insurance represent psychological readiness, as these are the most practical arrangements that people can make for death. As expected, Kalish and Reynolds report that older African-Americans are more likely to have made death arrangements than middle-aged or younger adults [3].

The African-American mourners, like the African mourners, were more likely to depend upon the church and the community (extended family) for support during bereavement and mourning [40]. Unlike the other ethnic groups surveyed, African-Americans were more likely to rely on friends, church members, neighbors, and non-relatives for practical assistance consistent with the finding that devout believers had less death anxiety, those active in churches had more tradition sources of spiritual and social support [3].

The social support of family and friends is important to those in mourning. Since a death is a significant event and the funeral is an important social occasion, social expectations require participation and some expression of condolence. It is a standard custom that if one cannot attend the funeral, flowers or other expressions of condolences should be sent. The African-American funeral is indeed a primary ritual and a focal occasion with a big social gathering after the funeral and the closest thing to a family union that might ever take place [32, 40, 43].

Kalish and Reynolds [3] report that the great majority of African-American respondents expressed opposition to elaborate funerals; did not expect friends to participate in covering funeral costs; preferred a funeral with only close friends and relatives; desired African-American clergymen and funeral directors; did not want a wake; wanted the funeral in the church; did not oppose an autopsy; and wanted to be buried. Overall, the African-American funeral is an important event characterized by a programmed atmosphere that is official, ritualistic, serious, and dignified.

ACKNOWLEDGMENTS

The author wishes to acknowledge Luvenia Morant Addison; Dorothy Addison Barrett; Deborah Freathy, Graduate Research Assistant, Loyola Marymount University; Elaine Nichols, Curator, South Carolina State Museum; Harri Close, President, National Funeral Directors & Morticians Association, Inc.; John Hill, III, Chief Administrator, Angelus Funeral Home; Chief Medical Examiner and Staff, Los Angeles County Coroners Office.

REFERENCES

1. R. Kastenbaum and B. R. Aisenberg, *The Psychology of Death*, Springer, New York, 1972.
2. E. Kübler-Ross, *On Death and Dying*, Macmillan, New York, 1969.
3. R. Kalish and D. Reynolds, *Death and Ethnicity: A Psychocultural Study*, Baywood, Amityville, New York, 1981.

4. J. Choron, *Death and Western Thought*, The Macmillan Company, New York, 1963.
5. R. Huntington and P. Metcalf, *Celebration of Death: The Anthropology of Mortuary Ritual*, Cambridge, Cambridge, 1979.
6. D. C. Rosenblatt, Grief in Cross-Cultural and Historical Perspective, in *Death and Dying*, P. F. Pegg and E. Metza (eds.), Pitman Press, London, 1981.
7. M. McGoldrick, P. Hines, E. Lee, and G. H. Preto, Mourning Rituals: How Culture Shapes the Experience of Loss, *Networker*, 1986.
8. W. R. Habenstein and M. W. Lamers, *Funeral Customs the World Over*, Bulfin, Milwaukee, 1963.
9. R. M. Leming and E. G. Dickinson, *Understanding Dying, Death, and Bereavement*, Holt, Rinehart and Winston, New York, 1985.
10. R. P. Cuzzort and W. E. King, *Twentieth Century Social Thought*, Holt, Rinehart and Winston, New York, 1980.
11. J. R. Averill, Grief: Its Nature and Significance, *Psychological Bulletin*, 70:61, 1968.
12. E. Durkheim, *The Elementary Forms of Religious Life*, Macmillan, New York, 1915.
13. M. C. Kearl, *Endings—A Sociology of Death and Dying*, Oxford, New York, 1989.
14. C. Geerty, *The Interpretations of Cultures: Selected Essays*, Basic Books, New York, 1973.
15. L. A. DeSpelder and L. A. Strickland, *The Last Dance: Encountering Death and Dying*, Mayfield, Mountain View, California, 1987.
16. A. M. Hocart, Death Customs, in *Encyclopedia of the Social Sciences 5*, E.R.A. Seligman and A. Johnson (eds.), Macmillan, New York, 1937.
17. P. G. Mandelbaum, Social Issues of Funeral Rites, in *The Meaning of Death*, H. Feifel (ed.), McGraw-Hill, New York, 1959.
18. T. A. Rando, *Grief, Dying and Death*, Research Press Co., Champaign, Illinois, 1984.
19. R. E. Kavanaugh, *Facing Death*, Penguin, Baltimore, Maryland, 1972.
20. H. Feifel, The Meaning of Death in American Society: Implications for Education, 1971.
21. G. Gorer, *Death, Grief & Mourning*, Crescent Press, London, 1965.
22. H. Feifel, *The Meaning of Death*, McGraw-Hill, New York, 1959.
23. J. Mitford, *The American Way of Death*, Simon and Schuster, New York, 1963.
24. H. C. Raether, The Place of the Funeral: The Role of the Funeral Director in Contemporary America, *Omega*, 2, pp. 136-149, 1971.
25. K. A. Opuku, African Perspectives on Death and Dying, in *Perspectives on Death and Dying*, A. Berger, P. Badham, J. Berger, V. Cerry, and J. Beloff (eds.), The Charles Press, Philadelphia, 1989.
26. C. M. Nangoli, *No More Lies About Africa*, African Heritage, East Orange, New Jersey, 1988.
27. J. S. Mbiti, *Introduction to African Religion*, Heinemann, London, 1975.
28. E. G. Parinder, *African Mythology*, Paul Hamlyn, London, 1967.
29. V. Mulago, Vital Participation: The Cohesive Principle of the Bantu Community, in *Biblical Revelation and African Beliefs*, K. Dickson and P. Ellingworth (eds.), Butterworth, London, 1979.
30. J. S. Mbiti, *African Religions and Philosophy*, Heinemann, London, 1969.
31. I. E. Metuh, *God and Man in African Religion: A Case of the Igbo of Nigeria*, G. Chapman, London, 1982.

32. E. Nichols (ed.), *The Last Miles of the Way: African American Homegoing Traditions 1890-Present,* Dependable, Columbia, South Carolina, 1989.
33. A. Chapman (ed.), *Black Voices: An Anthology of Afro-American Literature,* New American Library, New York, 1968.
34. J. E. Myers, H. Wass, and M. Murphey, Ethnic Differences in Death Anxiety among the Elderly, Death Education, 4, pp. 237-244, 1980.
35. D. S. Martin and L. Wrightsman, The Relationship between Religious Behaviour and Concern about Death, *Journal of Social Psychology, 65,* pp. 317-323, 1965.
36. A. Lomax, The Homogeneity of African-Afro-American Musical Style, in *Afro-American Anthropology,* N. E. Whitten and J. F. Szwed (eds.), Free Press, New York, 1970.
37. R. Koenig, N. S. Goldner, R. Kresojevich, and G. Lockwood, Ideas About Illness of Elderly Black and White in an Urban Hospital, *Aging and Human Development, 2,* pp. 217-225, 1971.
38. E. A. Fenn, Honouring the Ancestors: Kongo-American Graves in the American South, in *The Last Miles of the Way,* E. Nichols (ed.), Dependable, Columbia, South Carolina, 1989.
39. C. Connor, Archaeological Analysis of African-American Mortuary Behaviour, in *The Last Miles of the Way,* Dependable, Columbia, South Carolina, 1989.
40. H. U. Fielding, Mourning and Burying the Dead: Experiences of a Lawcountry Funeral Director, in *The Last Miles of the Way,* Dependable, Columbia, South Carolina, 1989.
41. H. Lewis, Blackways of Kent: Religion and Salvation, in *The Black Church in America,* H. M. Nelson, et al. (eds.), Basic Books, New York, 1971.
42. H. M. Nelson, et al. (eds.), *The Black Church in America,* Basic Books, New York, 1971.
43. W. B. Carter, Suicide, Death, and Ghetto Life, *Life-Threatening Behaviour,* L, 1971.

BIBLIOGRAPHY

Abrahamson, H., *The Origin of Death: Studies in African Mythology,* Almgvist, Uppsala, 1951.
Balandier, G. and Maguet, J., *Dictionary of Black African Civilization,* Leon Amiel, New York, 1974.
Boulby, J., Process of Mourning, *International Journal of Psycho-Analysis, 43,* pp. 314-340, Grune and Statton, New York. (Reprinted in G.E. Daniels (ed.), 1965, *New Perspectives in Psychoanalysis,* 1961.
Feifel, H., The Taboo on Death, *The American Behavioral Scientist, 6,* 1963.
Fulton, R., The Sacred and the Secular: Attitudes of the American Public toward Death, Funerals, and Funeral Directors, in *Death and Identity,* R. Fulton (ed.), Wiley, New York, 1965.
Goody, J., *Death, Property, and the Ancestors: A Study of the Mortuary Customs of the LoDagaa of West Africa,* Stock, London, 1962.
Harmer, R., Funerals, Fantasy, and Flight, *Omega, 2,* pp. 127-135, 1971.
Idowu, E.B., *African Traditional Religion,* SCM Press, London, 1973.

Jackson, M., The Black Experience with Death: A Brief Analysis through Black Writings, *Omega, 3,* pp. 203-209, 1972.

Kopytoff, E., Ancestors as Elders in Africa, *Africa, 41,* 1971.

Kutscher, A.H., *Death and Bereavement,* Charles C. Thomas, Springfield, Illinois, 1969.

Lindemann, E., Symptomatology and Management of Acute Grief, *American Journal of Psychiatry, 101.* Reprinted in R. Fulton (ed.) (1965) *Death and Identity,* Wiley, New York, 1944.

Lund, F.H., Why Do We Weep? *Journal of Social Psychology, 1,* 1930.

Opuku, K.A., Death and Immortality in the African Religious Heritage, in *Death and Immortality in the Religious of the World,* P. Badham and L. Badham (eds.), Paragon, New York, 1987.

Parinder, E.G., *African Traditional Religion,* SPCK, London, 1962.

Pinkney, A., *Black Americans,* Prentice Hall, Englewood Cliffs, New Jersey, 1969.

Ranum, P.M., *Western Attitudes toward Death: From the Middle Ages to the Present,* John Hopkins University Press, Baltimore, 1974.

Tegg, W., *The Last Act Being the Funeral Rites of Nations and Individuals,* William Tegg & Co., London, 1876.

Thomas, L.R., Litany of Home—Going—Going Forth: The African Concept of Time, Eternity and Social Ontology, in *The Last Miles of the Way,* E. Nichols, Dependable, Columbia, South Carolina, 1989.

Zahan, D., *The Religion, Spirituality, and Thought of Traditional Africa,* E. Martin and L. M. Martin (trans.), University of Chicago, Chicago, 1979.

CHAPTER 17

Funeral Customs in Thailand

Michael R. Leming and Sommai Premchit

Thailand is a nation of approximately sixty million people who live in a primarily rural-agricultural country roughly the size of the nation of France or the state of Texas. As a modern nation, Thailand has always been an independent constitutional monarchy with a representative form of government (including both parliament and prime minister).

Thais live in an extremely hierarchically stratified society where each person knows his or her relative social position. All Thais relate to each other in a patron-client or superior-subordinate relationship. Theravada Buddhism is a vital and visible force in daily Thai life where 95 percent of the population are Buddhists. In character the Thais are an easy-going, hospitable, and fun-loving people. They also have a strong pride and sense of national identity that springs from a long adherence to Buddhist traditions and independent national autonomy.

From a cross-cultural perspective, the understanding of death rituals, regardless of whether they call for festive or restrained behavior, allows us to understand the most important cultural values by which people live their lives and evaluate their experiences [1]. Life becomes transparent against the background of death, and fundamental social and cultural issues are revealed.

Ritual can be defined as "the symbolic affirmation of values by means of culturally standardized utterances and actions" [2]. A ceremony is a given complex of rituals associated with a specific occasion. People in all societies are inclined to symbolize culturally defined feelings in conventional ways. Ritual behavior, therefore, is an effective means of expressing or reinforcing these important sentiments.

The functions of rituals include validation and reinforcement of values, reassurance in the face of psychological disturbances, reinforcement of group ties, facilitation of status change by acquainting persons with their new roles, relief of psychological tensions, and restabilization of patterns of interaction disturbed by a crisis [2].

The Buddhist message of salvation, taught by Buddha in his first sermon, is "The Four Noble Truths." The first truth is that all human existence is characterized by pain and suffering in an endless cycle of death and rebirth. The second truth is that the cause of the agony of the human condition is desire for personal satisfaction, which is impossible to obtain. The third truth is that salvation comes by destroying these desires. By completely destroying ignorance, one experiences enlightenment and the cycle of transmigration of the soul is broken. Finally, in the fourth truth, one can experience perfect peace through the eightfold path to enlightenment. In the words of Pardue [3, p 168]:

> For this purpose the proper [meditation] is the "eightfold path," an integral combination of ethics (*sila*) and meditation (*samadhi*), which jointly purify the motivations and mind. This leads to the attainment of wisdo (*Prajna*), to enlightenment (*bodhi*), and to the ineffable Nirvana ("blowing out"), the final release from the incarnational cycle and mystical transcendence beyond all conceptualization.

Buddhism contends that while physical death causes one to experience life again in a transmigrated form, "death to this world" (via nirvana) provides the gateway for ultimate happiness, peace, and fulfilment. The ultimate goal of Buddhism is a state of consciousness and *not* a symbolic location for the disembodied soul.

Funeral prayers of the monks illustrate the "lesson of death"—that life is vanity. At funerals, Buddhist monks often read the following words from Buddha [4, p. 97]:

> The body from which the soul has fled has no worth. Soon it will encumber the earth as a useless thing, like the trunk of a withered tree. Life lasts only for a moment. Birth and death follow one another in inescapable sequence. All that live must die. That man indeed is fortunate who achieves the nothingness of being. All animal creation is dying, or dead, or merits to be dead. All of us are dying. We cannot escape death.

Cremation serves the function of promoting the process of liberation of the individual from the illusion of the present world. As a reflection of this orientation, Buddhist monks will recite these words prior to the final disposition of the body [4, p. 97-98]:

> O dead one, pursue your destiny. Flee to paradise. You will know rebirth into a better life. Do not linger to haunt those who remain here, and to share this life of invisible darkness which is the lot of the living. Those whom you leave behind reckon accurately your good fortune in your liberation. With happy

impatience they await their own turn. You neither want nor need them, and they are happy without you. Now follow your destiny.

During and after the funeral, family members will make offerings through the monk to the spirit of the deceased. They will also give ritual feasts for the priests and other mourners. As in other religious traditions, all of these funeral activities will emphasize the importance of the religious world view, promote community cohesiveness, and reincorporate chief mourners into the routine patterns of social life of the society.

CEREMONIES AT THE WAT

There are three parts of the Thai Buddhist funeral: ceremonies at the wat (temple), procession to the site of cremation, and the cremation. When a common person dies the body is cleaned and dressed and placed within a casket. The casket is kept either within the home or at the wat for a period of three days. During this period monks will come every evening to chant the Buddhist scriptures (*Abhidhamma*). Friends will attend these services and will offer as gifts floral tributes. Some of these wreaths will be rented and financial contributions will be made to charitable causes selected by the family of the deceased. On the fourth day the body will be taken to the charnel-ground (cremation site) which is usually a distance from the wat.

When a charismatic monk, high governmental official, member of the royalty, or another noble person of high prestige dies, the body will be kept for a longer period of time before final disposition is made. This period of time can vary from a few weeks to a period of many years determined by the status of the deceased. The fourth lunar month (corresponding to the month of March) is the preferred time for funeral ceremonies.

Bodies of high status people are embalmed and then bathed and dressed with new clothes. The entire face of the deceased (notably monks) is covered with gold leaves and then placed within a casket. Visitors will come to pay respect by offering floral tributes and pouring water on the deceased (*aab nam sob*).

The ceremony prior to cremation will last for several days and will typically be held at the big *vihara* at the wat compound. The casketed body will be placed within a larger gilded teak coffin called a *long tong* or outer coffin. The *long tong* will be placed on the right side of the *vihara* and surrounded by many items associated with the deceased (in the case of monks eg. bronze statues, certificates of title, the deceased's picture decorated with flowers, the honorific fan called a *kruang soong*, and the three tailed flag which is purported to be the refuge of the dead while traveling in the cycle of death and rebirth).

During these ceremonies held in the *vihara,* monks will chant important sutras from the *Tripitaka*—Buddhist scriptures. At the conclusion of the final service at the *vihara,* there will be a final tribute of flowers and three lighted candles presented to the deceased. The casket will then be removed from the golden case or *long tong* and removed from the *vihara*.

PROCESSION TO THE CREMATION SITE

The procession is a significant rite in the Thai Buddhist funeral. The casket is put on a carriage and taken from the wat compound to the cremation site. During the procession a long white cotton cord is attached to the casket and eight (the number is flexible) monks together with lay devotees will carry the cord. In the urban areas the carriage will be motorized, while in traditional funerals and/or funerals in rural areas the carriage will be pulled by walking members of the procession.

The procession is headed by the three-tail flag and followed by the monk's fan, the title certificate, the set of three yellow monk's robes, the deceased's picture, the bronze statue of the deceased, and the coffin, respectively. Upon arriving at the site of the cremation, the casket is carried around the crematorium three times which symbolizes the traveling in the cycle of death and rebirth. After the casket is then placed in front of the crematorium, the relatives will pose for pictures beside the casket, after which they will walk around the casket three times.

When the funeral is performed under royal patronage the *fai phra rajthaan* or the "Royal Fire" is brought to be used to light the cremation pyre. The royal fire is carried by a group of government officials dressed in the white official uniform, while the orchestra plays the Royal Anthem in salutation to the King of Thailand. During this time all mourners, dressed in black or white, will stand in respect to the King and royal fire.

As a final merit-making rite, five or ten important persons will come forward (one by one) and place a set of yellow robes on the long white cotton cord which is linked to the coffin, and then high-ranking monks will be invited to come forward and receive the robes on behalf of the *Sancta* (the Buddhist priesthood). The final act is when the most important person in the ceremony (e.g. Prime Minister) will place the last set of yellow robes on the cotton cord. The most senior monk will collect the robes after "contemplating symbolically the dead." According to religious practice in Buddhism, the contemplation of the corpse by Buddhist monks will bring merit to those who provide such opportunity for the monk to do so. And the merit earned can be dedicated further to the dead as well.

CREMATION

The stage is now set for the actual cremation. Just prior to the lighting of the fire, the biography of the deceased is read while *dok mai chan* is distributed to all in attendance. The *dok mai chan* is a sandalwood flower with one incense-stick and two small candles attached. The mourners are all invited to come forward and deposit the *dok mai chan* before the casket. By so doing, mourners are deemed participating in the actual cremation.

The chairman of the ceremony then ignites the fire and the casket is consumed. The next morning the ashes (several pieces of bones) are gathered and made into a shape of a human being with the head facing east. Four monks will attend this ritual which will culminate when the ashes are placed into a receptacle. Afterward the ashes will be enshrined in a reliquary built in the compound of the monastery.

Throughout the funeral ceremony sorrow or lamentation is not emphasized. Rather the focus is upon impermanence of all things. The funeral is primarily a social event that affirms community values and group cohesiveness. Furthermore, it is a time where people are expected to enjoy the fellowship surrounding the rituals. Typically there is entertainment (dancing and musical performances) associated with funeral rituals in order that sorrow and loneliness be dissipated. It is believed that this assists the bereaved to conceptualize the happy and pleasant paradise where the deceased will reside.

REFERENCES

1. R. Huntington and P. Metcalf, *Celebrations of Death: The Anthropology of Mortuary Ritual,* Cambridge University Press, Cambridge, 1979.
2. E. B. Taylor, *Cultural Ways,* 3rd Ed., Allyn and Bacon, Boston, 1980.
3. P. Pardue, Buddhism, in *International Encyclopedia of the Social Sciences, 2,* Macmillan, New York, 1968.
4. R. W. Habenstein and W. M. Lamers, *Funeral Customs the World Over,* Bulfin Printers, Milwaukee, 1974.

CHAPTER 18

Death and Bereavement among the Chinese in Asia

Jiakang Wu

Everybody dies; nobody lives forever. But do the Chinese address death and dying in ways which differ from the Western World? This chapter does not develop theory but addresses some perspectives about death and makes some observations about the following two questions:

1. Do the Chinese people talk about death?
2. How do the Chinese mourn the dead?

In preparing for this chapter, I circulated questionnaires to my friends and colleagues in China and Singapore, and those who are studying in Canada. Only one-third of the people returned their questionnaires. And all of those who answered my questionnaire wondered why I had chosen this subject. Why not? "Is there any problem?" I asked a Chinese student who seemed puzzled. "No," he said, "The topic is just so horrifying."

Why did I choose this subject? I guess the simplest answer is because it exists and it is a reality everybody faces sooner or later. I started to pay attention to this subject only six years ago in Singapore where I befriended people who were both religious and non-religious. Some, particularly the religious, liked to discuss life, and death, and after-life. Others did not want to talk about this subject. Our discussions never convinced people to change their beliefs, but these discussions aroused my interest in the topic of death.

In 1988, I went back to my hometown in Fujian province. My relatives took me to the mountain to visit the tombs of my grandfather, his brother, and my greatgrandfather. This was the first time I visited the tombs and saw the grave-stones of my relatives. The way the tombs were built, the positions they took, and the inscriptions attracted my attention and reinforced my interest.

DO THE CHINESE TALK ABOUT DEATH?

If a child asked you: "what happens when you die?," what would you say? Out of curiosity as a child I asked my father this question. To my surprise, my father told me to learn to ask only nice things. My father was angry, but I did not think I had done anything wrong. I could have asked, "What happens when people die?" But there were no taboos in my child's mind. To me, my parents were the most open-minded people among Chinese parents. I don't think they would mind me asking the same question, but I don't think I will ever ask it again, not because my father told me to say nice things or because I became superstitious, but probably because I was brought up in a culture in which people generally do not talk about death.

Not only do people not talk about it, some even avoid the word. Even words which have similar pronunciations are avoided. I remember once on my birthday, a friend sent me four balloons which I hung in my room. When another friend came, she asked me to take down one balloon. She said that *Si* (four) coincides with *Si* (die), although in the Chinese Language these two words have different tones. It just never occurred to me that four could mean die. I did not take any of the balloons down. But this situation reflects some of the discomfort the Chinese have about death. This is probably similar to the discomfort about death in the Western world.

I sent my survey to two of my Singapore friends and asked them to distribute the questionnaires among their friends. I received a reply only from one friend. In her letter, she told me that the reason she replied late was that my letter arrived in the midst of the Chinese New Year, and that she was reluctant to give the survey to her colleagues for fear of superstition. I realized that I had made a mistake! And now I wonder whether my letter and survey have offended my other friend because it also arrived during the Chinese New Year's time.

Although most people do not talk about death, some people do. Most Singaporean Chinese who spent time answering my questions said that they talk about death, although, to some, death is a taboo subject at home. But everybody in this group is Christian. One woman, in response to the question "Do you talk about death?," answered: "Not really," and then added, "except in a Christian way (because I am a Christian)—that we can be with the Lord." Only one person who is a Christian said that he does not talk about death and that death is a taboo subject at his home as well as among his friends.

In China, some people do talk about death and prepare for death. It seems that older people do so more often. People, like my grandmother in Fujian, would not be comfortable unless they could see their *houshi*—afterlife things—ready. When I was in Fujian Province in 1988, I found that many people of my grandmother's age had similar approaches to death. It comforts them when they have chosen their own coffins, brought them home, and placed them under their beds. The things they are to wear are also prepared well in advance. Filial piety also has a place here. Instead of interpreting it in a negative way, the parents or the older generation will feel content if their children and grandchildren prepare their *houshi*, as they know they have a place to go. Pre-arranged *houshi* give them a sense of belonging. This, of course, does not apply to everybody in my grandmother's generation. Her own brother, for instance, does not believe in this. Although he does talk about death, he has different opinions about it. "If I knew my day," he said, "I would dig my own grave and bury myself. A dead person is dead, it does not make any difference what a dead person wears and what coffin he or she has. Why bother spending so much time and money worrying about this?" *Houshi* preparation is more common in Fujian and Guangdong provinces than other places in China, and in the countryside than in the cities. So the practice exists more in the countryside but not in the cities. My other grandmother in Wuhan, for instance, would be furious if we put a coffin underneath her bed.

Pearl Buck, an American female writer, wrote many books about China [1]. In her novel, *The Good Earth,* the poor peasant Wang Lung gradually became rich because he married a woman who bore him sons. The following episode tells about Wang Lung's visit to his wife O-lan's grave [1, p. 310-311],

> . . . he wandered one day in a late spring, near summer, and he went over his fields a little way and he came to the enclosed place upon a low hill where he had buried his dead. He stood trembling on his staff and he looked at the graves and he remembered them every one. They were more clear to him now that the sons who lived in his own house, more clear to him than anyone except his poor fool (his daughter) and except Pear Blossom (his mistress). And his mind went back many years and he saw it all clearly, even his little second daughter of whom he had heard nothing for longer than he could remember, and he saw her a pretty maid as she had been in his house, her lips as thin and red as shred of silk—and she was to him like these who lay here in the land. Then he mused and thought suddenly,
>
> "Well, and I shall be the next."
>
> Then he went into the enclosure and he looked carefully and he saw the place where he would lie below his father and his uncle and above Ching (his neighbour, later his servant) and not far from O-lan. And he stared at the bit of earth where he was to lie and he saw himself in it and back in his own land forever. And he muttered,
>
> "I must see to the coffin."
>
> This thought he held fast and painfully in his mind and he went back to the town and he sent for his eldest son, and he said,
>
> "There is something I have to say."
>
> "Then say on," answered his son, "I am here"
>
> ". . . My son, I have chosen my place in the earth and it is below my father and his brother and above your mother and next to Ching, and I would see my coffin before I die."
>
> Then Wang Lung's eldest son cried on dutifully and properly,
>
> "Do not say that word, my father, but I will do as you say."

> Then his son bought a carved coffin hewn from a great log of fragrant wood which is used to bury the dead in and for nothing else because the wood is as lasting as iron, and more lasting than human bones, and Wang Lung was comforted. And he had the coffin brought into his room and he looked at it every day.

Although this story is set in the 1930s, it is still true to a great extent in the countryside in China today.

HOW DO THE CHINESE PEOPLE MOURN THEIR DEAD?

Since the 1950s cremation has been the main form of burial in China [2]. In fact, most of the participants of my survey preferred cremation. A few said they had no preference. One said that she would prefer whichever is convenient for the living. A school teacher in Singapore said when she dies she would like to be cremated, adding "better be ashes than to rot and have worms all over!"

But there are people who still prefer the old form of burial. An old lady from the countryside of Anhui Province settled down in the big city of Wuhan with her daughter's family. Although she enjoys city life immensely, she still wants to go back to her hometown to die. She does not want to be cremated. In her own words: "I am afraid to be burnt. It's very painful." According to my observation, the educated people usually prefer cremation.

In China the color red is associated with weddings and happiness, and white is associated with death, funerals and mourning. But there is a saying in Chinese *Hong Bai Xi Shi*, which states that happy events are associated with the colors of red and white. This is interesting especially when death is normally a sad and sorrowful event and a taboo subject. I must explain here that when people refer to *Bai Xi Shi*, the white happy event, they do not mean anybody who dies represents a happy occasion. They only mean old people who die a natural death, the so called *Shouzhong Zhengqin* die naturally in one's bedroom when one has lived long enough through his years. Although the saying does not apply to anybody who dies, white is the color to mourn the dead in the Chinese culture. This is also reflected in many of the films, for instance, "Bethune: the Making of a Hero."[1]

The fact that people are in white for the funeral does not mean that anyone wearing a white shirt or blouse is mourning the dead. But women or girls who wear a white flower (it could be real, but normally a paper flower), a bit of white

---

[1] A co-produced film by China and Canada. Norman Bethune was a Canadian doctor in China in the 1930s. He accidentally cut his finger on an operation table and died from blood poisoning not long after that. As the film starts, when the lines of people take Bethune's corpse to be buried, the basic color is white.

cotton, a white hair pin or hair band on their hair are usually mourning the dead. In the past in China, the bereaved dressed in burlap mourning clothes for several months after their loved ones died. But it is no longer done today. Nowadays many clothes are acceptable as long as they are not very colorful and bright. But people avoid red. In Singapore, Taiwan, some traditional families still dress in burlap clothes when they bury the dead. Today in mainland China, it is common to wear black crepe armbands. Normally these are worn for a month or so. The generations of the deceased could be distinguished by adding a little something to the armband. For instance if a grandparent dies, the grandchildren will have a small red piece of cloth or silk added to their armbands.

In China, at a memorial service at a funeral home, people will be able to see the dead in a casket. Wreaths are laid in the front of the hall close to the corpse. Special workers of the funeral home help dress and make up the dead. After the corpse is cremated, the family decides where and when to bury the ashes. Some families like to keep the ashes at home for a period of time.

When the dead or ashes are buried, there will be a tablet established. A tomb is not built for the dead everywhere. But in many places in Fujian Province, it is still built. What is interesting is that every tomb has a name. It is built in such a way that the dead would supposedly live a comfortable life in another world. So both my great grandfather and my grandfather's tombs have a front yard, a door to the house and windows. On their tombstones their birthdays and death dates are inscribed from upward to downward, and right to left. On my great grandfather's tombstone, his wife's name is seen beside his. She was so addressed as Lady Wu, and followed by her own name. All the names of family members, except female members, were inscribed on the stone. Females were considered outsiders, as eventually they would be married off to other families. But younger generation seems to be more open-minded, and would not object to adding female names onto the tombstone. What is more interesting is the fact that not only the names of the family members are inscribed, but also the members of the family are also inscribed. This is how it works:

The first grandson is named Guangzong, the second Guangyao and the third Guangzu. *Guang* means brighten, and bring honor to; *Zong* is ancestor; *Yao* means brighten, and bring honor to; and *Zu* is ancestor. It is up to the parents whether they name their children this way or not when the children are born in future. *Zong*

and *Zu* are often found in the names of those who come from very traditional families. This is because families and ancestors are important in Chinese culture. On my grandfather's tombstone, my grandmother's name and her birthday are next to her husband's. But since she is still living, her name is covered with tape.

In some rural areas, elaborate funeral ceremonies led by monks are still held; drums and trumpets are sounded as the ceremonies go on. In 1986, a friend of mine went to work in Anhui province, helping to upgrade the teaching level in that area. Once she wrote to tell me the "strange" customs she saw; "One day, at home she heard drums and trumpets outside getting closer and louder. It sounded so festive, but she could not figure out what holiday it was. She went out, only to find that someone had died. Mourners in special dress burn paper money for the dead to use in heaven or wave long narrow flags to call back spirits."

In China, Singapore and other areas where Chinese live, *Qing Ming Jie* (the Pure Brightness Festival), is a time when most people mourn their dead and worship their ancestors. This festival "was originally a celebration of nature's emergence from its long winter dormancy. People would take the opportunity to go on excursions outside of the city, 'treading the green grass' (*Ta Qing*) was how they described it" [3, p. 46]. It is on the third day of the third month of the Chinese lunar calender, the fourth or fifth day of April. People hold various traditional rituals to mourn their dead. The most common thing to do on this day is to sweep the graves (*Sao Mu* in Chinese). The whole area around the graves would be cleaned, weeds removed, fresh earth added to the graves, and flowers or trees planted. The lighting of firecrackers, the *kowtow* and the offering of food are also rituals frequently seen.

On *Qing Ming*, since many people go to visit the grave of the dead, the route to the graveyard is extremely crowded. Self-employed peddlers make money there selling silk flowers and plastic fruit to the mourners. Traffic police have a difficult time keeping the smooth flow of mourners.

THE CHANGES

Although traditional ways of mourning the dead are still very common among the Chinese, modern life has also found its way into the memorial ceremony. One should not feel surprised if an old man lights a cigarette and placed it in front of the tablet of his wife's tomb, because she loved to smoke while living; or a mother brings a tape-recorder with her to her son's grave, and plays his favorite music [2]. The way the Chinese mourn the dead tells much about our culture. But as society progresses, while tradition is still very much observed, one also finds that people's attitudes toward death, the rituals we perform to commemorate the deceased are changing.

REFERENCES

1. P. S. Buck, *The Good Earth,* The Modern Library, New York, pp. 310-311, 1931.
2. *China Daily,* April 9, 1991.
3. M. L. Latsch, *Chinese Traditional Festivals,* New World Press, Beijing, p. 46, 1984.

PART IV

Special Questions

CHAPTER 19

Hospice Future

Dame Cicely Saunders

The title was my own choice but it is a challenging one. The hospice movement is a kaleidoscope, not a neat package with a well set out destination. Indeed, we do not all use the same title. We respond locally, yet in spite of that, we have national and international recognition, impact and commitments. We have to answer to need with scientific and professional rigor knit together with personal compassion and yet we constantly have to worry about funds. We are a collection of very varied teams and individuals, continually on a learning curve. I have no crystal ball nor guide to the future, only some principles and hopes that as we began by paying attention to dying people, their families and the staff caring for them, so we will go on.

In July 1989 St. Christopher's organized an international conference, which included participants from thirty-seven countries, some struggling with little recognition or money. I think especially of the team from Halle in East Germany and two home care nurses from Guyana. In a sense they were saying to us, "We have only ourselves to offer but we can do that," and it was obvious that they work with the same principles and objectives as those of us in larger foundations. We all set out to maximize the potential of the patient as part of a family, in physical capacity, emotional truth and relationships in depth, to use the time given to find strengths within themselves and to affirm their own values and what they see as true beyond themselves. So far as possible this happens in their place of choice, whether it is their own home, a hospital in which they have had long trust or in a hospice bed. All this pre-supposes some facing of truth and a very careful following of the progress of the disease.

We remember first that unless symptoms are controlled, all else is hampered, and unless we monitor and search continually to improve in this area, we will fail those we serve. Symptom control in ten years time should be even better than it is now. Our responsibility is to be centers of enquiry, a phrase I prefer to centres of excellence. If we are to continue to offer our visitors from overseas and bodies such as the World Health Organization an objective basis for our teaching, we must go on with our commitment to research, each as we can in our own context.

Here I emphasize our commitment to inter-disciplinary work and enquiry. The *Journal of Palliative Medicine* is an important way of spreading information but we have to be ready to publish in general journals also. If we had not spent time in the 1950s and 1960s meeting with basic and clinical researchers in pain as we planned St. Christopher's early studies, there would not be the recognition now from the Royal College of Physicians and the Joint Board for Higher Medical Training and we would not be able to work alongside other specialties with such confidence.

I recently asked a well known oncologist if we would have done this if, in the 1960s, we had somehow managed to work within the National Health Service or the already established charities. The reply was that we needed to move out to demonstrate that whole person medicine included much more than anyone had imagined was possible at this stage of life.

The mention of the whole person recalls our commitment to the patient as part of his family, so another area for our development in the future is to learn more and more how to help people find their own strengths. This is an area not often recognized by the public, who do not realize how demanding is our involvement with split and conflicted families, with often angry teenagers and bereaved young children and the hours that have to be spent as communication opens up, relationships are repaired and the families find their own answers to their problems. Our hospice social workers have taught us all much in this area. Here too, we need to go on learning and sharing together and, of course, this is less easy to pass on to those working in general wards and general practice, who have less time than we do, than it is to give suggestions about symptom control. In our own ten year follow-up of a comparative study by Dr. Colin Murray Parkes, we found pain better controlled in the second general hospital group than in the first but that family anxiety was still a problem [1]. We need to show that we can offer special understanding and much greater time in this area so that the right people are referred, and referred in time for hospice home or in-patient care. In future, I hope to see our service used more perceptively.

Because we believe we have something special to offer we have to keep a careful balance between our enthusiasm and any hint of elitist self praise. Nowhere is this more of a challenge than with hospital support teams. They seem to me a very important area of future growth, and I would like to see one in every district general hospital and teaching hospital. The challenges there are unremitting and teams have succumbed. Most of their members need training first in special units. They are certainly not the places for learning on the job, with the constant questioning from other professionals. Team support here and elsewhere is another area for continued learning, both in understanding ourselves and sharing with our colleagues. I greatly admire individual pioneering nurses but I believe hospice care is essentially inter-disciplinary, with clear demands for a close knit team who have learned to understand and respect each other. I was recently giving tea to a visitor after an extensive whole day visit to the hospice. He had visited many hospitals and one of his comments after his day with us was "It seems to me that doctors are less important here." But he agreed with me that this was due to a levelling up of all the other disciplines, not a levelling down of the doctors' contribution. As a former nurse and social worker, I know the different questions and challenges that come to each profession. The medical input has been part of the strength of the work in the United Kingdom and one of the reasons why I still believe that we have some claim to be leaders in the field is that every profession has learned to recognize both their own contribution and that of others.

Are we in the hospice world working ourselves out of a job? After twenty-two years of in-patient care and twenty years of home care at St. Christopher's, we have found that demand is still increasing and that our patients come with ever more complex problems. We are more truly than ever a complementary local service. Should we be enlarging our commitment? I think that depends on local demand, although we must not forget that one of the reasons for our impact has been our focus and concentration on malignant disease. It is from that base that much has been spread by interchange with other medical specialties. Some of us have turned towards people with motor neurone disease, children and people with AIDS, and I am sure that our own local challenges will guide us here. However, we need to be careful to maintain our standards as we respond, monitor our practice and improve upon our special skills.

What of the financial future? We have to go on lobbying and presenting our case both nationally and locally, within and without Parliament. There been some hopeful straws in the wind but we continue to wait as political and other pressures are brought to bear. If we finally obtain more secure funding, I believe we will have to face some new demands to look at planning and audit. Our information service, like the Macmillan Cancer Relief Fund, has always emphasized to any new hospice group that they must talk at once to both regional and district health authorities and be part of the planning for terminal care demanded of them by the Department of Health. We have to show we are really needed if we want to start work and also look at the standards of care that we are going to offer. I know this has begun with the Sheffield Study but we need a further look at clinical standards and maybe should expect the sort of visitations that are made by the Joint Board for Higher Medical Training [2]. We now have various associations for the professions involved, who would surely help in this area. We have come a long way in recognition as a specialty, although our teams vary in size, commitment and possibilities but we need to remember also that this field is a general challenge, part of medicine and general practice as a whole.

And what of the spiritual dimension? Whether we like it or not every hospice worker will be faced with difficult questions as our patients and their families search for meaning, reach out beyond themselves and feel unable or unworthy to do so. We all need help. The spiritual dimension is wider than, although it includes, religion. We are all thrown back on whatever it is that convinces and enables us, even if we hesitate to use the word "faith." Although we will never pressure for our own point of view, we have a chance here to be bridge builders towards discovery for our patients and their families. When we are ready to let this area open up, an influence which I personally call "Grace" is ready to enter our dialogue and it is often a dialogue without words. I certainly would not have started out nor be here now without that, nor be looking to the future with anticipation. All of us have had to stay beside people in anguish, with no answers to give, only a conviction that there *is* an answer, that there is a future for them of growth through loss and a discovery of grace.

So our future as hospice or palliative or continuing care is both practical and spiritual, a match of compassion with tough clinical science built on research, training and teaching, enabled by competent, approachable administration, management and support. Hopefully more securely funded, but also more mature as a complementary service both where we are part of and where we are related to the Health Service. We will continue to belong to our communities yet be a recognizable part of a more general whole. I think we are a part song rather than a single voice, speaking from our local teams and refusing to be stereotyped. Yet we can come together as we do today to share what we have in common.

I have always thought of our hospice as a community of the unlike but we are one in our fundamental commitment to people facing mortal illness and parting. It is they who we speak for as it is they who hold us together. Their need and achievements will guide us to the future.

UPDATE

Developments in the United Kingdom have continued since late 1989 when this chapter was originally written. Numbers of units and teams have increased and there are now 178 inpatient units, mainly set up by independent charities but with a slowly increasing number fully within the National Health Service. There are presently about 740 nurses originally funded by Cancer Relief Macmillan Fund working with patients in their own homes. In addition Cancer Relief have initiated roughly 100 liaison hospital-based posts (including 25 breast care nurses and 14 paediatric nurses in teams around the country). The number of full multi-disciplinary teams and individual consulting appointments is now in excess of 160. The integration with the NHS both in the later stages of disease and increasingly earlier on continues with a number of important new teaching medical and nursing posts supported by the Cancer Relief Macmillan Fund. The Department of Health and Social Security has asked for plans from Districts concerning palliative and terminal care as their responsibility. How this will operate in the incoming era of contracts and emphasis on community care has yet to be seen.

Recognition as a medical specialty has led to an increasing number of posts being set up for experience and training although candidates for senior positions are in short supply and doctors move across from related specialties such as oncology. Educational developments in the nursing field include new courses leading to post graduate diplomas. The professional associations continue to encourage and monitor such progress.

Meantime the "part song" has come together as a more realistic single voice. After interest and pleas from the Department of Health and much debate, a forum has at last been established as The National Council for Hospice and Specialist Palliative Care Services. The independent charities and individual hospices will have their voice together with the professional associations. Interest in a greater proportion of Government funding was an incentive on both sides but in spite of welcome extra support an estimate of about 40 percent overall is still probably accurate. The tremendous support given by public and trust donations for nearly all capital expenditure and the remaining 60 percent of revenue continues in spite of the recession. Hospices come high on the overall list of charitable giving in the United Kingdom and reveals much personal support as well as effort by the charities and teams themselves.

The challenges and principles described above have been shown to flourish in different ways in many different cultures.

REFERENCES

1. C. M. Parkes and J. Parkes, "Hospice" versus "hospital" Care—Reevaluation after 10 Years as seen by Surviving Spouses, *Postgraduate Medical Journal, 60,* pp. 120-124, 1984.
2. R. Harper et al., *Good Practice in Terminal Care: Some Standards and Guidelines for Hospice In-Patient Units and Day Hospices,* University of Sheffield Medical School, Department of Community Medicine, 1988.

Contributors

RONALD K. BARRETT is a professor of psychology at Loyola Marymount University where he teaches a course on the Psychology of Death and Dying, facilitates grief support groups, and serves as a behavioral consultant for the Compton Unified School District and the Los Angeles County Coroner's Office. Dr. Barrett has researched cross-cultural patterns and is considered an expert on African-American attitudes towards death, dying and funeral rites and recently made presentations at the 1990 National Conference on Black Studies and the 1991 International Conference on Death and Dying at London's King College at the University of Western Ontario. Dr. Barrett's work on a major demographic study of homicide and suicide patterns in Los Angeles County was the subject for presentation at the 1990 National Conference on the State of the Black Male in Atlanta, Georgia and the lead articles in May and June 1991 publication *The American Black Male*. The results from his research in this area will be published in a chapter on homicidal violence in Lawrence Gary's (ed.) *Black Men* due for release early 1993. In addition, Dr. Barrett has specialized in working with young urban children experiencing trauma, grief and loss and has conducted a number of broadcasted and televised interviews on grief and bereavement as well as conducted a weekly radio broadcast for KTYM radio station in Los Angeles.

JEANNE QUINT BENOLIEL is one of the pioneer contributors to research and education on death and dying. Her research career began with a study of women's adaptations post-mastectomy (1961-1963). She then joined Anselm Strauss on a five-year sociological study of dying patients and hospital personnel (1962-1967) and began to publish the results of these efforts. Later at the University of Washington her research was focused on adaptations of lung cancer patients, spouse bereavement, and evaluation of home care and cancer prevention programs. In education she directed the Oncology Transition Services Program to prepare nurses for leadership in practice and offered a graduate course, "Death Influence in Clinical Practice," for 20 years (1970-1990). She has published extensively and is a charter member of the International Work Group on Death, Dying, and Bereavement. Awards and honors include recognition from the American Cancer Society and the Association of Death Education and Counseling.

GERRY R. COX is a Professor of Sociology at Fort Hays State University. His interest in death and dying initially began with teaching about death and dying over twenty years ago. He has led numerous bereavement sessions, workshops, and programs on various death and dying topics. He has authored, co-authored, and edited five books and over thirty chapters and articles.

JOHN DeFRAIN is Professor of family science at the University of Nebraska-Lincoln. Dr. DeFrain has co-authored several books on families and family crisis including *Secrets of Strong Families, Stillborn: The Invisible Death,* and *On Our Own: A Single Parent's Survival Guide.*

DEANNA EDWARDS is a composer, author and singer whose songs bring peace to the sick, the elderly and those who are grieving. A music educator, she is an adjunct faculty lecturer in Music Therapy at Utah State University. She conducts workshops throughout the United States and Canada, with recent tours in New Zealand and South Africa. She served for three years on the Foundation Board of Directors for the American College of Health Care Administrators. Her appearance on "Voice for the Hurting" with Sacred Heart Radio in St. Louis, Missouri, won the prestigious New York Radio Festival Award and the Religion-in-Media's Angel Award. She was selected by *Ladies Home Journal* as one of Fifty American Heroines in 1984. Her song, "Teach Me To Die" was used on the NBC News Special "On Death and Dying." She has recorded nine albums and written two books, and has been a contributing author to other books used in the helping professions. Her songs have been used in films by the American Journal of Nursing.

SANDRA ELDER is a grief counsellor certified by the Association for Death Education and Counseling, and has been in private practice for ten years. In addition to maintaining her practice and coordinating a "Learning Through Loss" program for grieving adolescents, Sandra is presently completing work on her doctoral dissertation in the Department of Psychological Foundations at the University of Victoria. She is doing a comparative study of the impact of father death on adolescents between the ages of twelve to sixteen. Sandra is a member of the Canadian Register of Health Service Providers in Psychology.

LINDA ERNST is an Assistant Professor in family resources at St. Olaf College in Northfield, Minnesota. Dr. Ernst has completed research and published in the areas of parent education, sudden infant death syndrome, and diversity in family education.

RONALD J. FUNDIS is Vice President of Jefferson College. His interest in death and dying emerged initially from his training in population studies and later from research, teaching, health and economic development project experiences in Mexico and Central America. The culture of poverty, hunger and death was/is ever present. A third influence came from criminology where suicide, homicide, and capital punishment are recurring themes. He has directed bereavement workshops and in-service training for teachers, clergy, counselors, and law enforcement personnel. He has authored, co-authored, and edited six books and over thirty articles.

NAN J. GIBLIN, Ph.D. is Chairperson and Associate Professor of the Department of Counselor Education at Northeastern Illinois University in Chicago, Illinois. She holds a B.A. degree in English Literature, a Master's Degree in Counselor Education and a Ph.D. from Loyola University in Counseling Psychology. At Northeastern she teaches courses including Family Counseling and Grief Counseling. As a licensed clinical psychologist she practices Grief Counseling with adults and children. She has written several articles on grief counseling and recently co-edited a book, *Family Counseling in School Settings.*

ROSS GRAY is a Psychologist Consultant to the Comprehensive Cancer Program at Sunnybrook Health Science Centre and the Toronto-Bayview Regional Cancer Centre. During 1989-1990 he served as special consultant to the suicide prevention program of the Department of Social Services, Northwest Territories.

EDWARD W. KEYSERLINGK is a University Professor in the Faculty of Medicine, Department of Humanities and Social Studies in Medicine, McGill University, Montreal, Canada. He is also a Member of the McGill Centre for Medicine, Ethics and Law, and an Associate Member of the McGill Centre for Studies in Aging. Professor Keyserlingk is also Director of the Contemporary Canadian Family Project, McGill University, Immediate Past-President (and Founding President) of the Canadian Bioethics Society, and a Member of the Permanent Consultative Group of Experts in Medical Law, Law Reform Commission of Canada.

MICHAEL R. LEMING is Professor of Sociology and Anthropology at St. Olaf College. He holds degrees from Westmont College (B.A.), Marquette University (M.A.), and the University of Utah (Ph.D.) and has done additional graduate study at the University of California in Santa Barbara. He is the co-author (with George E. Dickinson) of *Understanding Dying, Death, and Bereavement* (Holt, Rinehart, and Winston, 1985 and 1990) and *Understanding Families: Diversity, Continuity, and Change* (Allyn and Bacon, 1990). He is also the co-editor (with Raymond DeVries and Brendan Furnish) of *The Sociological Perspective: A Value-Committed Introduction* (Zondervan, 1989) and (with George E. Dickinson and Alan C. Mermann) *Annual Editions: Dying, Death, and Bereavement* (Dushkin Publishing Group). Dr. Leming is the founder and former director of the St. Olaf College Social Research Center, former member of the board of directors of the Minnesota Coalition on Terminal Care, steering committee member of the Northfield AIDS Response, and serves as hospice educator, volunteer, and grief counselor.

PENNY MacELVEEN-HOEHN is Professor in the Graduate School at the Union Institute and a founder of Hospice of Seattle and member of the Board since 1974. Selected publications include: "Sexual Assessment and Counselling" and "Understanding Sexuality in Progressive Cancer" both in *Seminars in Oncology Nursing,* Feb. 1985; "The Impact of Chronic Illness on the Family" in *Recent Advances in Nursing Series: Long-Term Care,* K. King (ed.); "Sexuality and

Cancer," in *Issues in Cancer Care,* R. McCorkle, and G. Honglardorum (eds.); Co-author, "Gay Clients with AIDS: New Challenges for Hospice Programs," *The Hospice Journal,* Spring 1988. Dr. MacElveen-Hoehn was honored by Hospice of Seattle as a Pioneer in Hospice Work (1991) for her seventeen years in the field.

KAREN MARTIN is a bereavement consultant and graduate student in the Department of Sociology at the University of Alberta in Edmonton. She is currently completing her master's thesis "Surviving SIDS: The Parents' Search for a Reason." She presented some of her findings at the Second SIDS International Conference in Sydney, Australia (1992). Her paper is being published in the conference proceedings. She was also a featured speaker at the annual conference of the Canadian Foundation for the Study of Infant Deaths.

JOHN D. MORGAN is Professor of Philosophy and Director of the Centre for Education about Death and Bereavement at King's College of the University of Western Ontario, London, Canada. Dr. Morgan has been teaching courses about death and bereavement since 1968 and has coordinated the King's College International Conferences on Death and Bereavement since 1982. Dr. Morgan is editor of *Thanatology: A Liberal Arts Approach; Suicide: Helping those at Risk; Death Education in Canada; The Dying and the Bereaved Teenager,* and *Young People and Death.* Dr. Morgan is the Consulting Editor for the Death, Value and Meaning Series published through Baywood Publishing Company. Dr. Morgan's research interests focus on issues of cultural attitudes related to death and bereavement.

MARY ANN MORGAN has been actively involved in death education with professionals, para-professionals, volunteers, students, and the community at large for over twenty years. She is a member of the International Work Group on Death, Dying, and Bereavement, a member of ADEC, and is certified as a death educator. She has edited several books in the field, authored chapters in texts, and written articles about death and bereavement for peer reviewed and popular publications. She has an undergraduate degree in nursing and a Master of Education in adult education. Presently she works as health promotion coordinator of population health strategies at Middlesex-London Health Unit in London Ontario where principles of empowerment guide her work with the community.

JUDY OAKS is a certified health educator and death educator. Dr. Oaks is Director of RENEW, Center for Personal Recovery in Berea, Kentucky.

RICHARD PAUL (Funeral Director) has been joined since 1986 by JOAN BURNETT (Palliative Care Volunteer), DAVID HOPPNER-HART (United Church Minister) and SUSAN PAUL-BRUSHEY (Funeral Director) in making an annual presentation to bereaved people at Christmas time. Over 600 people have been exposed to this educational format and the material in his chapter is a summary of the two seminars. The response from the participants is one of gratitude and growth throughout the year as the bereaved apply their learnings to manage their grief. The four presenters feel very strongly that the vast majority of bereaved people are unaware that they have any option but to grieve the way they always have. They also believe that it is the responsibility of everyone involved in a caregiving role to be a "Grief Educator." For further information about the format and production of this annual presentation, please feel free to contact the authors.

MARYSE PELLETIER, R.N., M.N., is an Assistant Professor in the Faculty of Nursing at the University of New Brunswick, Fredericton, New Brunswick, Canada.

SOMMAI PREMCHIT, an Associate Professor of Anthropology at the Faculty of Social Sciences, Chiang Mai University, Thailand, obtained an M.A. in Anthropology, UP, Diliman in 1971. He has been a pioneer in conducting extensive surveys of the palm-leaf manuscripts in Northern Thailand and microfilming them from 1973 through 1984. In 1992 he served as a Fulbright scholar in residence at the Department of Religion, Swarthmore College. With special interests in religious rites of passage and death-related customs, in 1992 he published, with the assistance of Amphay Dore, *The Lan Na Twelve-Month Traditions.*

RABBI DANIEL A. ROBERTS, M.A.H.L., is Senior Rabbi of Temple Emanu El in Cleveland, Ohio. He has lectured extensively on death and dying to adults and students of all ages. He has been instrumental in helping a local nursing home establish a hospice unit and in creating a community support group for widows and widowers. Rabbi Roberts produced a multi-media presentation on teenage suicide entitled, "Inside I Ache," which is distributed nationally by Mass Media Ministries of Baltimore, Maryland.

SISTER FRANCES RYAN, D.C., is a Daughter of Charity. She has an M.S.W. in social work from Saint Louis University (1961) and a Ph.D. in counseling psychology from Loyola University of Chicago (1983). She is currently an Associate Professor in the School of Education of DePaul University. She is in early childhood education and chair for the master's program in human services and counseling in the graduate division. Current publications include "The Video Child at Risk and Learning Theory," in *Children at Risk* (1989) and "A Philosophical Perspective: Can the Teacher-Counselor Express One's Values by Presence to the Student?" in *Children's Success in School* (1983). She has co-authored with Nan Giblin "Loss: A Cognitive and an Affective Process, *IACD Quarterly* (Fall 1986) and *Bereavement: Helping the Survivors* (Kings College, University of Western Ontario: 1987) and "Reaching the Child's Perception of Death," in *Helping Young People Cope with Death* (1989). She has been an executive member of the Vincentian Studies Institute since 1987.

JIAKANG WU is a graduate of the Beijing University of Foreign Studies, China. She is a Lecturer in Chinese and Modern Eastern Civilization at Huron College, affiliated with the University of Western Ontario, and a graduate student at the School of Library and Information Science at the University of Western Ontario.

Index